WORLDS WITHOUT END

The Art and History of the Soap Opera

Worlds

Harry N. Abrams, Inc., Publishers • The Museum of Television & Radio

Without End

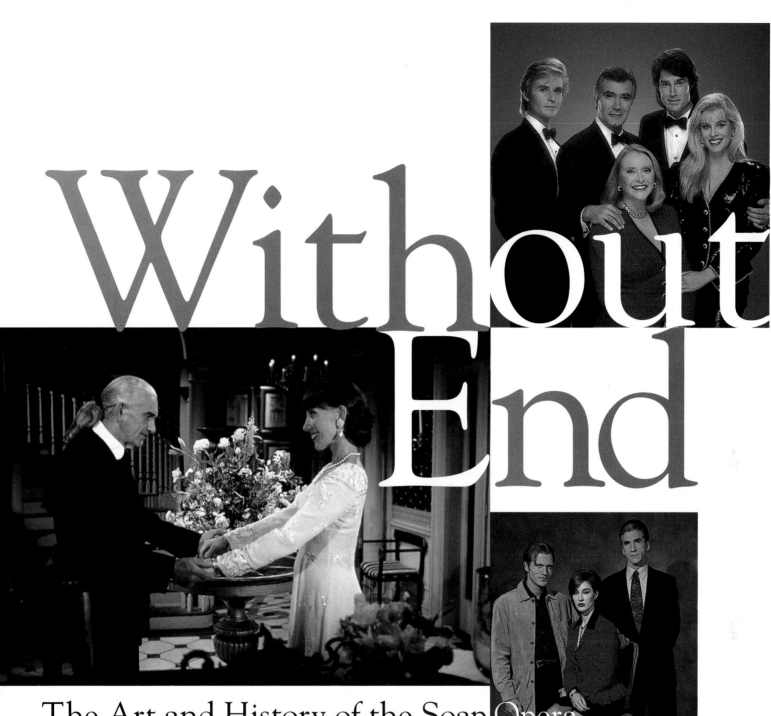

The Art and History of the Soap Opera

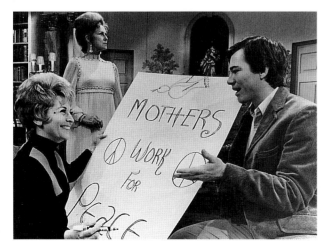

Editor's note:

The landscape of the soap opera world is constantly changing. This book offers a historic perspective on the genre as of September 1996. (Since then, *Sunset Beach* and *Port Charles* have debuted.) The interviews with producers, writers, directors, and actors of soap operas that are the basis for the extended quotes in this book were conducted in May, June, and July 1996. All titles and positions reflect the status of the individual at the time of the interview. Moreover, all discussions of the current plots of shows reflect the same time frame.

Worlds Without End: The Art and History of the Soap Opera is published in conjunction with an exhibition of the same title at The Museum of Television & Radio, New York and California, December 5, 1997– March 8, 1998

The exhibition is made possible by Procter & Gamble, with additional support from the American Federation of Television and Radio Artists (AFTRA)

The Museum of Television & Radio is located at 25 West 52 Street, New York, NY 10019-6106 and 465 North Beverly Drive, Beverly Hills, CA 90210-4654

For Harry N. Abrams, Inc.:
Editor: Robert Morton
Designer: Robert McKee

For The Museum of Television & Radio:
Director of Publications: Ellen O'Neill
Curator: Ron Simon
Photograph Editor: Roberta Panjwani
Art Director: Lou Dorfsman

Library of Congress Cataloging-in-Publication Data
Worlds without end: the art and history of the soap opera /
   the Museum of Television & Radio.
     p.   cm.
   Includes bibliographical references and index.
   ISBN 0–8109–3997–5 (cloth) / 0–8109–2777–2 (museum pbk)
   1. Soap operas—United States—History and criticism.
   I. Museum of Television and Radio (New York, N.Y.)
   PN1992.8.S4W67   1997
   741.45'6—dc21   97–307

 Harry N. Abrams, Inc.
100 Fifth Avenue
New York, N.Y. 10011
www.abramsbooks.com

Contents

7 Foreword by Robert M. Batscha,
   President of The Museum of
   Television & Radio

8 A Word from Procter & Gamble

11 Serial Seduction: Living in Other
   Worlds
   by Ron Simon

41 Essays from "Soapland"
   by James Thurber
      O Pioneers!
      Ivorytown, Rinsoville,
         Anacinburg, and Crisco
         Corners
      The Listening Women

67 Architects of the Afternoon
   by Robert J. Thompson

77 Watching Daytime Soap Operas:
   The Power of Pleasure
   by Louise Spence

89 Different Soaps for Different Folks:
   Conceptualizing the Soap Opera
   by Jane Feuer

99 Taking Issue: Social Themes
   in the Soaps
   by Laura Stempel Mumford

111 As the World Tunes In:
   An International Perspective
   by Robert C. Allen

121 The Classic Soap Operas

122 The Legacy of Irna Phillips:
   A Visualization

164 Notes

167 Select Bibliography

169 Acknowledgments

170 About the Contributors

171 Photo Credits

172 Index

On the General Hospital *set: Bobbie Spencer (Jacklyn Zeman), Dr. Noah Drake (Rick Springfield), Dr. Rick Webber (Chris Robinson), Mike Webber (David Mendenhall), and Dr. Lesley Williams Webber (Denise Alexander)*

Foreword

The place of soap operas in the history of broadcasting cannot be overstated. There are soap operas that have been carried into their fifth and sixth decades by generations of viewers, grandparents to parents to children—a compelling argument in itself that the serial fulfills some very real need in its audience. As often happens, though, popular appeal clouds and distorts perception of achievement and worthiness: the easiest way to discredit a situation in life and in art is to declare "It's just like a soap." This book and the accompanying screenings explore the hidden complexities of the soap opera, both in content and context, and in its extraordinary ability to attract loyal fans over decades, as well as the creative process behind the daily images on the screen.

As many critics and historians have recognized, the soap opera is rooted in the power of continuous storytelling. As Agnes Nixon has remarked, a good soap should "Make 'em laugh, make 'em cry, make 'em wait." To look at this phenomenon, television curator Ron Simon examines the roots of the serial narrative in literature, motion pictures, and comic strips and discusses how the soap opera developed on radio and television.

We turned to the academic community to examine various aspects of the genre. Louise Spence, who has interviewed many women who watch soap operas, reports on these discussions about the pleasure of soap watching. Jane Feuer offers a look at what it is that draws various "interpretive communities"—college students, housewives, academics—into soaps, beyond the cliché "they are at home." Laura Stempel Mumford explores how the genre has dealt with and responded over the years to social issues. Robert Allen focuses on the international aspect of the soap opera, and examines the vitality of the genre around the world.

To look more closely at the beginnings of the soap on radio, we are reprinting three essays by James Thurber from his five-part 1948 series in the *New Yorker* entitled "Soapland." Thurber captures the serial radio landscape of the time, from the pioneers Irna Phillips, Elaine Carrington, and Frank and Anne Hummert to the time-honored programs *Ma Perkins, The Romance of Helen Trent,* and *Pepper Young's Family.* Robert Thompson offers commentary on Thurber's essays, putting the opinions of 1948 into a historical perspective.

Behind the power and effect of the daytime soap lies a fascinating, Herculean creative process. To offer the voice of those who make the creative decisions that produce television soaps, Ron Simon and our director of publications Ellen O'Neill interviewed twenty-five people from the soap opera creative community in the spring of 1996. Their thoughts and opinions on their own work and the industry itself are offered alongside the essays of the academic community to provide very interesting insights.

An undertaking of this magnitude would not have been possible without the support of the soap opera's creative community and those who write and think about the soaps. I would like to thank our advisory committee for their time and their guidance: Robert Allen, Carolyn Culliton, Richard Culliton, Philip Dixson, Pat Fili-Krushel, Ken Fitts, Don Hastings, Claire Labine, Michael Laibson, Agnes Nixon, David Pressman, Millee Taggart, and Mimi Torchin.

For this endeavor, we would like to acknowledge the support of Procter & Gamble for underwriting this exhibition. Certainly their own history is inextricably linked to specific programs in the industry, but in their commitment to this project they have supported the value of understanding the history and significance of the entire genre. We would also like to thank the American Federation of Television and Radio Artists (AFTRA) for providing additional generous support, along with their great enthusiasm, for this exhibition.

We hope that this exhibition brings to light a new way for people to look at this seemingly simple yet deceptively complex area of daytime programming.

Robert M. Batscha
President, The Museum of Television & Radio

A Word from *Procter&Gamble*

The Procter & Gamble Company is pleased to share in The Museum of Television & Radio's first major exhibition exploring the art and impact of soap operas. In fact, Procter & Gamble was there in the earliest days of fifteen-minute continuing dramas on the radio with soap products as sponsors. One of the first, *Oxydol's Own Ma Perkins,* was an instant success in 1933 and popularized a new storytelling genre.

When television arrived as a commercial mass medium after World War II, it was just what the soaps needed. By 1959, P&G Productions, which had been incorporated to carve a niche in the new medium, had twelve soap operas on the air, on both television and radio, every weekday. And this year, one of them, *Guiding Light,* the only radio serial to make the transition to television and remain on the air today, celebrates sixty years of broadcasting—the longest running program in broadcast history.

What is the secret of the soaps' popularity? Perhaps it is that they deal with life as most of us know it— "often preposterous, always precarious, always infinitely precious." That's how Irna Phillips, probably the most important force in creating soap operas (including P&G's current serials *As the World Turns* and *Another World,* as well as *Guiding Light*) put it. Phillips also reminds us that "All our lives are serial stories, and the marriage ceremony outlines the plot for us: 'For better, for worse, for richer, for poorer, in sickness and in health.' Each day brings a new installment in our private soap opera, and no matter how bad yesterday was, who can resist tuning in tomorrow to find out what will happen next?"

The Procter & Gamble family is proud of the role it has played in the evolution of an American cultural phenomenon. We salute the Museum for its enthusiasm in organizing this extensive exhibition and thank our viewers for their continued devotion.

PROCTER & GAMBLE PRODUCTIONS, INC.

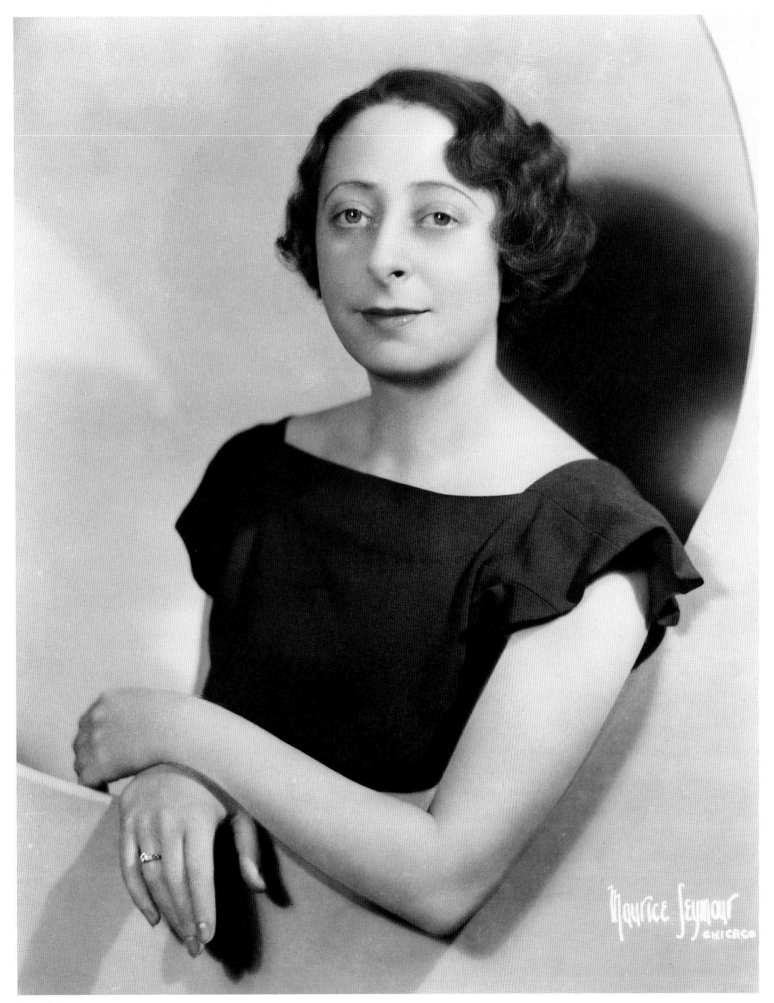

Irna Phillips

Serial

Seduction

Living in Other Worlds ◆ by Ron Simon

Prelude

Is it possible that Irna Phillips, the former schoolteacher who became the doyenne of the soap opera, was somehow influenced by philosopher George Santayana's dictum, "another world to live in . . . is what we mean by having a religion,"[1] as she created and then developed the daytime serial over forty years? Phillips certainly approached the genre with a spiritual discipline and intensity, and in 1964 even titled one of her creations *Another World*. More than any other art form, the soap opera creates an alternative world, where the characters and their environment seem to exist in a parallel dimension. Unlike individual works of art—a poem, novel, or film— which require Coleridge's temporary "suspension of disbelief," the serial demands ongoing belief and a daily commitment from the follower. Such surrender to an imaginative universe has engendered a loyalty and devotion that supersedes all rules of engagement: perhaps that is one reason why the soaps and their enthusiasts have been treated with suspicion, and sometimes contempt.

The well-made classical work of fiction is conscious of its structure: exposition in the beginning leads to a well-reasoned middle, culminating in the catharsis of the denouement. The never-ending soap, however, is a relentless series of beginnings and middles, without any final resolutions. The soap's characters take on a life of their own, often growing beyond the intentions, and even the lifetime, of the original author. When *Guiding Light* turned sixty in 1997, the serial had already outlived its creator, Irna Phillips, by twenty-three years. As they say, "life is short, and art is long," but how did an art get this long?

Since the beginning of mass culture at the turn of the nineteenth century, authors and entrepreneurs have tried to hook an audience and keep it coming back for more. Magazines, books, comic strips, and films have all employed a serial narrative to actively engage consumers. The soap opera was an invention of American radio, perhaps the only new form created by the media. Critic Gilbert Seldes thought that the serial was "[radio's] single notable contribution to the art of fiction."[2] This new form offered writers no temporal restrictions and thus the ability to achieve a whole new way of storytelling with a realism unheard of in any other art. Over time, the daily soap exploited the defining quality that made radio and then television distinct from other artistic experiences: their pervasive presence in the home, day in and day out. Characters could live, love, and die, experiencing the

Charles Dickens

The Young and the Restless: Sally McGuire (Lee Crawford) and Snapper Foster (William Grey Espy)

The Gumps comic strip from 1929

same happiness and hardships through the years as their audience. No doubt this is why a special kinship arose between soap characters and the listeners and viewers, a relationship so intense that psychologists have been analyzing the bond for more than fifty years.

It is certainly not the nature of a genre to have a single inventor, but the soap opera comes close, having been suffused from the beginning with the philosophy of Irna Phillips. More than sixty-five years after her first serial aired on radio, most of the television soaps can be traced back directly to Phillips and her disciples. How Phillips came to engender the serial tradition in broadcasting is a story worthy of the master herself. And like much that she wrote, it still continues today.

The Serial Narrative Before Radio

One can date the start of the serial narrative as we understand it from 1836, when publishers Chapman and Hall offered fledging newspaper columnist Charles Dickens the opportunity to sustain a story in monthly installments to accompany the illustrations of popular cartoonist Robert Seymour. Dickens was asked to write about the comic exploits of a metropolitan club whose members would include character types that mirrored the new urban population. Publishers had issued completed stories in serial installments before, but this was the first time that a story was published without the ending in sight. *The Pickwick Papers* became the 1830s equivalent of a pop culture phenomenon. The publishers had at first set a print run of four hundred copies; by the end they were printing forty thousand. One contemporary commentator wrote that "needy admirers flattened their noses against the booksellers' windows eager to secure a good look at the etchings and to peruse every line of the letterpress that might be exposed to view, frequently reading aloud to applauding bystanders . . . so great was the craze."[3] From that point on, the serial narrative combining the word and the image has thrived.

In America in 1850, *Harper's Monthly* magazine inspired the development of the serialized novel, and American readers found themselves immersed in the continuing tales of Nathaniel Hawthorne, Mark Twain, and Henry James. As in England, readers identified with the characters and actively sought out fellow subscribers to discuss what was going to happen next.[4] In fact, many publications had a regular forum that allowed readers to offer their feelings on the developing action. Such camaraderie has been part and parcel of the serial narrative ever since, as anyone in a soap opera chat room on the Internet can testify.

At the turn of the century the serial narrative was further popularized in daily newspapers through comic strips, descendants of the drawings that accompanied the Dickens installments. One of the earliest "funnies," *A. Mutt* (later to become *Mutt and Jeff),* was conceived by Harry Conway "Bud" Fisher and began running in the *San Francisco Chronicle* in 1907, appearing seven days a week. Fisher understood the power of the comics to bring readers back morning after morning. Increasingly, he showed his protagonist, compulsive gambler Augustus Mutt, engaging in activities that could be resolved in future strips.

The next advance in comic strip serials involved a penetrating look at everyday family life. Cartoonist Sidney Smith and his publisher Captain Joseph Patterson of the *Chicago Tribune* conceived *The Gumps* to be a visual equivalent of Theodore Dreiser's social-realist novels. The Gumps were a typical American family yearning to experience the prosperity of the Jazz Age. Smith wanted "everyday things to happen to them,"[5] which found a resonance in the audience. When one of the characters died after her wedding was disrupted, there was an outpouring of emotion across the nation.

Print and pictures also coalesced in a serial narrative for the movies. Charles Dwyer, editor of *The Ladies' World,* involved his magazine readers in a contest to predict the fate of virginal heroine Mary, whose fictional story, featuring a portrait by Charles Dana Gibson, appeared in a 1912 issue.[6] Dwyer joined forces with Thomas Edison's Kinetoscope Company, and Mary's adventures were soon presented monthly both in print and film. Noticing the public's enthusiasm, the *Chicago Tribune* combined a continuing newspaper scenario with a biweekly screen version of *The Adventures of Kathlyn,* spawning a cycle of women-in-peril imitations. The serial, thus, became a part of regular moviegoing, especially for adolescents, who enjoyed the continuing exploits of such heroes as Tarzan and Dick Tracy, who were also comic strip favorites.

The Serial Comes to Radio

Much of the mystique of radio derived from the compelling power of the individual voice. Think of the intimate chats of President Franklin D. Roosevelt, the crooning of Bing Crosby, or the harangues of Father Charles Coughlin. But no single person, regardless of how artful, can sustain an audience day in and day out. Dialogue between two people, however, has been the basis of daily radio serials for many years. The roots of the serial lie in the intimate conversation of two characters eavesdropped on by an entire nation: Amos and Andy, Ma Perkins and one of her daughters, Reverend Ruthledge and a parishioner of *The Guiding Light.*

The serial first came to radio in 1926, when the *Chicago Tribune* decided to bring a comic strip and its daily newspaper audience to its station, WGN. *The Gumps,* those middle-class

Amos 'n' Andy: *(Freeman Gosden and Charles Correll)*

1955
Guiding Light:
Joe Roberts
(Herb Nelson) and
Meta Bauer Banning
(Ellen Demming)

1995
As the World Turns:
Mike Kasnoff
(Shawn Christian)
and Rosanna Cabot
(Yvonne Perry)

1965
General Hospital:
Jessie Brewer
(Emily McLaughlin)
and Dr. Phil Brewer
(Roy Thinnes)

1990
Santa Barbara:
Eden Capwell
(Marcy Walker)
and Cruz Castillo
(A Martinez)

1954
Guiding Light:
The Bauers, Mike
(Glenn Walken),
Bert (Charita Bauer),
and Bill (Lyle Sudrow)

1996
Guiding Light:
Bridget Reardon
(Melissa Hayden)
with son Peter,
and Hart Jessup
(Marshall Hilliard)

1955
Search for
Tomorrow:
Jo Tate
(Mary Stuart),
with daughter Patti
(Lynn Loring)

1993
General Hospital:
Karen Wexler
(Cari Shayne) with
her mother Rhonda
(Denise Galik-Gurey)

1962
Guiding Light:
Bert Bauer
(Charita Bauer)

1996
The Young and
the Restless:
Katherine Chancellor
(Jeanne Cooper)

dreamers, were chosen. Two veterans of touring comedy and minstrel shows, Freeman Gosden and Charles Correll, were approached to lend their voices. The two performers, however, proposed another series more in keeping with their training. They suggested a serial about two poor black Southerners, Sam and Henry, who were forced to migrate to the big city. *The Gumps* went on the air without them, but for two years *Sam 'n' Henry* was broadcast six nights a week in ten-minute episodes. In 1928 Gosden and Correll wanted to syndicate the show nationally, so they left WGN to create a similar series, called *Amos 'n' Andy,* for a competing radio station, an NBC affiliate, owned by the *Chicago Daily News.* As audiences identified with the economic hardships of the two displaced Georgians, *Amos 'n' Andy* became broadcasting's first

mass phenomenon, a nightly ritual for most of the nation. Radio writers began to copy the *Amos 'n' Andy* formula and created programs with fictional locales peopled with characters who reflected universal emotions: Paul Rhymer evoked the entire small town of Crooper, Illinois, through his characters Vic and Sade; Carlton Morse delineated the Barbour clan of Sea Cliff, San Francisco, in *One Man's Family;* and Gertrude Berg, creator of *The Goldbergs,* made millions of listeners care about a poor Jewish family on New York's lower East Side.

Nearly all of this earliest radio programming was scheduled in the evening, because executives were concerned that housewives would not be able to concentrate on a program while performing their chores. During the formative years, radio was, as one scholar has noted, an "evening, family, and father-controlled entertainment."[7] That soon changed as the home products manufacturer General Mills looked for ways to integrate information about the home into an instructional program for women. In 1926 the food company created the character "Betty Crocker" to give daily hints on how to shop and take care of the home more efficiently. The late twenties saw a boom in these specialized programs for women. NBC created *The Women's Magazine of the Air* to combine ideas and entertainment of "genuine inspiration and help." Procter & Gamble became one of the main sponsors of the series and advertised three times during the week: health and beauty on Monday, underwritten by Camay soap; "Crisco Cooking Lessons" on Thursday, spotlighting "everyday dishes that are new, simple and different";[8] and Ivory Flakes' fashion trends on Friday. The manufacturer encouraged listeners to request companion guide booklets, which further connected the audience to the program.

Irna Phillips

Now enters Irna Phillips, the former teacher who was struggling to break into radio as an actress. She began her career as host of the inspirational show *Thought for a Day* for *Chicago Tribune*'s WGN in 1930. Station executives were not satisfied with her thespian talents and suggested that she take a crack at scriptwriting to create a serial along the lines of their previous successes, *The Gumps* and *Sam 'n' Henry*. Phillips melded several key elements in her work—the structure of the serial, the homey philosophy of the woman's program, and aspects of her own lonely, introspective life—to create one of the most resilient genres of broadcasting, the soap opera. Few writers would have such an impact on the history of radio and television: Phillips's disciples, Agnes Nixon and William J. Bell, have kept her paradigm going after more than sixty-five years. Despite this achievement, Phillips has gone largely unrecognized outside the scope of daytime radio and television broadcasting. She is not men-

---

On Irna Phillips

I guess I was around ten when I first heard Irna's name. I'd come home from school and mom would have soup and sandwich waiting for me. Inevitably the radio was on. Mom was a great fan of the serials, always listened, and before long I was hooked too. During my lunch hour, there was Our Gal Sunday, The Romance of Helen Trent, and Life Can Be Beautiful. The fourth serial was unique in that it mentioned the creator's name—"The Guiding Light, created by Irna Phillips."

The next semester I was on a different schedule and didn't hear the names Guiding Light or Irna Phillips for at least ten years. Even longer.

During the interim, I went to high school, spent twenty-one months in the Navy, attended college. Then I was hired by CBS in Chicago to write a daily comedy show.

I must have been at CBS a couple of years before I learned that a lady I had virtually forgotten about worked and lived less than a mile away from my office in the Wrigley Building. The lady, of course, was Irna Phillips. A short ten-minute cab ride away.

So I called her, talked to her secretary Rose Cooperman, asked that my name be put on a list whenever there was a job opening. I was totally blown away when Rose answered that I was in luck. One of the writers was moving to Florence! I was euphoric. I thought, "What fabulous timing!" But within twenty-four hours, I was totally bummed out to learn that the Florence-bound writer had changed his mind.

It was around three years later when Irna and I finally met for the first time. That was after I had met and married the first lady of Chicago television, my wife, partner, and future mother of our three terrific kids, Lee Phillip.

I worked with Irna first on Guiding Light, a fifteen-minute show—live, as all serials were at that time. Ultimately, Irna switched me to As the World Turns, which was the very first half-hour serial. Several years later, Irna and I created Another World.

About Irna. She was one of the most talented, complex, fascinating persons I ever met. Brilliant. A tough lady! Very tough! A lonely lady! Dictated every word she ever wrote.

I spent every day of the ten or so years we worked together at Irna's apartment, planning each and every script. I learned a lot from this great lady. Exciting, demanding, challenging, occasionally devastating days, all filled with creative challenge. There was only one Irna. There will never be another.

William J. Bell
Creator, The Young and the Restless *and*
The Bold and the Beautiful
Cocreator, Another World

Irna Phillips

tioned in Eric Barnouw's sweeping history of the mediums, and her one-time bosses, David Sarnoff at NBC Radio and William S. Paley of CBS Television, give no credit to one of their key moneymakers in their autobiographies.

Phillips's first series, *Painted Dreams,* debuted unsponsored in the fall of 1930. In it, she formed the bedrock of all the soaps that followed—a core family surviving the trials and tribulations of daily life. Phillips focused on the role of Mother Moynihan, a part she played herself, who oversaw a large family and ran a boardinghouse. The scripts emphasized the domestic sphere and personal relationships; Mother Moynihan's biggest worry was the future of her youngest daughter Irene, who fancied herself a modern girl, ambitious for a successful career very much like the creator herself. The tensions between the old and new ways of life were played out in a series of interlocking story lines as characters grasped for their own happiness. Phillips was also shrewd enough to develop ideas that might interest potential sponsors, arguing that for any radio series to be a "utility to its sponsor, [it] must

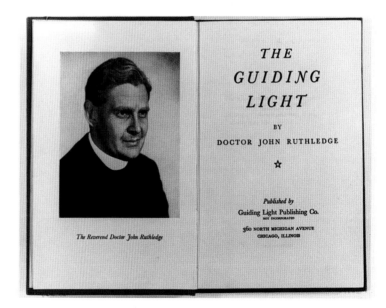

Irna Phillips supervised a companion book, "told by the Reverend Dr. John Ruthledge," that traced the backstory of The Guiding Light

actually sell merchandise; otherwise the object of radio advertising has failed."[9] Among other story elements, Phillips conceived of an engagement and wedding that offered the possibility for product tie-ins.

With a good head for business, Phillips saw the national possibilities for her daily serial and wanted to sell it to one of the networks. She took WGN to court over their claim to the copyright of *Painted Dreams,* but lost the case. Then, acting as an independent producer, she retooled her concept for the NBC Chicago affiliate WMAQ and created *Today's Children* for national network broadcast. The program's opening epigram delineates a major principle of all soap opera: "And today's children with their hopes and dreams, their laughter and tears, shall be the builders of a brighter world tomorrow." Mother Moynihan became Mother Moran, but in Phillips's mind both were modeled on her own mother. So closely were reality and the fictional world intertwined for the creator that when her mother died in 1938, a heartbroken Irna Phillips decided to do the unthinkable in the soap world—she canceled her own serial.

In 1937 Phillips, wanting to capture "life as most of us know it," created her "never-ending" saga, *The Guiding Light,* which has become the longest-running drama in broadcasting history. In the first incarnation of the serial—the life and times of a nonsectarian minister, Dr. John Ruthledge, and his flock in small-town Five Points—Phillips fully realized the essence of the soap opera: a continuous series of first and second acts, with a complex juggling act of dominant and secondary stories that never reach a final denouement. A year after the series began Phillips supervised publication of a companion volume for fans that traced the backstory (the unwritten history that exists before a soap goes on) of *The Guiding Light,* "authored" by the fictitious Dr. Ruthledge. In it she made clear that each character's pain and confusion is interlocked with others in the community. Rose Kransky, for example, born of Jewish parents but refusing to define herself by orthodox rules (very much a reflection of Irna herself), was nurtured by her friendship with Mary Ruthledge, the Reverend's daughter. If Phillips felt the pain of Rose Kransky, her alter superego was Ruthledge, whose philosophy was that

Our Gal Sunday: *Sunday Brinthrope (Vivian Smolen; also played by Dorothy Lowell)*

"no matter how difficult your problems may be . . . others have been faced with the same obstacles, and with faith and determination and courage have managed to overcome them."[10]

By the early forties Irna Phillips was assigned the mantle "Queen of the Soap Opera" by the press. She served as independent producer of her work, packaging entire programs for a sponsor, generally Procter & Gamble, the genre's leading impresario. Working on several serials at the same time, she was generating two million words a year, the equivalent of approximately twenty-five novels. When five serials became too taxing, Phillips hired assistant writers to fill in the dialogue after she blocked the story, but she continued to be the wellspring of plot devices, one of which became a staple of the genre, the amnesia story line. To get them to tune in again, she once said she liked to "cliff-hang" her audience.

There was such a defined universe to a Phillips serial that three of her stories were programmed consecutively to constitute *The General Mills Hour,* which ran for one year in 1945. Within this larger narrative framework Phillips allowed her characters to drift from serial to serial. One of the remaining examples of this experiment of running together programs that are connected by the characters and themes of one creator is a remarkable self-reflexive deliberation on the nature of the soap opera. In the broadcast of May 7, 1945, the eve of V-E Day, Phillips has a character, a World War II veteran, produce a radio drama about his own disability. The fictitious broadcast is listened to and discussed by the other characters in all three serials, who comment that radio stories "taken out of life" can help make "their own" lives better.

The Hummerts and the Serial Factory

Frank and Anne Hummert provide a fascinating contrast to Irna Phillips. Frank Hummert had been working in copywriting and advertising when he noticed "the success of serial fiction in newspapers and magazines."[11] In the early thirties, he decided to translate that serial narrative to the infant medium of radio. He wanted his radio dramas to accommodate the daily pattern of the homemaker, but at the same time to offer a release into the world of romance and fantasy—very different from the "real" world of Irna Phillips. He worked with his assistant Anne Ashenhurst (whom he married in 1935) and writer Charles Robert Douglas Hardy Andrews to devise fantasies to help alleviate the boredom and repetition of ritualistic housework. By the midforties the Hummerts were producing twelve serials a day and were operating what was derided as a soap opera mill, which now might be considered the prototype for a television soap opera's writing staff, where various

Frank and Anne Hummert (both wearing glasses) during production of one of their radio serials

aspects of the scripts are written by different people. [For more on the background and working methods of the Hummerts and other serial writers, see James Thurber's essays on pages 41–64.]

Each Hummert serial answered a basic rhetorical question, around which multiple plots were woven. For *Our Gal Sunday* the question was "can this girl from a small mining town in the West find happiness as the wife of a wealthy and titled Englishman?" In *Backstage Wife* the audience learned what it meant for Mary Noble, the small-town Iowa girl, "to be the wife of a famous Broadway star, dream sweetheart of a million other women." Most of the Hummert plots focused on the gap between the wealthy and the aspiring middle class, bringing comfort to millions of listeners who were struggling with the reality of deprivation, first during the depression years and then World War II. A notable example is the Hummerts'

1938 adaptation of the 1937 film *Stella Dallas*. In the Barbara Stanwyck movie, the self-sacrificing mother is resigned to wait outside the gates of a mansion, feeling she is not good enough to attend her daughter's wedding to the son of the wealthy family. The Hummerts reconcile that disjunction in their fantasy world, and the mother, still obviously from a lower class, feels right at home in the grand Grosvenor mansion and helps both the upstairs and downstairs characters with their problems. Thus, the Hummerts did not try to reflect reality, but rather to improve it, or, as Frank Hummert stated, to paint "against the canvas of everyday American life."[12]

The Daytime Controversy

During the early forties there were more than seventy daytime serials on the air, listened to by approximately half of all women at home. Beginning in 1939, the genre was regularly referred to as "soap opera" by the press,[13] mocking these sentimental tales that were sponsored almost exclusively by manufacturers of household products, especially cleansers. Educators and psychologists were disturbed by the morbid content of the soaps, also called "washboard weepers," and tried to analyze why the audience was habitually addicted to endless stories of calamity and unhappiness. As the country prepared for war, cultural critics theorized that all the suffering on the airwaves was undermining the moral fiber of American womanhood. New York psychiatrist Dr. Louis Berg compared the repetitiveness of the soaps to Hitler's propaganda machine, claiming that each was corrupting the human nervous system.

In the wake of the widespread success of the soaps, a small industry trying to understand the effects of long-term listening began to flourish. Paul Lazarsfeld, director of the Office of Radio Research at Columbia University, discovered two almost contradictory gratifications that women received from the soaps: the first, pure escapism, removed the listener from the drudgery of daily life; and the second, moral guidance, helped the housewife solve her own personal problems. In examining the audience, various studies sponsored by the networks proved that there was little difference in social and cultural activities between listeners and nonlisteners.

Although fantasy remained a consistent aspect of soaps, during World War II the radio serial matured to create more story lines about the realities of wartime. Stella Dallas worked in a munitions factory; one of Ma Perkins's sons died on the European battlefield. The real change in the radio serial, however, came after World War II, and not from reformers but from the television industry, when major daytime sponsors such as General Mills and Pillsbury were lured to the new medium, leaving a major vacuum in the radio schedule. Without the backing of a single advertiser, radio networks experimented with programs that attracted multiple sponsors, including talk and variety programs. By the midfifties, many broadcasting executives felt the serial was a product of depression America and had outlived its usefulness, although the radio soap lingered on until 1960.

The Soap Opera on Television

Despite the serial's proven success in magazine publishing, at the movies, and on radio, there was genuine resistance by television executives to employ the form. One of the visionaries of early television, NBC president Sylvester "Pat" Weaver, felt that the old radio soap opera technique would not work in a visual medium "because of the higher absorption and tension demands of television over radio."[14] Prime-time entertainment first hit its stride in 1948 with the success of Milton Berle's translation of vaudeville to television; it would take at least three more years for the soap opera to successfully adapt to the new technology.

While the established networks, CBS and NBC, concentrated on weekly programs for their nightly schedules, it was newcomer DuMont that experimented with the low-budget serial. In 1944 Lever Brothers sponsored television versions of two radio soaps, *Big Sister* and *Aunt Jenny's True Life Stories*, on DuMont's New York affiliate, and two years later DuMont created the serial *Faraway Hill* especially for the network. Its producer, David P. Lewis, searched for techniques that would not require total viewer attention, allowing the housewife time "to turn away and go on peeling potatoes or knitting."[15] He devised a stream-of-consciousness technique, an offscreen voice that probed the interior motives of the series heroine, Karen St. John, a widow searching for emotional refuge in the country. The most successful television programs immediately after World War II, however, were live remote broadcasts, especially boxing, and the studio-bound *Faraway Hill* faded after three months. Even Irna Phillips failed in her initial attempt, a reworking of her first radio serial *Painted Dreams*,

During the early forties there were more than seventy daytime serials on the air, listened to by approximately half of all women at home

A promotional photo for Aunt Jenny's True Life Stories: radio announcer Dan Seymour and Aunt Jenny (Edith Spencer; also played by Agnes Young); (young actress unknown)

On the early days of Search for Tomorrow

It was a marvelous time! I think one of the big reasons is because we had so little to work with. It brought out the best in everybody. When we went on the air, we had no sets. We were playing in front of a black cyclorama. Picture and door frames hung in thin air. We had almost no props.

We had to create a reality, out of almost nothing. The stories moved so slowly that to fill the time, to fill the reality, to make the relationships real required so much from all of the actors. All we had was each other so it was all in the listening, in the faces.

It was partly because the writers came from radio and they didn't know how to write television. I remember Charles Irving going right through the roof one day, over a scene at the mailbox. And that's all the script said, "This scene takes place at the mailbox." And he said, "What is behind the mailbox? Where is the mailbox? You can't just say—the mailbox." Just like you couldn't, as they used to do in radio, have somebody knock on the door on Monday and it was Wednesday before anybody answered it. It's so obvious now, but in the early days, the writers were just learning.

Mary Stuart
"Jo Tate," Search for Tomorrow

Search for Tomorrow: *Jo Tate (Mary Stuart), Stu Bergman (Larry Haines), and Marge Bergman (Melba Rae)*

because she made no concessions to the visual medium.

One influential experiment from Chicago, a production center noted for its low-key realism, was *Hawkins Falls*, a self-proclaimed television novel about a typical small town that wistfully evoked an earlier America whose way of life was being transformed by the fifties flight to the suburbs. Although this rural community with a population of 6,200 was too far removed from the contemporary American experience to make the show successful in terms of the great soaps (*Hawkins Falls* ran three months in prime time and four years in the afternoon), the genre had finally found a template that would be developed further by cocreator Roy Winsor. In 1951 a veteran of the Hummerts' *Ma Perkins*, Winsor used the dominant heroine archetype from his predecessors' tradition to build the first viable soap, *Search for Tomorrow*, around one female character, Jo Tate. (Jo was played by the indomitable Mary Stuart from day one until the serial ended in 1986.) Winsor insisted on a bare-stage technique for his series and emphasized the close-up to connect his characters to the audience. There was no need for elaborate sets or long shots, since most of the action took place in the living room or kitchen, key places in the geography of a soap. The critical

On As the World Turns

Whenever you think back to World, you have to remember Ted Corday, because he and Irna and Agnes Nixon created the show together. It was the very first half-hour television serial. It's ironic to remember how skeptical the industry was about a half-hour serial. There was enormous skepticism that an audience would commit to a half-hour show. "Too long! It'll never work!"

I should mention that Edge of Night also premiered on the same day with a half-hour show. But it was more of a detective story, not the traditional family-oriented serial. World was really the test case. The show quickly emerged as the number one daytime show and ultimately achieved a 64 percent share of the audience, something that will never again be equaled.

William J. Bell
Creator, The Young and the Restless *and* The Bold and the Beautiful
Cocreator, Another World

Director Ted Corday (left) on the television set of Guiding Light *with associate producer Lucy Rittenberg, producer David Lesan, and a representative from the Compton Advertising Agency*

On an old scene technique

Years ago we used to play more stream-of-consciousness scenes, where we would stand looking pensive and our inner voice would be played on tape. *Strange Interludes.* That's what Ted Corday used to call them. We all hated it. The best, though, was one day I exited a scene in the doctors' lounge, and Henderson Forsythe, who was Dr. Stewart, was still onstage. The camera dollied in, so you knew a stream of consciousness was coming, and I thought, "Gee, when Dr. Stewart thinks, he sounds just like Dr. Cassen [played by Nat Polen]." Of course, they had played the wrong tape.

Don Hastings
"Bob Hughes," *As the World Turns*

The Doctors: *Maggie Powers (Lydia Bruce)*

As the World Turns: *Chris and Nancy Hughes (Don MacLaughlin and Helen Wagner)*

Guiding Light: *Bert Bauer (Charita Bauer) with, at left, Ed Bauer (Martin Hulswit), and Mike Bauer (Don Stewart)*

Doris and Frank Hursley

On Procter & Gamble

P&G controlled the majority of daytime serials and naturally wanted to exercise that control. People like Bob Short and Ed Trach are P&G legends. There would be meetings every three or four months, more often if necessary, although it rarely was. Sometimes we'd meet at Irna's apartment in Chicago. Sometimes in her suite at the Drake Hotel in New York. More often than not, the meetings lasted for an afternoon during which Irna and I would present our story thrusts for the months ahead. There would be comments, suggestions, discussions about new characters and old. In short, very stimulating meetings.

Bob and Ed never once mandated that writers develop stories that didn't excite them or ones that in any way they had misgivings about. They realized what so many producers and network executives don't: that a head writer worthy of the name knows his characters and story better than anyone.

William J. Bell
Creator, The Young and the Restless *and*
The Bold and the Beautiful
Cocreator, Another World

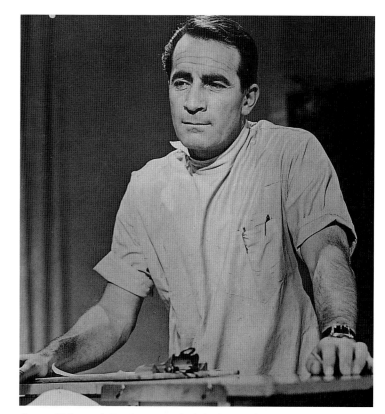

General Hospital: *Dr. Steve Hardy (John Beradino)*

importance of *Search for Tomorrow* is that it found an audience that was emotionally invested enough to make a daily commitment, which proved that the serial had a future on daytime television.

Ten months after *Search*, Irna Phillips brought *The Guiding Light* to television. Reverend Ruthledge and his family had been written out of the series years before, and "the guiding light" in the title no longer had religious connotations, but rather the camaraderie of a loving family in times of upheaval. The core family was now the Bauers, a German-American brood trying to find a better life, first in Selby Flats, a fictionalized West Coast suburb, and later in Springfield, the prototype for the midwestern towns that would provide a haven for most of the soap world.

When Phillips first brought the show to television, the series followed the fifteen-minute format of the ongoing radio program. Up to this point, soaps had always run fifteen minutes, which came to formalize the way a story progressed. Then, in 1956, she created *As the World Turns* and threw out the rules of the radio serial. With this new series she pioneered the first thirty-minute drama, and in the process, reconceived the genre for the visual medium. Few people at the time realized that the thirty-minute serial revolutionized the dynamics of serial storytelling. The longer format allowed Phillips to underline two central tenets: that the heart of the serial is the exchange of feeling and memories between two characters; and that any incident should not affect a handful of characters but the whole community. Serial tellers now had the time to go beyond the core family and explore two families from different social classes, reflecting the search for the American dream of advancement and happiness.

Phillips's other groundbreaking work came in creating the visual look for the entire genre. She worked with her producer/director from radio, Ted Corday, to create an intimate style that emphasized the interior lives of her characters. Slow, lingering close-ups during intimate revelations became the visual paradigm of the serial and presented many possibilities for character revelation.

Days of Our Lives: *Tom and Alice Horton (Macdonald Carey and Frances Reid)*

As the World Turns was structured around the patrician Lowells and the solidly middle-class Hugheses, a clan whose ambitions and frustrations would be a motif for over forty years. It also provided the dominant story line of the late fifties, the romance between Penny Hughes and Jeff Baker, played by Rosemary Prinz and Mark Rydell, who later became a film director. The impetuous Penny and the spoiled Jeff, whom many consider soap's first "supercouple," gave youth its own reasons in the television soap. Phillips, with a new generation of writers, was able to reflect the rebellion and disillusionment of the developing youth culture, while still keeping the family-oriented serial intact.

On Erica versus Rachel

Erica was a very unique character. Rachel on Another World was her precursor to the public, but in fact I created Erica first, since I had written the bible for All My Children before I started head writing Another World. Rachel was a lower-class Erica, her mother was a cleaning woman, and her goals were not nearly so stratospheric as Erica's. Rachel just wanted to marry Russ or somebody with money.

What Erica and Rachel have in common is they thought if they could get their dream, they'd be satisfied. But that dream has been very elusive.

Agnes Nixon
Creator, One Life to Live, All My Children, Loving

On love triangles

Triangles work like gangbusters as a story line. When Jim Riley [head writer, Days of Our Lives] does a show where one sister is about to marry the guy and the minister asks, "Is there any reason someone should object to this?" And the other sister comes down the aisle and says, "Yeah, because I'm pregnant, and he's the father." Hello? You've got three years of story there. At least.

Gary Tomlin
Director, One Life to Live

Another World: *Liz Matthews (Irene Dailey) and Rachel Davis (Victoria Wyndham)*

All My Children: *Nancy Grant (Lisa Wilkinson) and Dr. Christina Karras (Robin Strasser)*

On the genre

I am very proud to be a part of this industry.

My heart and soul for the love of performing and style were formed with the kinds of movies that were made in the thirties and forties. Today, in the absence of the studio system, there is daytime television; we have all of that drama, that style, that panache that you don't often see on other television.

Robin Strasser
"Dorian Lord"
From One Life to Live seminar at
The Museum of Television & Radio,
July 8, 1993

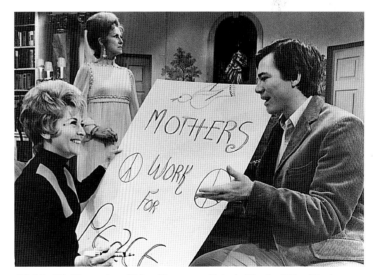

All My Children: *Amy Tyler (Rosemary Prinz), Phoebe Tyler (Ruth Warrick), and Phillip Brent (Richard Hatch)*

Agnes Nixon

All My Children: *Wally McFadden (Jack Magee), Devon Shepherd (Tricia Pursley)*

One Life to Live: *Nora Buchanan (Hillary B. Smith), Hank Gannon (Nathan Purdee), Rachel Gannon (Sandra P. Grant), Drew Buchanan (Victor Brown), R.J. Gannon (Timothy Stickney)*

William J. Bell

Daytime Versus Early Prime Time

Whatever the ultimate root of the critical prejudice against the television soap opera, it is interesting to note that it existed from the beginning, even when daytime and prime-time dramas were much closer in tone and style. During the fifties, daytime serial and live drama shared many of the same aesthetic values: both emphasized psychology of character and the power of the revelatory close-up; both employed actors who had training in the theater and writers working in the realistic tradition of the Broadway problem play; both were performed live, solidifying their association with a theatrical experience. The phrase that defined the apogee of anthology drama, Chayefsky's "this marvelous world of the ordinary,"[16] could equally apply to the best of Irna Phillips. Yet whereas the masters of live drama—Paddy Chayefsky, Rod Serling, and Gore Vidal—were praised for authenticity and depth, there was little critical appraisal of any kind for daytime.

By the end of the decade, serial and prime-time television were on divergent paths. West Coast studios were producing the evening schedule, and television was no longer live but recorded on film, with Hollywood production values. (Soaps were broadcast live until the late sixties and then performed as if live, on tape.) The first genre to conquer prime time, the Western, underlined the rigid dichotomy between television in the afternoon and in the evening—the soap opera and the horse opera. Daytime was the province of perceived feminine values, talk and negotiation; prime time was the arena for masculine resolve, on the range or in the streets. Soaps catered to character growth and memory—Bert Bauer matured from an anxious housewife into *Guiding Light's* philosophical matriarch—while prime time was an existential wilderness, where lead characters acted without the past as a guide. The new heroes of prime time, Cheyenne and Matt Dillon, discovered themselves anew each week, continuing characters without the benefit of the soap's connecting memories.

A Look at Sponsorship

Throughout the fifties the most successful serials were put together by advertising agencies for a sponsor. This sponsor-originated formula had its roots in radio and ceded production control to the agency, which in theory better understood the needs of its intended audience. CBS dominated the daytime ratings because of its alliance with Procter & Gamble, which worked directly with the early soap auteurs, Irna Phillips and Roy Winsor. September 3, 1951, proved to be a defining day for P&G: it not only debuted *Search for Tomorrow,* but also marketed two new products, Joy and Spic and Span, to its largely female audience. With the sponsor owning the production, the network's role was passive, pro-viding the airwaves and exercising little creative authority.

To compete with P&G's tightly controlled schedule on CBS, both ABC and NBC decided to package their own soaps, assuming greater control over daytime programming. After several misfires by both networks, in 1963 ABC hired Frank and Doris Hursley, longtime writers of *Search for Tomorrow,* to create a "daytime *Ben Casey,*"[17] the popular evening series starring Vince Edwards. The hospital, that dramatic intersection where personal and professional spheres collided, had been a fixture on radio serials. Irna Phillips had remarked that doctors especially were "an integral part of everything I have written,"[18] introducing the first serial surgeon on *The Road of Life* in 1937. It is ironic that in the early sixties daytime executives were looking to prime time for inspiration, instead of the soap's own considerable history on radio.

The Hursleys' creation, *General Hospital,* was produced at the ABC facilities in Hollywood and brought a new element to the soap. Until then most of the serials had been produced in New York, with roots in the city's performing arts heritage. Beginning with *General Hospital,* soap producers on the West Coast started their own tradition, using videotape, but searching for the more polished look and artful camera angles associated with the movies. Casting directors now searched for actors who had performed on film, whether in the movies or on television. The star of *General Hospital,* John Beradino, had previously been featured in the syndicated series *I Led Three Lives* and worked in such genre series on film as *Cheyenne* and *The Untouchables.* In 1965 the collaboration between Hollywood and the serial was further solidified when Columbia Pictures Television became a partner in another medical soap, *Days of Our Lives.* Although created by Irna Phillips and Ted Corday, an East Coast team, *Days* featured Hollywood leading man Macdonald Carey. It was the first serial to be broadcast in color, although for NBC, which had pioneered color technology in the early fifties, this was late in the game for bringing color to the daytime soap.

Agnes Nixon and William J. Bell

Irna Phillips taught her most gifted progeny, Agnes Nixon and William J. Bell (who were toddlers when the domestic soaps began), not only story structure and character development, but, more importantly, a respect for the métier. In Nixon's words, from this respect emerges "the ability and capacity to develop one's craft and perhaps even raise the standards of the form."[19] Both Nixon and Bell served an arduous apprenticeship under Phillips, and emerged with the belief that soap opera had meaning and relevance in the turbulent world of the late sixties.

Nixon began as a dialogue writer on Phillips's *Woman in White*, a radio serial about the checkered romance between a nurse and a fledgling surgeon. She wrote scripts for early television anthologies and developed the inaugural stories for *Search for Tomorrow*. Returning to the Phillips fold, she wrote for *Guiding Light* for thirteen years, eight as head writer, and cocreated the defining television soap, *As the World Turns*. During these years with Phillips the Nixon touch emerges in her treatment of Bert Bauer, the "tentpole" character of *Guiding Light*. Bert, played by Charita Bauer for thirty-five years, had matured into the homey philosopher of the series by the early sixties, and viewers were stunned when she underwent treatment for uterine cancer. Nixon had struggled with P&G executives and network censors to have Bert first undergo a Pap smear test. Capitalizing on the temporal quality of the serial, Nixon played the cancer story line out over many months, educating her public about the necessity of medical prevention. The soap form and the pedagogical story coalesced perfectly, and the positive viewer reaction suggested a more sophisticated audience than the industry had realized.

All My Children: *Dimitri Marick (Michael Nader) and Erica Kane (Susan Lucci)*

On Susan Lucci and Erica

Susan Lucci has been able to invest her enormous talent in Erica. It's such a mercurial, quixotic thing, when a character becomes so beloved over so many years. Susan has been able to maintain her feistiness and indomitable spirit, no matter what she's gone through. And it's amusing and outrageous and encouraging to women. Women understand Erica because what made her the way she is, was a tragedy. She has a severe abandonment complex.

Agnes Nixon
Creator, One Life to Live,
All My Children, Loving

While she was head writing *Guiding Light*, Nixon had created the bible for what would become *All My Children*. Procter & Gamble was not able to find a slot for it, but offered her head-writing duties on a struggling show, *Another World*, which Phillips and Bill Bell created in 1964. Much has been written about Nixon's ability to dramatize topical issues, but here she displayed her mastery of traditional soap fundamentals. Nixon revived *Another World* with a romantic triangle that sustained itself for more than seven years. With the success of *General Hospital* on ABC, the network allowed Nixon to create a signature series, *One Live to Live*, allowing her to realize a personal ambition to take soap operas out of WASP Valley.[20] She conceived a multicultural community of ethnic types and challenged her audience to confront their prejudices. While prime-time television was receiving con-

The Bold and the Beautiful: *Taylor Hayes (Hunter Tylo), Ridge Forrester (Ronn Moss), and Brooke Logan (Katherine Kelly Lang)*

gratulations for starring Diahann Carroll as the innocuous black nurse on *Julia*, Nixon developed a black character, Carla Gray, who was passing for white. In superb use of dramatic irony, the audience was clued in to her heritage before her suitors, a white doctor and a black intern.

Nixon consolidated soap traditions and advanced the respectability of the genre. While she maintained the theatrical base of her mentor, having all her serials produced in New York facilities, her work has made creative use of videotape. (Two important examples are the exploration of the fantasies and desires of lead characters, notably the split personality of Victoria Lord, and going on location outside the studio, as for the unscripted Odyssey House sequences for *One Life to Live*.) Most importantly, she sustained the moral seriousness that characterized Phillips's creations. When her story of a peace activist was debated in the *New York Times*, Nixon brought daytime to a critical plateau it never had reached.[21] Her examinations of the generation gap and sixties politics predated by several years prime time's breakthrough series, *All in the Family*.

Bill Bell was in advertising before Irna Phillips made him dialogue writer on the *Guiding Light* in 1957. Working in the same room with Phillips he cowrote *As the World Turns* for nine years, where he developed the ability to capture an audience with expansive storytelling, and to allow stories to go on past the traditional breaking points. Remaining in Chicago, Bell was appointed head writer of *Days of Our Lives* on the West Coast in an effort to salvage one of Phillips's floundering cocreations. Sensing a potential audience fascination with abnormal psychology, Bell ventured into sexual territories hitherto unexplored anywhere in television. His signature story line for *Days* was the return of an amnesiac Korean War veteran, whose looks had been horribly disfigured in captivity. Having undergone plastic surgery, he returns unrecognized to the nurturing community of Salem and falls in love with his sister. Integrating such sexual taboos as incest and rape into the narrative of the soap has remained Bell's specialty.

Where the center of Phillips's soap universe had been the kitchen and the living room, Bell staked his claim to the bedroom. His first creation with his wife, Lee Phillip Bell, *The Young and the Restless*, took for granted the sexual revolution that was sweeping America. Although he appropriated from Phillips the two-family schemata that he knew so well, Bell focused on the sexual desires and entrapments of the younger characters. *The Young and the Restless*, packaged by Columbia Pictures Television, furthered the integration of Hollywood production values into the serial. Bell and his production team cast glamorous model types for lead roles and pho-

tographed his stars in senuous lighting. There was no mistaking a Bell close-up; its lingering caress would have made Garbo or Dietrich proud. In 1987 Bell underscored the Hollywood connection with his next creation, *The Bold and the Beautiful*, by setting the serial in Los Angeles, one of the few specific sites in the soap world, and by concentrating on the chic fashion industry.

One of the many defining legacies of the Phillips-Nixon-Bell collaboration is the soap archetype that transformed and defined the entire genre: the bitch goddess. Since the sixties no character has energized more plots than the girl from the wrong side of the tracks who will stop at nothing to achieve material happiness. The once-passive Cinderella of radio serials, a lowly commoner waiting to be swept off her feet, was transformed in the early sixties into a hurricane of lustful desires. Phillips and Bell conspired with actress Eileen Fulton to create the prototypical home-wrecking villainess of unlimited ambition, Lisa Miller on *As the World Turns*. Nixon revitalized Phillips and Bell's *Another World* with the Bitch of Bay City, Rachel Davis, who lusted after power and privilege. Rachel was modeled on a character that Nixon envisioned for her own soap, which took five years to find a sponsor. When that serial, *All My Children*, was finally produced in 1970, Nixon unleashed Erica Kane as a conniving teenage vixen. After years of amorous escapades and serial marriages, Susan Lucci's character has become the femme fatale incarnate. For Nixon and Bell, who have led the way in exploring family problems, the avenging goddess archetype borrows from the Hummerts' tradition an element of pure fantasy, thereby giving their work the possibility of outrageous fun and exaggerated melodrama that is missing from their mentor's.

The Monty Revolution

By the midseventies most soaps had expanded into an hour every day. As production became more costly and complex, the role of the executive producer became as crucial as the head writer's. It fell to the producer to fuse the writing and production teams into a unified whole, sustaining the look and rhythm of a specific soap world, day in and day out, fifty-two weeks a year. Producing the equivalent of more than 100 movies, the executive producer was like the mogul of old, overseeing a highly coordinated studio.

The producer who epitomized this new power was a long-time veteran of the field, Gloria Monty. A director of Roy Winsor's *The Secret Storm* for sixteen years, Monty left, and experimented with ways to make daytime drama less studio-bound. She directed the first daytime special shot entirely on location, *This Child of Mine*, but when she was put in charge of *General Hospital* she changed all the rules. During her first meeting with Tony Geary, the actor confessed, "I hate soap opera." Monty replied: "Honey, so do I. I want you to help me change all that."[22]

Monty subverted all the strictures that she had learned during her live television days in New York. For one thing, she wanted the pacing of a prime-time program, so she eliminated the long pauses of the serial and ordered more than twice the number of scenes per episode of the average soap. In addition to redesigning the sets and costumes, she challenged the form itself. She romantically paired troubled teen Laura Vining with the streetwise, antihero Luke Spencer. United by a problematic rape scene, which Monty labeled a "choreographed seduction,"[23] but which others saw as unmitigated violence, Luke and Laura spent the summer of 1980 on the lam, an unprecedented story line that liberated the characters from the established community. Monty enlivened the escapades with homages to Hitchcock and, particularly, to Frank Capra's *It Happened One Night*. With the new look capturing a youthful and collegiate audience, *General Hospital* became a cultural phenomenon; a benchmark equal to anything in the history of television.

Serial Memory

For almost fifty years, beginning in radio, the techniques and strategies of the daytime serial were rejected by evening entertainment. Prime time's major experiment with the serial, *Peyton Place* (1964–69), had limited appeal; only the heavily promoted first season reached the Nielsen top twenty-five programs. Nighttime's most successful use of the genre was parody, epitomized by "As the Stomach Turns," a series of sketches on *The Carol Burnett Show*, and the almost surrealistic serials *Mary Hartman, Mary Hartman* and *Soap.*

In the late seventies, with competition from the cable industry, network producers began looking for new ways to capture an audience. They reconsidered the form of the soap opera, a genre that they had derided for years. Both *Dallas* and *Dynasty* employed the cliff-hanger to engage an audience in the continuing sagas of greed and lust in a core family, the Ewings and Carringtons, respectively. In the eighties, the writers of episodic television, wanting to find more dimensions for their characters, experimented with stories that lingered over many episodes and with characters who had a consciousness of their own histories. Several prime-time series did pioneering work in employing the serial structure, including *St. Elsewhere, Cheers,* and *L.A. Law.* But the place it really all began for nighttime was *Hill Street Blues.*

Whereas Joe Friday of the fifties *Dragnet* seemed to have neither a personal life nor any memories of his previous cases, Captain Frank Furillo entered the landscape of *Hill Street Blues* with a complicated backstory: a son and an ex-wife, a job in turmoil, and a budding romance with the district attorney. Importantly, Furillo's history was not just a premise. Cocreator Steven Bochco used the details of the character's life to spin story lines that explored the private and public turmoils of Furillo's life each week, interlocking those situations with equally rich vignettes of ten or more characters. This soap opera structure forms the basis for the powerful storytelling that characterizes Bochco's series. The audience is drawn deeper and deeper into the world of the Hill Street station, gathering memories of the series and its characters over many years.

Time and memory for both the characters and the audience are at the heart of the soap opera. While prime-time programming since *Hill Street* has incorporated the serial as a sustaining narrative element, there is no way that evening drama can match how familiar a character can become to a soap opera viewer: the combined run of *Hill Street Blues* and *Cheers* equals approximately one year's worth of any hour-long soap. Moreover, the very narrative structure of the soap demands that the viewer bring memories of the pain and joy and subtle emotional nuances to each scene.

When characters with such rich, penetrating histories as Victor Newman and Nikki Reed on *The Young and the Restless* or Alan and Monica Quartermaine on *General Hospital* confront each other, the viewer fills in the sustained silences and piercing reaction shots that characterize the genre with a keen knowledge of their pasts, thus becoming an important partner in the scene. This deep, emotional involvement in a story that is unfolding day by day over years

General Hospital *producer Gloria Monty with Robert Scorpio (Tristan Rogers), Laura Spencer (Genie Francis), and Luke Spencer (Anthony Geary)*

is ultimately the triumph of the soap opera. No other art form can achieve, much less sustain, this kind of connection with an audience for so long in such a deeply satisfying way.

The audience for the daytime serial is following in the footsteps of Dickens's passionate admirers, who likewise embraced fictionalized characters as another family: that has been the essential quality of the serial, linking story with audience. The history of the soap opera on radio and televi-sion, lasting more than sixty-five years, is in itself a continu-ing story, with the work of Irna Phillips being carried forward by Agnes Nixon and William J. Bell. As new creative forces enter the world of daytime, whoever carries on the work of Nixon and Bell well into the twenty-first century will by lin-eage have some connection to Irna Phillips, no doubt reaf-firming her vision that "we do not live in this world alone, but in a thousand other worlds."

The Young and the Restless: *Nikki and Victor Newman (Melody Thomas Scott and Eric Braeden)*

Essays From

"Soapland"

In 1948 James Thurber wrote a series of five articles about radio soap operas for the *New Yorker*. The articles are "O Pioneers!" (May 15, 1948), "Ivorytown, Rinsoville, Anacinburg, and Crisco Corners" (May 29, 1948), "Sculptors in Ivory" (June 12, 1948), "The Invisible People" (July 3, 1948), and "The Listening Women" (July 24, 1948). Three of these essays are reprinted on the following pages.

The New Yorker, *May 15, 1948*

Anne and Frank Hummert

O PIONEERS!
by James Thurber

In the intolerable heat of last August, one Ezra Adams, of Clinton, Iowa, strode across his living room and smashed his radio with his fists, in the fond hope of silencing forever the plaintive and unendurable chatter of one of his wife's favorite afternoon programs. He was fined ten dollars for disturbing the peace, and Mrs. Adams later filed suit for divorce. I have no way of knowing how many similarly oppressed husbands may have clapped him on the back or sent him greetings and cigars, but I do know that his gesture was as futile as it was colorful. He had taken a puny sock at a tormentor of great strength, a deeply rooted American institution of towering proportions. Radio daytime serials, known to the irreverent as soap opera, dishpan drama, washboard weepers, and cliffhangers, have for years withstood an array of far more imposing attackers, headed by Dr. Louis I. Berg, a New York psychiatrist and soap opera's Enemy No. 1.

A soap opera is a kind of sandwich, whose recipe is simple enough, although it took years to compound. Between thick slices of advertising, spread twelve minutes of dialogue, add predicament, villainy, and female suffering in equal measure, throw in a dash of nobility, sprinkle with tears, season with organ music, cover with a rich announcer sauce, and serve five times a week. A soap opera may also contain a teaser ("Be sure to tune in next Monday for a special announcement"), a giveaway ("Send a box top and twenty-five cents for a gorgeous lovebird brooch"), a contest offer ("Complete this sentence and win a Bendix washer"), or a cowcatcher or hitchhike, that is, a brief commercial for another of the sponsor's products, such as a Kolynos plug on an Anacin program. It is the hope of every advertiser to habituate the housewife to an engrossing narrative whose optimum length is forever and at the same time to saturate all levels of her consciousness with the miracle of a given product, so that she will be aware of it all the days of her life and mutter its name in her sleep.

Beginning at ten-thirty in the morning and ending at six o'clock in the evening with the final organ strains of "Front Page Farrell," thirty-six soap operas are now being broadcast from New York stations Monday through Friday. Sixteen of N.B.C.'s run one after another, and C.B.S. has a procession of thirteen. Eight or ten other serials, without New York outlets, bring the nation's present total to around forty-five. The average is closer to fifty, and at one time before the war sixty-five such programs overburdened the air waves and the human ear. Soap opera has an estimated audience of twenty million listeners, mainly women in the home, for whose attention the serials' sponsors—Procter & Gamble, Lever Brothers, General Mills, General Foods, and other big manufacturers of household products—pay a total of nearly thirty-five million dollars a year. The average serial costs about eighteen thousand dollars a week, of which three thousand is for talent and fifteen thousand for network time. The latter figure includes basic time costs, plus a fifteen-per-cent cut for the advertising agency handling the show. Serials are variously owned, most of them by individuals or radio-production firms, some by sponsors, advertising agencies, networks, and local stations.

The headquarters of soap opera is now in New York and has been for a dozen years or so, but serials originated in Chicago. No other city has ever disputed Chicago's half-proud, half-sheepish claim to the invention of the story-coated advertising medium that either fascinates or distresses so many millions of people. Since soap opera is a form of merchandising rather than of art, the records of its beginnings are somewhat vague. It waited fifteen years for serious researchers, and it has had few competent critics. Almost none of the serial writers has saved his scripts. If the more than four thousand scripts (eight million words) of "Just Plain Bill," the oldest serial now on the air, had been saved, they would fill twenty trunks, and the entire wordage of soap opera to date, roughly two hundred and seventy-five million words, would fill a good-sized library.

The idea of a daytime radio program that would entertain the housewife and sell her a bill of goods at the same time was in the air in Chicago around 1928, "give or take a year," as one serial writer puts it. During the next four years, a dozen persons fiddled and tinkered with the ancient art of story-telling, trying to adapt it to the cramped limitations of radio, the young, obstreperous, and blind stepsister of entertainment. The principal figures in this experimentation were (not necessarily in the order of their appearance or importance) Mrs. Gertrude Berg, a matronly, warm-hearted woman, sincerely dedicated to the task of dramatizing Jewish family life; Mrs. Elaine Carrington, a magazine writer whose market had declined with the depression; Irna Phillips, a Dayton, Ohio, schoolteacher; Paul Rhymer, a young network executive; Frank Hummert, a smart advertising man; his young assistant, Mrs. Anne S. Ashenhurst; and Hummert's star writer, Robert D. Andrews, an able Chicago *Daily News* reporter who was destined before he quit, in 1942, to write thirty million words for radio (give or take three million). The progress of the serial pioneers was slow. There were major handicaps to overcome: the wariness of advertisers, mainly, and the thin resources of talent in the Middle West. But there was a smell of gold in Chicago, and the pioneers were indefatigable. In the field of radio narrative, continuous from day to day and week to week, they had one famous and successful nighttime model to study—"Amos 'n' Andy." It was a comedy program, of course, and the pioneers didn't want that; it had created, in George (King Fish) Stevens, a character worthy of a place in the fabulous line of rascals that extends from Sam Slick to Donald Duck, and the pioneers didn't want anything as difficult and wonderful as that; but it had proved that Americans like a continued story on the air, fifteen minutes a day, five days a week, and the pioneers did want that.

Mrs. Berg, a New York woman who did some of her early writing in Chicago, was one of the first of the pioneers to come up with a popular and durable soap opera, "The Goldbergs," which began as a nighttime show twenty years ago and took to the daytime air several years later. It ran until 1945, when Procter & Gamble, who had had it since 1937, dropped it. This incredibly long and loving saga of Molly Goldberg, her family, and her friends had become such an important part of Gertrude Berg's life that she was lost and bewildered when the serial ended its run. She herself had played Molly Goldberg and had come to identify herself completely with the character. For sixteen years, she had been known to her intimates as Molly. She found it impossible to give up the Goldbergs, and two years ago she set about putting them on the stage. In "Me and Molly," the old family reached Broadway last February, with Mrs. Berg in the leading role. She demonstrated, even to those critics who saw no art or significance in her play, why her beloved family had lasted for nearly two decades on the air. Mrs. Berg, as author and actress, had transferred to the stage the simplicity, honesty, and warm belief in common humanity that had distinguished her serial, for all its faults. "In her code of values," wrote Brooks Atkinson, "Mrs. Berg is more nearly right than Noel Coward, who is a more expert playwright; and her family makes better company than the overcivilized family J. B. Priestley introduced to us in 'The Linden Tree.' " Soap opera, last February, thus won the applause, however mild, of gentlemen who up to that point had probably said of "The Goldbergs"

no more than "Shut that damn thing off before I throw it out the window." Clarence L. Menser, later chief of program production for N.B.C. in Chicago, likes to feel that he had an influence on the early scripts of "The Goldbergs," but Mrs. Berg wrote them herself and the serial bore the lusty stamp of her own vitality. At about the same time, Paul Rhymer, a member of the N.B.C. staff in Chicago, began to turn out a serial called "Vic and Sade," which was eventually to become just as popular as "The Goldbergs." "Vic and Sade" began in June, 1932, and lasted more than thirteen years. A half-dozen old-timers fell by the wayside during the war years, along with "The Goldbergs" and "Vic and Sade," owing to retrenching

The Goldbergs: *Molly Goldberg (Gertrude Berg)*

Myrt and Marge: Myrt (Myrtle Vail; also played by Alice Yourman) and Marge (Donna Damerel Flick; also played by Helen Mack and Alice Goodkin)

by advertisers and other commercial factors. More than a score of the serials that were on the air in 1940 have since disappeared. "Vic and Sade," like another favorite, called "Myrt and Marge," differed from most serials in that it was basically humorous. Edgar Lee Masters, I am told, once said that the Rhymer serial presented the best American humor of its day.

Elaine Carrington, another of the pioneers, had sold many short stories to women's magazines in the nineteen-twenties. They dealt with the frustrations, heartbreaks, kindliness, nastiness, cruelties, and tragedies of the middle class. She created little men, cold women, and thankless children to the taste of various editors. Her dialogue was frequent and facile. She felt that radio might be more profitable than magazine writing in the depression years, and in 1932 she decided to take a crack at it. Her first program, "Red Adams," was put on by N.B.C., as a half-hour nighttime show, once a week. It was broadcast on a sustaining basis; that is, it had no sponsor and the network paid the production costs. Mrs. Carrington got seventy-five dollars a script. At the end of three months, the Beech-Nut Company decided to sponsor "Red Adams," as a

daytime serial. They agreed to pay Mrs. Carrington a hundred dollars apiece for three scripts a week. They also wanted the title changed. Adams is the name of a Beech-Nut rival celebrated for the singing commercial that begins, "I like Chiclets candy-coated chewing gum." Mrs. Carrington changed the name to "Red Davis." In 1936, Procter & Gamble offered Mrs. Carrington twice as much money per script for five scripts a week. She accepted, and the name was changed again, this time to "Pepper Young's Family." Under the aegis of Procter & Gamble, Mrs. Carrington prospered and proliferated. "Pepper Young's Family" is still going, and she now is responsible for "Rosemary" and "When a Girl Marries," too.

Mrs. Carrington's original radio income of seventy-five dollars a week has grown to an estimated forty-five hundred. Unlike the majority of serial authors, who are merely hired to

Elaine Carrington

Irna Phillips

write soap operas and are known disparagingly as "dialoguers," Mrs. Carrington was wise and firm enough to retain the ownership of her literary properties. She leases broadcasting rights to the sponsors. Most dialoguers get credit on the air only once a week, but Mrs. Carrington's name is mentioned before and after each of her shows. Today she lives in a penthouse apartment in the West Fifties and a country place in Bridgehampton. Aided by only a few notes on a sheet of memo paper, she dictates her scripts into a dictaphone, usually standing. Her working hours are from 10 A.M. to 4 P.M., with time out for a long lunch. She never bothers about hearing a playback. Her secretary takes the record off the machine and transcribes the dialogue at her own office. Mrs. Carrington rarely listens to one of her soap operas—she prefers to call them daytime serials—and has never heard a broadcast of any of her colleagues' serials. She is known as

the Member in Mink to the other members of the Radio Writers Guild, which she helped to found and on whose committees she has frequently served. When the Guild threatened to go out on strike in April, 1947, for recognition, reasonable rights, basic minimum pay, and a general "area of dignity," Mrs. Carrington agreed to walk out with her less prosperous co-workers. The networks finally consented to enter into negotiations with the Guild, and the strike was called off. The Guild won most of its demands from the networks but is now engaged in a grim battle with the American Association of Advertising Agencies.

No other woman writer of soap operas has written as many words as Irna Phillips, or made as much money. Miss Phillips, a brown-haired, blue-eyed native of Chicago now in her middle forties, became studio-struck after she graduated from the University of Illinois. She had originally decided to become a teacher, and after a year and a half at William Woods College, in Missouri, she was made an instructor at a normal school in Dayton, Ohio, where she specialized in storytelling and dramatics for children. In 1930, at the age of twenty-eight, she went back to Chicago on a visit and made a tour of its broadcasting studios, which still held a strong fascination for her. At WMAQ, she was mistaken for someone seeking an audition. A book was thrust into her hands and she was asked to read Eugene Field's "The Bow-Leg Boy." She was offered a job as an actress on the spot, but when she found out that she wouldn't be paid, she returned to her school in Dayton. In the days before the American Federation of Radio Artists and the Writers Guild were formed, the broadcasting industry took an easy and cynical advantage of actors and authors, many of whom, for the sake of a foothold, worked for nothing. On a later trip to Chicago, she was asked to write a script for a free half hour on one of the station's Memorial Day schedules. She did the job with considerable speed and also read it over the air. She was not paid for either her writing or her performance, but radio was now definitely in her blood and she came back to work for nothing throughout her summer vacation. She had her trunks packed for her return to Dayton in September when somebody at WGN asked her to write a family serial. When she discovered, to her surprise, that she would get fifty dollars a week for this, she unpacked and went to work. She spent the next seven months writing a serial called "Painted Dreams," and her salary rose to a hundred dollars a week. It wasn't long before the ambitious lady learned that the studio intended to peg her salary permanently at fifty-two hundred dollars a year. She instantly resigned and went to work for N.B.C. in Chicago, once again for no money at all but with the hope and determination to make a financial success of her writing and acting this time.

Miss Phillips began to write, and to act in, a serial called "Today's Children," which is still on the air. Once she got into the swing of things, she invented story lines with such facility that she could dictate six scripts a day. Soap operas involving family life were easy for her, since she was one of ten children. "Painted Dreams" had been ignored by the sponsors of soap operas for many months, but "Today's Children" was snapped up by a sponsor almost at once, and so were her subsequent ones—"Woman in White," "Right to Happiness," "The Guiding Light," "Road of Life," and "Lonely Women." All of them except "Lonely Women" are still being broadcast. Miss Phillips learned to dictate her scripts to a stenographer while sitting on the arm of a chair or pacing back and forth, acting out each part. In the beginning, she had typed her scripts, and then she sometimes ran so close to the broadcast deadline that pages were whipped out of her typewriter, mimeographed, and handed to the actors without editing. When she took up dictating, she could turn out sixty thousand words a week, or around three million a year. She learned a lesson in the tough field of radio when WGN and the Chicago *Tribune,* which owns that station, claimed the ownership of "Painted Dreams" and were sustained by the courts. She had copyrighted several of the scripts of this serial, but her claim that it was her property was disallowed, since it was held that she had been hired to write the serial and had not actually created it. This technical point has been a source of disagreement and litigation ever since soap operas began. Facing the hard commercial world, Miss Phillips developed a shrewd business personality. Her forthrightness used to frighten into numbed silence William Ramsey, of Procter & Gamble, perhaps the biggest sponsor's man in radio. They later became friends. Ramsey, some years ago, bought the rights to three of her serials— "Right to Happiness," for seventy-five thousand dollars, and "Road of Life" and "The Guiding Light," for fifty thousand dollars each, and the first two of these have since been written by others. The "Painted Dreams" case had taught Miss Phillips the art of establishing beyond legal doubt her rights to her own material. At the height of her production, in the middle nineteen-thirties, she is said to have made in some years as much as a quarter of a million dollars. The vast volume of scripts eventually became too much for her to handle by herself, and she hired a staff of assistants.

Miss Phillips' troubles were not over yet, however. In 1944 Emmons C. Carlson, promotion manager for N.B.C. in Chicago, filed suit against her for an accounting of her income on "The Guiding Light," asserting that he had helped originate the material. A lower court decided in favor of Miss Phillips, but a superior court, on appeal, reversed the decision, and Mr. Carlson received a large amount of money in a final settlement of the case. The sponsors of "The Guiding Light" at the time the suit was filed were General Mills, but they subsequently dropped the program. Ramsey grabbed the show for Procter & Gamble. In 1945, Miss Phillips returned to Northwestern, where she had studied for a year, to teach classes in the writing of radio serials on the side, and shortly afterward she moved to California. Her serials have been described as vehicles of evil and also as documents sincerely devoted to public welfare. Miss Phillips now writes only "The Guiding Light," for a thousand dollars a week.

In 1927, Frank Hummert, one of the most influential figures in the history of soap operas, became a vice-president of Blackett & Sample, a Chicago advertising agency. The Messrs. Blackett and Sample wanted to round out their firm with a topflight idea man. Hummert was one of the best-paid men

Vic and Sade: *Sade and Vic Gook (Bernardine Flynn and Art Van Harvey)*

in advertising. He had been chief copy writer for Lord & Thomas in New York since 1920 and was the white-haired boy of the company's president, Albert Lasker. Hummert is an extreme example of that variety of human being classified by Dr. William Herbert Sheldon as the cerebrotonic ectomorph—the thin, unmuscular type, thoughtful, sensitive, quiet to the point of shyness. He had been a reporter for a while in his younger days, but his recessive temperament was not suited to that aggressive calling. He liked to work at home, and during his seven years as a copy writer he rarely showed up at the office. He had hit on the idea of writing advertising as if it were feature news, and the idea was successful. The one thing he enjoys remembering from the old advertising days is the work he did on behalf of the Brunswick New Hall of Fame, which brought new voices to the operatic and concert stages. Blackett & Sample became Blackett-Sample-Hummert, though the new man was not a partner. The change was made because it was felt that his name would lend a certain prestige to the agency, and he began to build up a unit of his own in the company for the production of radio programs.

Sample introduced Hummert, one day, to a small, smartly dressed young woman named Anne S. Ashenhurst and later suggested to him that she might develop into a useful assistant. Hummert said he was skeptical, but he was persuaded to give the young woman a trial. Mrs. Ashenhurst was a graduate of Goucher and had been a reporter for the Baltimore Sun and the Paris Herald. She was the wife of John Ashenhurst, a reporter she had met on the Herald. Her lack of radio and advertising experience was offset by what proved to be a sound understanding of how to catch and hold the ear of the woman radio listener. Like Hummert, she had an inventive mind and could make up a story line and write nimble dialogue. Hummert and Mrs. Ashenhurst figured that the largely fallow daytime air of twenty years ago could be transformed into valuable advertising time.

Things moved slowly at first. Advertisers favored evening hours, because they were convinced that radio entertainment would not be popular during the day. Most men and many women, they pointed out, worked from eight or nine in the morning until five in the afternoon. They admitted that the millions of American housewives acted as purchasing agents for the home, but they did not see how this peripatetic mass of busy women could be made into an attentive audience. The housewife was notoriously all over the place, upstairs and down, indoors and out, feeding the children, cleaning the house, hanging up clothes in the yard, talking on the phone. Hummert and his assistant decided to invent a daytime program first and then try to adjust it to the ambulant nature of

the housewife. What they needed to begin with was a young writer with an indestructible typewriter, strong wrists, a story sense, and the knack of stringing out words. They came up finally with a young man beyond their dreams of stamina and fluency, who was eventually to become one of radio's legendary figures, Charles Robert Douglas Hardy Andrews.

Andrews was a reporter on the Chicago Daily News and editor of its Midweek magazine. If Hummert was a perfect ectomorph, Andrews was a superb example of what Dr. Sheldon has called the mesomorph—big, strong, sanguine, energetic, and inclined more to activity than to contemplation. He was almost six feet tall, weighed two hundred pounds, and boasted a chest measurement of forty-six inches. He dressed better than most reporters, liked to wear rings, and always carried a cane. He was once described in the now defunct Chicagoan as "a pen-and-ink illustration of a college-graduated heavyweight champion in a love story in a slick-paper magazine." The cathedral calm of the sound-proof office had no allure for Andrews. He could pound a typewriter in a room with a dozen other people pounding typewriters, and he could write in his bedroom while the neighbors' children bawled and radios blared. The attention of Hummert and Mrs. Ashenhurst had been called to a serial story in the Daily News entitled "Three Girls Lost" and signed Robert D. Andrews. Andrews had, on a bet, batted out "Three Girls Lost" in seven days, writing about fifteen thousand words every night. The friend who didn't think he could do it must have been unaware that Andrews had once won a typing contest sponsored by the Royal Typewriter Company. Andrews was later to turn out a hundred thousand words a week over a period of years, without losing a pound or whitening a hair.

The Hummert office phoned Andrews one day at the News and asked him to come up for a conference. Andrews' first serial for Hummert was "The Stolen Husband," and it was read over the air by an actor impersonating the author, a device that was not successful, in spite of the fact that, in passages of dialogue, the actor changed his tone and accent for the various characters, in an effort to build the interest up. The audience response was not enthusiastic, so the final chapters were done with several actors. Meanwhile, Grosset & Dunlap had decided to publish "Three Girls Lost" as a novel, and the Fox Film Corporation had bought the movie rights for a new young actress named Loretta Young. Andrews' breakneck writing speed was mentioned with a trace of awe by a columnist or two. A gossip journalist, digging into the past of the demon writer, revealed that at the age of sixteen he had rattled off, for a hundred and fifty dollars, a hundred-thousand-word serial story for a newspaper-contest promoter and that he had been city editor of the

Minneapolis *Journal* before he was twenty-one. When Andrews hit his stride and began to turn out five radio scripts a day, the author of a book called "How to Write for Radio" declared that he was not one man but three or four. "Charles Robert Douglas Hardy Andrews," said the author, "is a syndicate."

Hummert's second radio venture, "Bill the Barber," is still on the air, under the title of "Just Plain Bill." The story of the barber, his daughter, and his son-in-law and their mixups with the good people and the bad was written by Andrews for its first ten years. He was next set to writing "Ma Perkins," which *Variety* held to be "Just Plain Bill" in skirts. Bill was a widower, Ma was a widow. Each was a kindly and respected figure in a small town, and both could hold their own, in the end, with a series of spiteful women, deceitful men, powerful bankers, and tough gangsters. "Ma" was another enduring hit. Hummert and Mrs. Ashenhurst had found a formula that worked.

Hummert now proposed to General Mills that they sponsor daytime serials for children. General Mills boldly agreed to give the idea a try. Andrews wrote two of them, "Terry and Mary" and then "Skippy," the latter based on the famous cartoon character created by Percy Crosby, who was paid a thousand dollars a week for the radio rights. The kiddies loved "Skippy," and Wheaties became a household word. Andrews formed a secret society of the air for the young followers of Skippy, got up a code book based on the old "Gold Bug" cryptogram, and drew a diagram of a secret grip that he had stolen from a national fraternity. You could get this paraphernalia by sending in box tops, or facsimiles, and a signed statement from your mother that you ate Wheaties twice a day. A popular but somewhat unfortunate contest was staged, and the young winner, who got a free trip to Chicago and a week of entertainment, turned out to be a difficult brat who hated Wheaties and whose many brothers and sisters had helped him send in more facsimiles of the Wheaties box top than any other contestant.

Not all listeners were as enchanted as the children and General Mills. A Scarsdale woman told a meeting of her Parent-Teacher Association that "Skippy" was a dangerous and degrading form of entertainment, and newspapers everywhere printed her charges. A panel of psychologists hired by Hummert pooh-poohed the Scarsdale lady's fears and said that the loud and rambunctious adventure serial was a good thing for America's over-cloistered young. A kidnapping sequence in the story aroused criticism. Although it was written long after the Lindbergh case, indignant ministers and editorial writers denounced it as an attempt to profit by exploiting a tragedy. A new story line was instantly devised,

Just Plain Bill: *Bill Davidson (Arthur Hughes)*

and Andrews wrote twenty-five scripts in five days to catch up. Percy Crosby, who had been moaning and wringing his hands over his mild little character's lost innocence, breathed easier. But "Skippy" was not to last much longer. General Mills were disturbed when they heard that Andrews was not only a newspaperman but a writer of books; the chances were they had a drinking fellow and a bohemian on their hands, and this might get to the listening women and distress them. To forestall old wives' tales and young mothers' fears, Andrews had himself photographed eating Wheaties and sliced bananas with the child actors of "Skippy." He swears today that these actors once gave him a cocktail shaker and two bottles of Scotch for Christmas. The excitement over "Skippy" didn't last long, but it at least had the effect of diverting the public's mind from serials for adults.

By the middle thirties, most of the pioneers had set up shop in New York. Clarence L. Menser came along a little later, and a year ago he became famous as the vice-president of N.B.C. who cut Fred Allen off the air, a gesture as foolhardy as an attempt by your nephew to strike out Ted

Williams. Chicago was no longer the center of daytime radio serials but just another outlet. Hummert and Mrs. Ashenhurst formed a production company of their own in New York. In 1935, they were married. They have prospered and are now the producers of thirteen soap operas and six half-hour shows, five of them musicals and the sixth a mystery, "Mr. Keen, Tracer of Lost Persons," for which Mrs. Hummert selected a beautifully apt theme song, Noel Coward's "Some Day I'll Find You." The Hummert firm is the largest and most successful concern of its kind. The Hummerts choose the casts for all their shows. Men known as supervisors or script editors act as liaison officers between the Hummerts and their staff of writers, who are occasionally shifted from one serial to another when they show signs of running dry or muttering to themselves after too long a stretch with the same group of characters. One writer, Marie Baumer, has worked on eight serials in the last ten years, and another, Helen Walpole, has dialogued six since 1939.

The Hummerts have employed two hundred serial writers since they went into radio. They have fourteen on the staff now, and they can call on a reservoir of thirty others. The Hummerts think up their own ideas for serials. When they do, Mrs. Hummert writes an outline of the plot, suggesting incidents for the first three months or so and indicating key dialogue. Copies of this are given to five writers, and the one whose sample script seems to hit it off best is picked to do the serial. He is given an opportunity to write at least five scripts in advance, and from then on is supposed to stay that far ahead. When Ned Calmer, now a news commentator, was writing a Hummert serial, "Back Stage Wife," he built up a backlog of nineteen scripts so that he could take a trip to Mexico. When the story line was suddenly changed, for some reason or other, he had to cancel his vacation and start all over again. For the last year, Mrs. Hummert has delegated some of her work, but before that she personally kept the story lines of all the serials going by turning out synopses for her writers.

Let us now turn back to Robert Andrews and see what became of him, in order to complete this survey of the pio-

neers' progress. Until 1932, when he came to New York, Andrews wrote radio scripts at night and worked on the Chicago *Daily News* during the day, and he somehow found time to turn out a novel, "Windfall," which was made into the movie called "If I Had a Million." When he got to New York, he wrote radio scripts in a penthouse on Central Park West, typing from noon to midnight seven days a week. He smoked as many as five packs of cigarettes a day and drank forty cups of coffee. For a long period, he kept seven radio shows going, and he rarely had fewer than five, most of them soap operas. He has had a hand in more than twenty-five programs during his radio career. He averaged well over a hundred thousand words a week for years, and his sprint record was thirty-two thousand in twenty hours. In 1935, he decided he needed an outside interest, and he began an intensive research into various periods of history, with the idea of writing a dozen or so novels. One dealing with Daniel Defoe was published in 1945 and one dealing with the era of Alexander Hamilton will be out next year. One morning in April, 1936, Andrews decided to have a fling at writing for the movies, and the next day he was on a train for Hollywood and Warner Brothers. He wrote twenty-seven radio scripts on the train. For a while, he continued to do six serials, and he did four for several years after he got to Hollywood, now working at the studio during the day and batting out the radio scripts at night. He kept at "Bill" until October, 1942. This was his last radio stint. He has written, alone or in collaboration, forty-five movies in the last twelve years, including "Bataan," "The Cross of Lorraine," and "Salute to the Marines." It will come as no surprise to you that he has recently found time to write a novel about his old occupation, soap opera.

Andrews answered a brief telegraphic query of mine some weeks ago with a letter, no doubt written between teatime and the cocktail hour, that ran to eight thousand words. In it, he advanced an astounding explanation for giving up the writing of radio scripts. "I just got tired," he said. Why, Charles Robert Douglas Hardy Andrews!

The New Yorker, *May 29, 1948*

IVORY TOWN, RINSOVILLE, ANACINBURG, AND CRISCO CORNERS
by James Thurber

The last time I checked up on the locales of the thirty-six radio daytime serials, better known as soap operas, that are broadcast from New York five days a week to a mass audience of twenty million listeners, the score was Small Towns 24, Big Cities 12. I say "score" advisedly, for the heavy predominance of small towns in Soapland is a contrived and often-emphasized victory for good, clean little communities over cold, cruel metropolitan centers. Thus, daytime radio perpetuates the ancient American myth of the small town, idealized in nov-els, comedies, and melodramas at the turn of the century and before, supported by Thornton Wilder in "Our Town," and undisturbed by the scandalous revelations of such irreverent gossips as Sherwood Anderson and Edgar Lee Masters. Soapland shares with the United States at least five actual cities—New York, Chicago, Boston, Washington, and Los Angeles—but its small towns are as misty and unreal as Brigadoon. They have such names as Hartville, Dickston, Simpsonville, Three Oaks, Great Falls, Beauregard, Elmwood,

Rosemary: *Rosemary Dawson (Betty Winkler) and Peter Harvey (Sidney Smith)*

Oakdale, Rushville Center, and Homeville. "Our Gal Sunday" is set in Virginia, but no states are mentioned for the towns in the other serials.

The differences between small-town people and big-city people are exaggerated and oversimplified by most serial writers in the black-and-white tradition of Horatio Alger. It seems to be a basic concept of soap-opera authors that, for the benefit of the listening housewives, distinctions between good and evil can be most easily made in the old-fashioned terms of the moral town and the immoral city. Small-town Soaplanders occasionally visit, or flee to, one of the big cities, particularly New York, out of some desperation or other, and they are usually warned against this foolhardy venture by a sounder and stabler character in tones that remind me of such dramas of a simpler era as "York State Folks" and "The County Chairman." A few months ago, Starr, a young, selfish, and restless wife who ornamented "Ma Perkins" with her frets and tears, ran away to New York. She promptly met two typical Soapland New Yorkers, a young woman who talked like Miss Duffy in "Duffy's Tavern" and an underworld gent with a rough exterior and a heart of gold. This type of semi-gangster threads his way in and out of various serials, using

such expressions as "on the up-and-up," "baby doll," and "lovey-dovey stuff," and, thanks to some of the women writers, the fellow has become a kind of extension of Editha's burglar. In "Rosemary," a conniving chap named Lefty actually conceived a fond and pure devotion for a little girl. But the Soaplanders do not have to come to New York, as we shall see, to become entangled with the Misses Duffy and the Lefties and all the rest.

A soap opera deals with the plights and problems brought about in the lives of its permanent principal characters by the advent and interference of one group of individuals after another. Thus, a soap opera is an endless sequence of narratives whose only cohesive element is the eternal presence of its bedevilled and beleaguered principal characters. A narrative, or story sequence, may run from eight weeks to several months. The ending of one plot is always hooked up with the beginning of the next, but the connection is unimportant and soon forgotten. Almost all the villains in the small-town daytime serials are émigrés from the cities—gangsters, white-collar criminals, designing women, unnatural mothers, cold wives, and selfish, ruthless, and just plain cussed rich men. They always come up against a shrewdness that outwits them or destroys them, or a kindness that wins them over to the good way of life.

The fact that there are only two or three citizens for the villains to get entangled with reduces the small town to a wood-and-canvas set with painted doors and windows. Many a soap town appears to have no policemen, mailmen, milkmen, storekeepers, lawyers, ministers, or even neighbors. The people live their continuously troubled lives within a socio-economic structure that only faintly resembles our own. Since the problems of the characters are predominantly personal, emotional, and private, affecting the activities of only five or six persons at a time, the basic setting of soap opera is the living room. But even the living room lacks the pulse of life; rarely are heard the ticking of clocks, the tinkling of glasses, the squeaking of chairs, or the creaking of floor boards. Now and then, the listener does hear *about* a hospital, a courtroom, a confectionery, a drugstore, a bank, or a hotel in the town, or a roadhouse or a large, gloomy estate outside the town limits, but in most small-town serials there are no signs or sounds of community life—no footsteps of passersby, no traffic noises, no shouting of children, no barking of dogs, no calling of friend to friend, no newsboys to plump the evening papers against front doors. A few writers try from time to time to animate the streets of these silent towns, but in general Ivorytown and Rinsoville and Anacinburg are dead. This isolation of soap-opera characters was brought about by the interminability of daytime serials, some of which began as authentic stories of small-town life. The inventiveness of writers flagged under the strain of devising long plot sequences, one after another, year after year, involving a given family with the neighbors and other townsfolk. Furthermore, the producers and sponsors of soap opera and the alert advertising agencies set up a clamor for bigger and wider action and excitement. The original soap-opera characters are now often nothing more than shadowy and unnecessary *ficelles,* awkwardly held on to as confidants or advisers of the principal figures in the melodramas that come and go in chaotic regularity. Even "Mrs. Wiggs of the Cabbage Patch" followed the formula and degenerated into radio melodrama after six months. Its heroine spent her time dodging the bullets of gangsters and the tricks and traps of other scoundrels from the city.

If the towns in Soapland are not developed as realistic communities, neither are the characters except in rare instances—developed as authentic human beings. The reason for this is that the listening housewives are believed to be interested only in problems similar to their own, and it is one of the basic tenets of soap opera that the women characters who solve these problems must be flawless projections of the housewife's ideal woman. It is assumed that the housewife identifies herself with the characters who are most put-upon, most noble, most righteous, and hence most dehumanized. Proceeding on this theory, serial producers oppose the creation of any three-dimensional character who shows signs of rising above this strange standard. Advertising agencies claim—and the record would appear to sustain them—that a realistically written leading woman would cause the audience rating of the show to drop. The housewife is also believed to be against humor in the daytime in spite of the long success of the truly funny "Vic and Sade"—on the ground that comedy would interfere with her desire to lose herself in the trials and tribulations, the emotional agonies and soul searchings, of the good women in the serials. The only serial that deliberately goes in for comedy now is "Lorenzo Jones," whose narrator describes it as "a story with more smiles than tears." The lack of humor in most of the others is so complete as to reach the proportions of a miracle of craftsmanship.

The principal complaint of audience mail in the early days of the serials was that they moved so swiftly they were hard to follow. Surveys showed that the housewife listens, on an average, to not more than half the broadcasts of any given serial. Plot recapitulation, familiarly called "recap," was devised to slow down the progress of serials. "We told them what was going to happen, we told them it was happening, and we told them it had happened," says Robert D. Andrews. The listeners continued to complain, and action was retarded still further, with the result that time in a soap opera is now an amazing technique of slow motion. Compared to the swift flow of time in the real world, it is a glacier movement. It took one male character in a soap opera three days to get an answer to the simple question "Where have you been?" If, in "When a Girl Marries," you missed an automobile accident that occurred on a Monday broadcast, you could pick it up the following Thursday and find the leading woman character still unconscious and her husband still moaning over her beside the wrecked car. In one sequence of "Just Plain Bill," the barber of Hartville said, "It doesn't seem possible to me that Ralph Wilde arrived here only yesterday." It didn't seem possible to me, either, since Ralph Wilde had arrived, as mortal time goes, thirteen days before. Bill recently required four days to shave a man in the living room of the man's house. A basin of hot water Bill had placed on a table Monday (our time) was still hot on Thursday, when his customer stopped talking and the barber went to work.

Soap-opera time, by an easy miracle, always manages to coincide with mortal time in the case of holidays. Memorial Day in Hartville, for example, is Memorial Day in New York. Every year, on that day, Bill Davidson, Hartville's leading citizen, makes the Memorial Day address, a simple, cagey arrangement of words in praise of God and the Republic. One serial writer tells me that the word "republic" has been slyly suggested as preferable to "democracy," apparently because "democracy" has become a provocative, flaming torch of a word in our time. For Soapland, you see, is a peaceful world, a political and economic Utopia, free of international unrest, the menace of fission, the threat of inflation, depression, general unemployment, the infiltration of Communists, and the problems of racism. Except for a maid or two, there are no colored people in the World of Soap. Papa David, in "Life Can Be Beautiful," is the only Jew I have run into on the daytime air since "The Goldbergs" was discontinued. (Procter & Gamble sponsored "The Goldbergs" for many years, and the race question did not enter into its termination.) Lynn Stone and Addy Richton, who have written several serials, were once told by a sponsor's representative to eliminate a Jewish woman from one of their shows. "We don't want to antagonize the anti-Semites," the gentleman casually explained. They had to take out the character.

Proponents of soap opera are given to protesting, a little vehemently, that serials have always promoted in their dialogue an understanding of public welfare, child psychology, and modern psychiatric knowledge in general, and that this kind of writing is supervised by experts in the various fields. There was an effective lecture on the dangers of reckless driving in "The Guiding Light" one day, and I have heard a few shreds of psychiatric talk in a dozen serials, but I have found no instances of sustained instruction and uplift in soap opera. During the war, it is true, at the behest of government agencies, many writers worked into their serials incidents and dialogue of a worthy sociological nature. Charles Jackson, the author of "The Lost Weekend," who wrote a serial called "Sweet River" for more than two years, brought to his mythical town factory workers from the outside and presented the case for tolerance and good will. Social consciousness practically disappeared from serials with the war's end, and Soapland is back to normalcy. Three weeks after Charles Luckman's food-conservation committee had begun its campaign, Ma Perkins invited a young man who had not been satisfied by a heavy breakfast to "fill up on toast and jam." It was just a slip. The script had been written before the committee started work. But, after all, there is plenty of bread in Soapland, which never has scarcity of production.

A study of the social stratification of Soapland, if I may use so elegant a term, reveals about half a dozen highly specialized groups. There are the important homely philosophers,

Life Can Be Beautiful: *Toby Nelson (Carl Eastman) and Carol "Chichi" Conrad (Teri Keane; also played by Alice Reinheart)*

male and female. This stratum runs through "Just Plain Bill," "Ma Perkins," "David Harum," "Life Can Be Beautiful," and "Editor's Daughter," a soap opera not heard in the East but extremely popular in the Middle West, whose male protagonist enunciates a gem of friendly wisdom at the end of every program. ("Life Can Be Beautiful," by the way, is known to the trade as "Elsie Beebe." You figure it out. I had to.) Then, there are the Cinderellas, the beautiful or talented young women of lowly estate who have married or are about to marry into social circles far above those of their hard-working and usually illiterate mothers. (Their fathers, as a rule, are happily dead.) On this wide level are Nana, daughter of Hamburger Katie; Laurel, daughter of Stella Dallas; and my special pet, Sunday, of "Our Gal Sunday," who started life as a foundling dumped in the laps of two old Western miners and is now the proud and badgered wife of Lord Henry Brinthrop, "England's wealthiest and handsomest young nobleman." Christopher Morley's famous Cinderella, Kitty Foyle, also lived in Soapland for some years. Mr. Morley was charmed by the actors and actresses who played in "Kitty," but he says that he never quite gathered what the radio prolongation of the story was about. Kitty eventually packed up and moved out of Soapland. The late Laurette Taylor received many offers for the serial rights to "Peg o' My Heart," which was written by her husband, J. Hartley Manners, but it is said that she rejected them all with the agonized cry "Oh, God, no! Not that!" On a special and very broad social stratum of Soapland live scores of doctors and nurses. You find scarcely anyone else in "Woman in White," "Road of Life," and "Joyce Jordan, M.D." The heroes of "Young Dr. Malone," "Big Sister," and "Young Widder Brown" are doctors, and medical men flit in and out of all other serials. The predominance of doctors may be accounted for by the fact that radio surveys have frequently disclosed that the practice of medicine is at the top of the list of professions popular with the American housewife.

A fourth and highly important group, since it dominates large areas of Soapland, consists of young women, single, widowed, or divorced, whose purpose in life seems to be to avoid marriage by straight-arming their suitors year after year on one pretext or another. Among the most distinguished members of this group are Joyce Jordan, who is a doctor when she gets around to it; Helen Trent, a dress designer; Ellen Brown, who runs a tearoom; Ruth Wayne, a nurse; and a number of actresses and secretaries. For some years, Portia, the woman lawyer of "Portia Faces Life," belonged to this class, but several years ago she married Walter Manning, a journalist, and became an eminent figure in perhaps the most important group of all, the devoted and long-suffering wives whose mar-

David Harum: *(Cameron Prud'homme in the title role; also played by Wilmer Walter and Craig McDonnell),* *Aunt Polly (Charme Allen; also played by Eva Condon),* and *Susan Price Wells (Joan Tompkins)*

riages have, every hour of their lives, the immediacy of a toothache and the urgency of a telegram. The husbands of these women spend most of their time trying in vain to keep their brave, high-minded wives out of one plot entanglement after another.

All men in Soapland must be able to drop whatever they are doing and hurry to this living room or that at the plaint or command of a feminine voice on the phone. Bill Davidson's

one-chair barbershop has not had a dozen customers in a dozen years, since the exigencies of his life keep him out of the shop most of every day. In eight months, by my official count, Kerry Donovan visited his law office only three times. He has no partners or assistants, but, like Bill, he somehow prospers. The rich men, bad and good, who descend on the small town for plot's sake never define the industries they leave behind them in New York or Chicago for months at a

Young Dr. Malone: *Dr. Jerry Malone (Sandy Becker; also played by Alan Bunce, Carl Frank, and Charles Irving)*

time. Their businesses miraculously run without the exertion of control or the need for contact. Now and then, a newspaper publisher, a factory owner, or a superintendent of schools, usually up to no good, appears briefly on the Soapland scene, but mayors, governors, and the like are almost never heard of. "The Story of Mary Marlin," just to be different, had a President of the United States, but, just to be the same, he was made heavily dependent on the intuitive political vision of his aged mother, who, in 1943, remained alive to baffle the doctors and preserve, by guiding her son's policies, the security of the Republic.

The people of Soapland, as Rudolf Arnheim, professor of psychology at Sarah Lawrence, has pointed out, consist of three moral types: the good, the bad, and the weak. Good women dominate most soap operas. They are conventional figures, turned out of a simple mold. Their invariably strong character, high fortitude, and unfailing capability must have been originally intended to present them as women of a warm, dedicated selflessness, but they emerge, instead, as ladies of frigid aggressiveness. The writers are not to blame for this metamorphosis, for they are hampered by several for-

midable inhibitions, including what is officially called "daytime morality," the strangest phenomenon in a world of phenomena. The good people, both men and women, cannot smoke cigarettes or touch alcoholic beverages, even beer or sherry. In a moment of tragedy or emotional tension, the good people turn to tea or coffee, iced or hot. It has been estimated that the three chief characters of "Just Plain Bill" have consumed several hundred gallons of iced tea since this program began, in 1932. Furthermore, the good women must float like maiden schoolteachers above what Evangeline Adams used to call "the slime"; that is, the passionate expression of sexual love. The ban against spirituous and amorous indulgence came into sharp focus once in "Just Plain Bill" when the plot called for one Graham Steele to be caught in a posture of apparent intimacy with the virtuous Nancy Donovan. He had carelessly upset a glass of iced tea into the lady's lap and was kneeling and dabbing at her dress with his handkerchief—a compromising situation indeed in Soapland—when her jealous husband arrived and suspected the worst.

The paternalistic Procter & Gamble, famous for their managerial policy of "We're just one big family of good, clean folks," do not permit the smoking of cigarettes at their plants during working hours except in the case of executives with private offices. This may have brought about the anti-cigarette phase of daytime morality, but I can adduce no evidence to support the theory. The supervision of Procter & Gamble's eleven soap operas is in the tolerant hands of the quiet, amiable William Ramsey, who smokes Marlboros. In daytime radio, the cigarette has come to be a sign and stigma of evil that ranks with the mark of the cloven hoof, the scarlet letter, and the brand of the fleur-de-lis. The married woman who smokes a cigarette proclaims herself a bad wife or an unnatural mother or an adventuress. The male cigarette smoker is either a gangster or a cold, calculating white-collar criminal. The good men may smoke pipes or cigars. A man who called on the hero of "Young Dr. Malone" brought him some excellent pipe tobacco and announced that he himself would smoke a fine cigar. As if to take the edge off this suggestion of wanton sensual abandon, a good woman hastily said to the caller, "Don't you want a nice, cold glass of ice water?" "Splendid!" cried the gentleman. "How many cubes?" she asked. "Two, thank you," said the visitor, and the virtue of the household was reëstablished.

Clean-living, letter-writing busybodies are unquestionably to blame for prohibition in Soapland. When Mrs. Elaine Carrington, the author of "Pepper Young's Family," had somebody serve beer on that serial one hot afternoon, she received twenty indignant complaints. It wasn't many, when you con-

Ma Perkins: *Virginia Payne in the title role*

sider that "Pepper" has six million listeners, but it was enough. The latest violation of radio's liquor law I know of occurred in "Ma Perkins," when a bad woman was given a double Scotch-and-soda to loosen her tongue. Letters of protest flooded in. The bad people and the weak people are known to drink and to smoke cigarettes, but their vices in this regard are almost always just talked about, with proper disapproval, and not often actually depicted.

As for the sexual aspect of daytime morality, a man who had a lot to do with serials in the nineteen-thirties assures me that at that time there were "hot clinches" burning up and down the daytime dial. If this is so, there has been a profound cooling off, for my persistent eavesdropping has detected nothing but coy and impregnable chastity in the good women, nobly abetted by a kind of Freudian censor who knocks on doors or rings phones at crucial moments. Young Widder Brown has kept a doctor dangling for years without benefit of her embraces, on the ground that it would upset her children if she married again. Helen Trent, who found that she could recapture romance after the age of thirty-five, has been tantalizing a series of suitors since 1933. (She would be

going on fifty if she were a mortal, but, owing to the molasses flow of soap-opera time, she is not yet forty.) Helen is soap opera's No. 1 tormentor of men, all in the virtuous name of indecision, provoked and prolonged by plot device. One suitor said to her, "After all, you have never been in my arms"— as daring an advance as any of her dejected swains has ever made in my presence. Helen thereupon went into a frosty routine about marriage being a working partnership, mental stimulation, and, last and least, "emotional understanding." "Emotional understanding," a term I have heard on serials several times, seems to be the official circumlocution for the awful word "sex." The chill Miss Trent has her men frustrated to a point at which a mortal male would smack her little mouth, so smooth, so firm, so free of nicotine, alcohol, and emotion. Suitors in Soapland are usually weak, and Helen's frustration of them is aimed to gratify the listening housewives, brought up in the great American tradition of female domination. Snivelled one of the cold lady's suitors, "I'm not strong, incorruptible, stalwart. I'm weak." Helen purred that she would help him find himself. The weak men continually confess their weakness to the good women, who usually manage to turn them into stable citizens by some vague and soapy magic. The weak men and the good men often confess to one another their dependence on the good women. In one serial, a weak man said to a good man, "My strength is in Irma now." To which the good man replied, "As mine is in Joan, Steve." As this exchange indicates, it is not always easy to tell the weak from the good, but on the whole the weak men are sadder but less stuffy than the good men. The bad men, God save us all, are likely to be the most endurable of the males in Soapland.

The people of Soapland are subject to a set of special ills. Temporary blindness, preceded by dizzy spells and headaches, is a common affliction of Soapland people. The condition usually clears up in six or eight weeks, but once in a while it develops into brain tumor and the patient dies. One script writer, apparently forgetting that General Mills was the sponsor of his serial, had one of his women characters go temporarily blind because of an allergy to chocolate cake. There was hell to pay, and the writer had to make the doctor in charge of the patient hastily change his diagnosis. Amnesia strikes almost as often in Soapland as the common cold in our world. There have been as many as eight or nine amnesia cases on the air at one time. The hero of "Rosemary" stumbled around in a daze for months last year. When he regained his memory, he found that in his wanderings he had been lucky enough to marry a true-blue sweetie. The third major disease is paralysis of the legs. This scourge usually attacks the good males. Like mysterious blindness, loss of the use of the legs may be either temporary or permanent. The hero of "Life Can Be Beautiful" was confined to a wheel chair until his death last March, but young Dr. Malone, who was stricken with paralysis a year ago, is up and around again. I came upon only one crippled villain in 1947: Spencer Hart rolled through a three-month sequence of "Just Plain Bill" in a wheel chair. When their men are stricken, the good women become nobler than ever. A disabled hero is likely to lament his fate and indulge in self-pity now and then, but his wife or sweetheart never complains. She is capable of twice as much work, sacrifice, fortitude, endurance, ingenuity, and love as before. Joyce Jordan, M.D., had no interest in a certain male until he lost the use of both legs and took to a wheel chair. Then love began to bloom in her heart. The man in the wheel chair has come to be the standard Soapland symbol of the American male's subordination to the female and his dependence on her greater strength of heart and soul.

The children of the soap towns are subject to pneumonia and strange fevers, during which their temperatures run to 105 or 106. Several youngsters are killed every year in automobile accidents or die of mysterious illnesses. Infantile paralysis and cancer are never mentioned in serials, but Starr, the fretful and errant wife in "Ma Perkins," died of tuberculosis in March as punishment for her sins. There are a number of Soapland ailments that are never named or are vaguely identified by the doctors as "island fever" or "mountain rash." A variety of special maladies affect the glands in curious ways. At least three Ivorytown and Rinsoville doctors are baffled for several months every year by strange seizures and unique symptoms.

Next to physical ills, the commonest misfortune in the world of soap is false accusation of murder. At least two-thirds of the good male characters have been indicted and tried for murder since soap opera began. Last year, the heroes of "Lone Journey," "Our Gal Sunday," and "Young Dr. Malone" all went through this ordeal. They were acquitted, as the good men always are. There were also murder trials involving subsidiary characters in "Portia Faces Life," "Right to Happiness," and "Life Can Be Beautiful." I had not listened to "Happiness" for several months when I tuned in one day just in time to hear one character say, "Do you know Mrs. Cramer?", and another reply, "Yes, we met on the day of the shooting." Dr. Jerry Malone, by the way, won my True Christian Martyr Award for 1947 by being tried for murder and confined to a wheel chair at the same time. In March of this year, the poor fellow came full Soapland circle by suffering an attack of amnesia.

The most awkward cog in the machinery of serial technique is the solemn, glib narrator. The more ingenious writers cut his intrusions down to a minimum, but the less skillful craftsmen lean upon him heavily. Most soap-opera broadcasts begin with the narrator's "lead-in," or summary of what has gone before, and end with his brief résumé of the situation and a few speculations on what may happen the following day. The voice of the narrator also breaks in from time to time to tell the listeners what the actors are doing, where they are going, where they have been, what they are thinking or planning, and, on the worst programs, what manner of men and women they are: "So the restless, intolerant, unneighborly Norma, left alone by the friendly, forgiving, but puzzled Joseph . . ."

Another clumsy expedient of soap opera is the soliloquy. The people of Soapland are constantly talking to themselves. I timed one lady's chat with herself in "Woman in White" at five minutes. The soap people also think aloud a great deal of the time, and this usually is distinguished from straight soliloquy by being spoken into a filter, a device that lends a hollow, resonant tone to the mental voice of the thinker.

In many soap operas, a permanent question is either implied or actually posed every day by the serial narrators. These questions are usually expressed in terms of doubt, indecision, or inner struggle. Which is more important, a woman's heart or a mother's duty? Could a woman be happy with a man fifteen years older than herself? Should a mother tell her daughter that the father of the rich man she loves ruined the fortunes of the daughter's father? Should a mother tell her son that his father, long believed dead, is alive, well, and a criminal? Can a good, clean Iowa girl find happiness as the wife of New York's most famous matinee idol? Can a beautiful young stepmother, can a widow with two children, can a restless woman married to a preoccupied doctor, can a mountain girl in love with a millionaire, can a woman married to a hopeless cripple, can a girl who married an amnesia case—can they find soap opera happiness and the good, soap-opera way of life? No, they can't—not, at least, in your time and mine. The characters in Soapland and their unsolvable perplexities will be marking time on the air long after you and I are gone, for we must grow old and die, whereas the people of Soapland have a magic immunity to age, like Peter Pan and the Katzenjammer Kids. When you and I are in Heaven with the angels, the troubled people of Ivorytown, Rinsoville, Anacinburg, and Crisco Corners, forever young or forever middle-aged, will still be up to their ears in inner struggle, soul searching, and everlasting frustration.

The New Yorker, *July 24, 1948*

THE LISTENING WOMEN
by James Thurber

During the nineteen-thirties, radio daytime serials were occasionally sniped at by press and pulpit, and now and then women's clubs adopted halfhearted resolutions, usually unimplemented by research, disapproving of the "menace of soap opera." Husbands and fathers, exacerbated by what they regarded as meaningless yammering, raised their voices against the programs, and some of them, pushed too far, smashed their sets with their fists, like Mr. Ezra Adams, in Clinton, Iowa. But it wasn't until 1942 that the opponents of

the daytime monster discovered in their midst a forceful and articulate crusader to lead the assault on the demon of the kilocycles. He was Dr. Louis I. Berg, of New York, psychiatrist and physician, author, and, according to *Who's Who*, medicolegal expert. In a report published in March, 1942, and widely quoted in the press, Dr. Berg confessed that he had been unaware of the menace of the radio serial until late in 1941. His examination of several female patients undergoing change of life had convinced him that radio serials were a main cause of relapses in the women. He thereupon made a three-week study of two of the aggravations, "Woman in White" and "Right to Happiness." He found these serials guilty of purposefully inducing anxiety, dangerous emotional release, and almost everything else calculated to afflict the middle-aged woman, the adolescent, and the neurotic. "Pandering to perversity and playing out destructive conflicts," Dr. Berg wrote, "these serials furnish the same release for the emotionally distorted that is supplied to those who derive satisfaction from a lynching bee, who lick their lips at the salacious scandals of a *crime passionnel*, who in the unregretted past cried out in ecstasy at a witch burning." Hitting his stride, Dr. Berg referred to "the unwitting sadism of suppurating serials." The Doctor then admitted, "There are several excellent ones," and added, somewhat to my bewilderment, since he had set himself up as a critic, "Naturally, an analysis of them has no place in a study of this kind." In a later report, Dr. Berg set down such a list of serial-induced ailments, physiological and psychological, as would frighten the strongest listener away from the daytime air. It began with tachycardia and arrhythmia and ended with emotional instability and vertigo.

Dr. Berg's onslaught was not unlike the cry of "Fire!" in a crowded theatre, and a comparable pandemonium resulted. The uneasy radio industry decided to call in experts to make a study of the entire field. Professors, doctors, psychologists, research statisticians, and network executives were all put to work on the problem. In the last five years, their findings have run to at least half a million words. This vast body of research covers all types of programs, and an explorer could wander for weeks just in the section devoted to soap opera. Among the outstanding investigators are Dr. Paul S. Lazarsfeld, of Columbia University, whose Bureau of Applied Social Research has the dignified backing of the Rockefeller Foundation, and Dr. Rudolf Arnheim, professor of psychology at Sarah Lawrence College, who, for *his* three-week study of serials, had the fascinated assistance of forty-seven students at Columbia University. C.B.S. appointed Mrs. Frances Farmer Wilder, a former public-relations director in radio, as program consultant with special reference to the investigation of daytime serials. Both N.B.C. and C.B.S., the only national networks that broadcast soap opera, appointed research committees, and were cheered up by their reports, which admitted that soap opera could be greatly improved, but decided that its effect on the listening woman was more likely to be benign than malignant. The cry of "whitewash" went up from the enemy camp, but the networks were able to prove that the data of their specialists agreed in general with studies made by independent researchers in the field. It is not always easy to distinguish between independent investigators and the ladies and gentlemen whose work is stimulated by the networks, and I am not even going to try.

In 1945, Mrs. Wilder summarized the findings of the C.B.S. experts in a pamphlet called "Radio's Daytime Serial." If you have been worried about America's womanhood left home alone at the mercy of the daytime dial, you will be relieved to know that forty-six out of every hundred housewives did not listen to soap opera at all. This figure was approximately confirmed a year later by checkers working for the United States Department of Agriculture, which had presumably become worried about the effect the serials were having on the women in small towns and rural areas of the country. Estimates differ as to how many serials the average addict listens to each day. Mrs. Wilder puts the figure at 5.8. She also points out that a housewife listens to a given serial only about half the time, or five programs out of every ten. On the other hand, a survey by an advertising agency indicates that the ladies listen to only three broadcasts out of every ten.

There have been all kinds of measurements of the social stratification of the listening women, and all kinds of results. There is a popular notion that only ladies of a fairly low grade of intelligence tune in soap operas, but some of the surveys would have us believe that as many as forty per cent of the women in the upper middle class, or the higher cultural level, listen to soap opera. The most interesting specimen that the scientists have examined in their laboratories is the habitual listener who has come to identify herself with the heroine of her favorite serial. Many examples of this bemused female have been tracked down by Dr. Arnheim and other workers, and a comprehensive analysis of the type was completed last year by Professor W. Lloyd Warner and Research Associate William E. Henry, both of the University of Chicago, at the instigation of the Columbia Broadcasting System. They made a study of a group of listeners to "Big Sister," using as subjects mostly women of the lower middle class, and found that almost all of them were "identifiers," if I may coin a pretty word. Let us take a look at the summary of their conclusions about the nature of the serial and its impact on its audience. "The 'Big Sister' program arouses normal and adaptive anxiety in the women who listen," wrote Warner and Henry. "The 'Big Sister' program directly and indirectly condemns neurotic and non-adaptive anxiety and thereby functions to curb such feelings in its audience. This program provides moral beliefs, values, and techniques for solving emotional and interpersonal problems for its audience and makes them feel they are learning while they listen (thus: 'I find the program is educational'). It directs the private reveries and fan-

Right to Happiness: *Carolyn Kramer (Claudia Morgan; also played by Eloise Kummer)*

tasies of the listeners into socially approved channels of action. The 'Big Sister' program increases the women's sense of security in a world they feel is often threatening, by reaffirming the basic security of the marriage ties (John's and Ruth's); by accentuating the basic security of the position of the husband (Dr. John Wayne is a successful physician); by 'demonstrating' that those who behave properly and stay away from wrong-doing exercise moral control over those who do not; and by showing that wrong behavior is punished. The 'Big Sister' program, in dramatizing the significance of the wife's role in basic human affairs, increases the woman's feeling of importance by showing that the family is of the highest importance and that she has control over the vicissitudes of family life. It thereby decreases their feeling of futility and makes them feel essential and wanted. The women aspire to, and measure themselves by, identification with Ruth, the heroine; however, the identification is not with Ruth alone, but with the whole program and the other characters in the plot. This permits sublimated impulse satisfaction by the listeners, first, unconsciously identifying with the bad woman and, later, consciously punishing her through the action of the plot. Unregulated impulse life is condemned, since it is always connected with characters who are condemned and never related to those who are approved."

"Big Sister" is written by two men, Robert Newman and Julian Funt, and they have made it one of the most popular of all serials. For more than two years it has dealt with a moony triangle made up of Ruth Wayne, the big sister of the title, her estranged husband, Dr. John Wayne, and another doctor named Reed Bannister. The authors, I am told, plan to tinker with the popular old central situation, but they are aware that they must proceed with caution. The identifiers are strongly attached to the status quo of plot situation, and to what psychologists call the "symbols" in soap opera—serial authors call them "gimmicks"—and they do not want them tampered with. Thus, the soap-opera males who go blind or lose the use of both legs or wander around in amnesia are, as the psychologists put it, symbols that the listening women demand. As long as the symbols are kept in the proper balance and the woman is in charge and the man is under her control, it does not seem to make a great deal of difference to the female listeners whether the story is good or not.

We come next to that disturbing fringe of the soap-opera audience made up of listeners who confuse the actors with the characters they play. These naïve folk believe that Bill Davidson, the kindly Hartville barber of "Just Plain Bill," is an actual person (he is, of course, an actor, named Arthur Hughes), and they deluge him with letters in the fond belief that he can solve their problems as successfully as he does those of the people in the serial. James Meighan and Ruth Russell, who play the husband and wife in "Just Plain Bill," have had to lead a curious extra-studio life as Mr. and Mrs. Kerry Donovan. When it became apparent to the listening audience, some thirteen years ago, that Mrs. Donovan was going to have her first child, the network and local stations received hundreds of gifts from the devoted admirers of the young couple—bonnets, dresses, bootees, porringers, and even complete layettes were sent by express to the mythical expectant mother—and when, several years later, the child was killed in an automobile accident, thousands of messages of sympathy came in. Such things as this had happened before, and they still happen, to the bewilderment and embarrassment of network executives. In 1940, when Dr.

John Wayne married the heroine of "Big Sister," truckloads of wedding presents were received at the C.B.S. Building on Madison Avenue. This flux of silver, cut glass, and odds and ends presented the exasperated broadcasting system with a considerable problem. Gifts for babies had always been disposed of by sending them to children's hospitals and orphanages, but the wedding gifts were another matter. Since network men are a little sheepish about the entire business, they are inclined to change the subject when the question of the misguided largesse of listeners is brought up.

The quandary is enlarged when, in addition to gifts for the nursery, parlor, and dining room, checks, paper money, and even coins arrive for this serial hero or that who has let it out over the air that he is in financial difficulties. The money, like the presents, cannot very well be returned to the senders, for fear of breaking their naïve hearts, and the sponsors have adopted the policy of giving it to the Red Cross and other charities. In addition to the newly married, the pregnant, and the broke, soap-opera characters who are single and in the best of health and circumstances receive tokens of esteem, in a constant, if somewhat more moderate, stream. One young actress who plays in a Procter & Gamble serial estimates that she is sent about three hundred pounds of soap every year, much of it the product of her sponsor's rivals. The year 1947 was the Big Year for live turtles and alligators, and radio listeners from all over the country bombarded the studios with gifts of hundreds of these inconvenient creatures.

Mrs. Carrington's "Pepper Young's Family" used to have a recurring scene in which a man and his wife were heard talking in bed—twin beds, naturally. When the man playing the husband quit and was replaced by another actor, indignant ladies wrote in, protesting against these immoral goings on. Equally outraged was the woman who detected that Kerry Donovan, the husband in "Just Plain Bill," and Larry Noble, the husband in "Backstage Wife," were one and the same man. This pixilated listener wrote Kerry Donovan a sharp letter revealing that she was on to his double life and threatening to expose the whole nasty mess unless the bigamous gentleman gave up one of his wives. The key to this particular scandal is simple. One actor, James Meighan, plays both husbands. A woman in the Middle West once wrote to N.B.C. asserting that the wrong man was suspected of murder in her favorite serial. She said she was tuned in the day the murder took place and she knew who the real culprit was. She offered to come to New York and testify in court if the network would pay her expenses.

Even the listening women who are shrewd enough, God bless them, to realize that serial characters are not real people but are played by actors and actresses expect superhuman

Backstage Wife: (character actor Dave Gothard), Betty Burns (Patricia Dunlop), Larry Noble (Ken Griffin; also played by James Meighan and Guy Sorel), Mary Noble (Vivian Fridell; also played by Claire Niesen), and (character actor Alice Patton)

miracles of their idols. They never want them to take vacations, but usually the weary players manage to get away for a few weeks in the summer. Sometimes they are replaced by other performers, but often the characters they play are "written out" of the script for the periods of their absence. Thus, the housewives who love Mary Noble, the heroine of "Backstage Wife," are not told that Claire Niesen, who plays the role, is taking her annual vacation. Instead, the script arranges for Mary Noble to visit her sick mother in San Diego for a while or travel to Bangkok to consult a swami who has the secret of the only known cure for that plaguey summer rash of hers. Now and then, a serial audience hears one of its favorite characters complain of a severe headache. This is almost always a symptom of brain tumor. It means that the part is going to be written out of the soap opera for-

ever, perhaps because the player wants to go to Hollywood, or the author is bored with the character, or the producer has to cut the budget. In any case, the listeners become slowly adjusted to the inevitable, and when the character finally dies, many of them write letters of condolence, often bordered in black.

The gravest real crisis in years came a few months ago when Lucille Wall, who plays Portia in "Portia Faces Life," was critically hurt in a fall in her Sutton Place apartment. Until her accident, Miss Wall had taken only one vacation in eight years, and her devoted audience was alarmed when her replacement, Anne Seymour, went on playing Portia week after week. The news that Miss Wall was in the hospital in a serious condition spread swiftly among her followers, and letters, telegrams, flowers, and gifts poured in. Because of this evidence of her popularity, Miss Wall improved rapidly, to the amazement and delight of her doctors, who had told her that she could not go back to work for a year. When she got home from the hospital, Miss Wall spoke to her listeners at the end of a "Portia" broadcast one day over a special hookup at her bedside, thanking them for their kindness and promising to be back soon. She repeated this message on the Thursday before Mother's Day, and again, some time later, while she was still recuperating. On June 14th, after being away less than four months, she began to play Portia again.

This reporter is too tired, after more than a year of travel in Soapland, and too cautious in matters of prophecy, to make any predictions about the future of soap opera. One thing, though, seems certain. The audience of twenty million women has taken over control of the daytime serial. The producers must give them what they want and demand. The formula has been fixed. The few serious writers who have tried to improve on it are gradually giving up the unequal struggle. It is probable that superior serials, like "Against the Storm," winner of a Peabody Award for excellence, are gone from the air forever, and that only the old familiar symbols and tired plots will survive.

Your guess is as good as mine about the effect that television will have on the daytime serial. The creeping apparition called video has already made several experiments with continuous narratives. Two of them have been dropped, but one called "The Laytons," the story of a family, though off the air at the moment, will be back next month. It differs from soap opera in that it is a half-hour nighttime show once a week, but the agent I sent to watch a performance at the WABD studio at Wanamaker's reports that it has the basic stuff of the daytime serials, even if the producer is horrified at the mention of such a thing. Just how television could manage to put on a fifteen-minute program five times a week, I have no idea, but from what I know of American technological skill, I wouldn't bet that it can't be done. There is a problem, however, that the wizards of television may find insurmountable if they attempt to transpose any of the current radio serials to the screen. The researchers have discovered that the listening women have a strong tendency to visualize the serial heroine and her family. Some of them even go so far as to describe to their interviewers what the different women characters wear. If their favorites did not come out to their satisfaction on television (imagine their dismay if they find that the tall, handsome hero of their daydreams is really a mild little fellow, five feet four), the ladies might desert the video versions by the million. The way around that, of course, would be to invent entirely new soap operas for telecasting, and "The Laytons" may well be the first lasting adventure in this field.

It is hard for one who has understood the tight hold of "Just Plain Bill," "Big Sister," and some of the others to believe that their intense and far-flung audience would ever give them up easily. If soap opera did disappear from the air (and I see no signs of it), the wailing of the housewives would be heard in the land. I doubt that it could be drowned out even by the cheers and laughter of the househusbands dancing in the streets.

I took the train from Hartville one day last week, waving good-bye to Bill Davidson and his family, and vowing—I hope they will forgive me—to put my radio away in the attic and give myself up to the activities and apprehensions of the so-called real world. I have also put away the books and pamphlets dealing with the discoveries of the serial researchers. In closing, though, I think you ought to know that Benton & Bowles, an advertising agency, recently employed a system invented by Dr. Rudolph Flesch, of New York University, to determine mathematically the comparative understandability, clarity, and simplicity of various kinds of prose and poetry. The agency wanted to find out just how easy it was to understand that old and popular serial of Elaine Carrington's called "When a Girl Marries." The results of Dr. Flesch's formula showed that this soap opera is as easy to understand as the Twenty-third Psalm and a great deal clearer than what Abraham Lincoln was trying to say in the Gettysburg Address. I don't know about you, but when the final delirium descends upon my mind, it is my fervent hope that I will not trouble the loved ones gathered at my bedside by an endless and incoherent recital of the plot of "When a Girl Marries." It will be better for everyone if my consciousness selects that other clear and famous piece of English prose, and I babble of green fields.

When a Girl Marries: *Harry Davis (John Raby; also played by Robert Haag, Whitfield Connor, and Lyle Sudrow)*

Afternoon

by Robert J. Thompson

For all its 100 million-plus viewers worldwide, the American soap opera remains shrouded in anonymity. Production credits do not even appear on most daily installments, and, unlike episodes in prime-time series, even the names of the stars of the soaps are not identified in the opening sequences. Although many devotees of daytime serials follow the creative processes as they are reported in fan magazines and Web sites, many others have little idea who created their favorite stories, much less who writes, produces, and directs them. Strangely enough, the only truly famous soap personage, Susan Lucci, made her way into the American consciousness through the phenomenal string of Emmy awards she didn't win.

None of this, of course, should come as any surprise. With some notable exceptions, the people who make mass media entertainment do so, as far as most consumers are concerned, incognito. The widespread recognition of the behind-the-scenes people who make movies did not really begin in any significant way until a group of French critics developed the auteur (authorship) theory in the fifties. This theory advances the idea that the director of a film could be seen as the author, that is, the driving creative force, even in the seemingly anonymous workings of the Hollywood studio system. Over time this critical perspective has become a useful way to look at the primary creative force behind other forms of popular entertainment, including television. As for radio, although profiles of and interviews with prolific artists such as Orson Welles and Norman Corwin appeared in the popular press during the years they were active in the medium, a systematic study of radio authorship never developed.

Pepper Young's Family: *Sam Young (Jack Roseleigh; also played by Bill Adams, Thomas Chalmers, and Bill Johnstone), Mary Young (Marion Barney), Peggy Young (Elizabeth Wragge), and Larry "Pepper" Young (Curtis Arnall; also played by Lawson Zerbe, Mason Adams, and Peter Fernandez)*

The Secret Life of Soap Operas: James Thurber as Broadcasting Auteur

Which brings us to James Thurber, a writer ahead of his time in both the harm and the good that he did in helping Americans to understand the soap opera. On the one hand, as a major author writing in a major national magazine, Thurber consolidated and perpetuated the glib generalizations that were already circulating about the daytime serial. Thurber set the tone for the shallow treatments of the soap opera that are very much in evidence to this day by taking the soap as an easy target for facile humor based on its complicated plot descriptions and affinity for narrative contrivances such as amnesia.

He also did something in his five-part 1948 *New Yorker* series that has some real historic significance: he launched the series with "O Pioneers!," a piece that identifies the real people who were churning out thousands of words per week in the very popular but already intellectually disdained form of the daytime radio serial. By refraining from treating these programs, as most others did, and still do, as something that materialized out of thin air, Thurber himself was a pioneer of sorts.

The elevation of popular culture creators to the status of subjects for serious studies is not a particularly fashionable strategy among many intellectuals. Many believe that attention and legitimacy given to individual artists distracts us from the social and economic factors that are so crucial to the production of mass-media entertainment. In the case of the soap opera, programs were developed by station and network executives, advertising agencies, writers, and producers to serve the commercial needs of big businesses which, many argue, ultimately determined the form the soap would take. Robert C. Allen wrote in *Speaking of Soap Operas* that "the force exercised by individual genius in the origins of the soap opera was slight, despite the roles played in its early development by such figures as Irna Phillips and the Hummerts."[1]

Although the early radio soaps were indeed very much in the service of their sponsors' marketing needs—characters would hawk products within the narrative of the show and story lines were developed around the sponsors' goods—we still must remember that individuals, not industries, ultimately create programming. Thurber seemed to recognize the need to identify both the people and the context in which they worked. After introducing the major creative players in his first essay, he goes on to discuss the roles of sponsors, actors, and audiences in subsequent essays. Thurber doesn't reduce the study of soaps merely to the study of single individuals; rather, he identifies individuals who work within a swirl of competing commercial and creative forces.

As we might expect in essays written so long ago, Thurber's prescient auteurist leanings had their limits. Though he does supply brief career profiles of several radio artists, he never really gets around to identifying individual creative styles. We learn, for example, that the prolific soap creator Elaine Carrington dictated her scripts into a tape recorder while standing up (although later accounts say she dictated them while smoking in bed). Thurber, however, tells us little about her style. His comments that her dialogue was "frequent and facile" and that she liked to deal with "the frustrations, heartbreaks, kindliness, nastiness, cruelties and tragedies of the middle class" appear in a description of the short stories she wrote for women's magazines, not of her subsequent work in radio soaps. Thurber says nothing about the gushing romance and unpretentious, prosaic narratives that distinguished Carrington's programs such as *Red Adams,* which evolved into the immensely popular *Pepper Young's Family,* from the work of other suppliers. All he gives us on Paul Rhymer, the creator of the hit serial *Vic and Sade,* was that his material was funny, and, for all of Thurber's fascination with itinerant writer Robert H. Andrews, we are left knowing little more than the fact that he wrote really fast.

Thurber, like most people who write and think about soaps, identified Frank and Anne Hummert and Irna Phillips as the two founding forces of the broadcast soap opera. Phillips usually gets credit for creating the first local radio soap, *Painted Dreams,* which began airing on WGN in Chicago in 1930, while the first national soap opera is usually attributed to the Hummerts' *Betty and Bob,* which debuted on NBC's Blue network in 1932. Phillips would create a legacy that is still active today; the Hummerts would disappear with the coming of television.

We Remember Irna

Of all the soap artists Thurber mentions, only Irna Phillips still remains much on the American mind. A prime-time celebration of the genre on CBS in 1994, for example, included a loving, eight-minute panegyric to the "queen of the soaps" and two of her protégés. In the entire two-hour program, the Hummerts, Robert Andrews, and Elaine Carrington get not a single mention. While unknown by most Americans, Phillips's name continues to come up with some frequency in everything from Ph.D. dissertations to soap digests.

The principal reason for this is that Irna Phillips's radio serials had a distinct and unique style that was adaptable to the new medium of television, while none of the other radio soap creators were able to make this transition. Unfortunately, Thurber's essays are not much help in determining what this style was. In his second installment, "Ivorytown, Rinsoville, Anacinburg, and Crisco Corners," Thurber defines the genre by lumping all the soaps together and coming up with a list of conventions and characteristics common to the form. Overall, it's a pretty good survey of the art in 1948, but it doesn't recognize how different producers and writers used these conventions in unique and individual ways. Thurber identifies the soaps' predilection for small town settings, for example, but he then fails to distinguish the difference between a Hummert small town and a Phillips small town.

He does, however, give us a place from which to start. Many of the stylistic differences between the leading soap suppliers were the result of differences in production philosophies. The Hummerts were, primarily, manufacturers. Starting out as employees of an ad agency, they produced not only serials, but mysteries and dramas as well, selling them to sponsors and taking the finished product to the networks, from whom they needed nothing but airtime. According to radio historian John Dunning, the Hummerts were buying as much as 8 percent of available network time slots at the peak of their assembly-line production.[2] While Anne Hummert did some of her own writing and apparently dictated plotlines, the Hummerts were known for employing a stable of dialoguers, who wrote most of the actual scripts. Robert Andrews was one of their most productive employees, a "hack" on a colossal scale.

Serial historian Raymond W. Stedman suggests that the Hummerts nudged out the possibility of a higher aesthetic standard in daytime drama. "If one serial factory had not been in such a dominant position [in the second half of the 1930s]," he argues, "a few more Carringtons, or [Gertrude] Bergs, might have begun writing daytime serials. As it happened, the genre had little attraction for good writers because of the relatively narrow opportunity to place worthwhile dra-

Irna Phillips

mas on the air."[3]

If the Hummerts were producers and Robert Andrews was a hired gun writing for someone else's creations, Irna Phillips was a true candidate for the status of broadcast auteur. Like Carrington, she created worlds, then produced and wrote about them herself. The Hummerts created the production style of the soaps, explain sociologists Muriel Cantor and Suzanne Pingree in their book *The Soap Opera*, but Phillips developed modern soap opera content.[4]

Phillips was first and foremost a writer, and she remained intimately involved in the stories she created. She not only wrote 520 scripts for her first creation, *Painted Dreams*, she also acted in the program. Once her product was in high demand, she used a system similar to the one developed by the Hummerts: plotting shows and approving scripts but employing others to write some of the dialogue. She continued to do much of her own writing, however, some two to three million broadcast words per year during her prime.

Radio historian J. Fred MacDonald wrote in 1979 that "unlike the massive operation of the Hummerts, which could have as many as a dozen different series broadcast weekly, Phillips confined her efforts to four or five quality serials per season. She also avoided the fantasy that sometimes entered the Hummert product, and preferred dramas about people caught up in more realistic predicaments."[5] Stedman agrees, arguing that Phillips was a principal creator of a style of soap opera that "displayed literary quality beyond that turned out by the 'dialoguers.'"[6] Phillips sought to present what she saw as the ultimate goal of American women: a safe and secure family. "The foundations of all dreams of all the men and

women in the world," declared the matriarch of *Today's Children*, Phillips's second soap, are "love, family, home."

Phillips knew, of course, that all drama needed conflict, but in a 1972 interview in the trade magazine *Broadcasting*, she pointed out that conflict between characters didn't need to be sordid to be interesting. Dramatic tension could be achieved by introducing realistic threats to the ideal family situation. "I'm trying to get back to the fundamentals," she explained. "For example, the way in which a death in the family or serious illness brings members of the family closer together, gives them a real sense of how much they're dependent on each other."[7]

The Hummerts also claimed that they "painted against the canvas of everyday American life"[8] and we see plenty of homespun material in Thurber's descriptions of many of the soaps from the forties. But the degrees of realism in the homey settings of the soaps could vary dramatically. Stedman points out that "the canvas of American life was not filled with so many crimes, trials, strange diseases, lost mates, and causes for extended suffering as was the canvas of the daytime serial, especially as painted by Frank and Anne Hummert."[9] The Cinderella story, for example, was one of the Hummerts' favorite fairy-tale inspirations. *Our Gal Sunday* concerned an orphan girl from a depression-era mining camp in Silver Creek, Colorado, who goes on to marry England's richest, most handsome lord. In *Backstage Wife*, a stenographer from rural Iowa marries a matinee idol beloved by a million other women.

Phillips's serials, on the other hand, were less exaggerated, less melodramatic, and less fantastic than those of the Hummerts. Her characters and their problems were more like those that listeners might actually encounter, both personally and professionally. Thurber lamented that "Many a soap town appears to have no policemen, mailmen, milkmen, storekeepers, lawyers, ministers, or even neighbors" and that while we might hear about a hospital or a courtroom, we seldom saw one.[10] This wasn't, in fact, true of many contemporary soaps, and it certainly wasn't true of those made by Phillips. Both *Guiding Light* and *The Brighter Day* were centered around a clergyman, and professional settings like hospitals and courtrooms would become a Phillips trademark, especially in her later television work.

Screen Test

Irna Phillips thrived during the soap opera's move from radio to television. The worlds that she brought to television on *Guiding Light, As the World Turns, Another World,* and *Days of Our Lives,* are still on the air today. *Guiding Light,* which effortlessly went to television after fifteen years on the radio and four years simulcast on both radio and television, has been running for sixty years, the longest continuous story ever told. Of the ten soaps currently on the air, nine were created by Phillips or people who started out working on Phillips's soaps. The work of the Hummerts, on the other hand, never made it out of radio.

Only two radio soaps, in fact, met with any long-term success when they were moved to television. Both *Guiding Light* and *The Brighter Day* were concocted by Phillips, who has been identified by popular culture expert Carol Traynor Williams as "one of the few (and best) radio writers to be energized by television."[11] Phillips's television work continued

to emphasize realistic presentations of family life, professional settings, and rich characterizations that drove the narrative. Her homey realism was consistent with the small screens and claustrophobic settings of fifties television. Her characters' bent toward amateur philosophy and psychotherapy provided a perfect opportunity for the use of long, lingering close-ups that television was so good at providing. Some of the less realistic creations of the Hummerts, though, could never have worked on television. In *The Romance of Helen Trent,* for example, Helen remains somewhere on the far side of thirty-five for more than twenty-seven years. Even with modern makeup, this could never have been pulled off on television.

Furthermore, Irna Phillips trained a new generation of soap creators that would move the genre to places Thurber could never have imagined. Agnes Nixon was a Phillips protégé and employee who would bring the television soap into the relevance era of the sixties, seventies, and beyond, with creations that include *All My Children, One Life to Live,* and *Loving.* Nixon took the basic formula that she had learned from Phillips and added contemporary social issues. Announcing that she wanted her soaps to educate and inform as well as to entertain,[12] she introduced topical stories concerning race, abortion, infertility, depression, child abuse, AIDS, and a host of other subjects that would have turned crimson the cheek of her Victorian mentor (who had once quit her job as a consultant on *Peyton Place* because the subject matter was too risqué). An extended story line on *Loving* in 1984 explored the plight of Vietnam veterans three years before prime-time television would introduce its first dramatic series about the war.

William J. Bell, another former employee of Irna Phillips, and his wife, Lee Phillip Bell, followed a path similar to Nixon's. *The Young and the Restless,* like the Nixon soaps, injected topical issues (its 1975 story about breast cancer was especially notorious) and, in so doing, brought an increasingly younger audience to the soap opera. As Nixon had introduced a new visual style to the soap by occasionally taking her shows on location (St. Croix, the streets of New York), the Bells offered an element of glamour with the glitzy costuming on *The Bold and the Beautiful,* which was set in the fashion industry of Los Angeles. For all their updated subject matter, however, neither Agnes Nixon nor the Bells ever saw the need to stray far from the Irna Phillips formula. In most cases, their soaps continued to center around two families in small cities, and the basic narrative structure that Phillips had developed back in the radio days remained intact.

The Guiding Light: *Charlotte (Lesley Woods; also played by Gertrude Warner and Betty Lou Gerson) and Ray Brandon (Staats Cotsworth; also played by Donald Briggs and Willard Waterman)*

A word from Irna Phillips

None of us is different, except in degree. None of us is a stranger to success and failure, life and death, the need to be loved, the struggle to communicate with another human being, a corroding sense of loneliness. My life is completely different from the average woman's; yet because we share the same essential hopes and fears, what is true of her is true of me.

> Irna Phillips
> from "Every Woman's Life Is a Soap Opera"
> McCall's, March 1965

On the early days

I started my P&G saga on Edge of Night in 1956—the day As the World Turns went on, Edge of Night premiered too. After four and a half years, the part I was playing [Jack Lane] was being written out, and all of the sudden, I heard through people at P&G that Irna Phillips wanted me to play Bob Hughes. It was surprising because I had never had any contact with her.

Since in live television changes can happen very quickly, I was on Edge of Night on Monday and Tuesday, and then World Turns, Thursday and Friday in the same week in 1960.

> Don Hastings
> "Bob Hughes," As the World Turns

Insight, Foresight, Hindsight

Although James Thurber had the insight to recognize the soaps' creators and introduce them to the wide readership of the *New Yorker*, his decision not to flesh out the unique ways in which each of those creators used a set of formulaic dramatic ingredients in the end left his readers without much of an idea that individual style matters, even in a commercially driven, factory-produced art form like the soap opera. Unfortunately, the most-often quoted bit from the five essays reveals their greatest weakness: a tendency to define all soap opera with generalizations. "A soap opera is a kind of sandwich," Thurber writes in the first essay, "whose recipe is simple enough, although it took years to compound. Between thick slices of advertising, spread twelve minutes of dialogue, add predicament, villainy, and female suffering in equal measure, throw in a dash of nobility, sprinkle with tears, season with organ music, cover with a rich announcer sauce, and serve five times a week."[13]

Comments like this perpetuate our inability to make distinctions of quality between the products in our most popular media. John Ford's Westerns, of course, had horses and cacti

Guiding Light: *Dick Grant (James Lipton) and Kathy Roberts Holden (Susan Douglas)*

On his career and Irna Phillips

I started out as an actor. I had the pleasure, perhaps the questionable pleasure, of acting on As the World Turns when Irna Phillips, the head writer who was the queen of all soaps, was back to write it for awhile.

At that point, I did not know that Irna Phillips was an institution, and a saint, and famous. But it was a period in Irna's life where I do not think she was terribly happy writing the show. And we were not too happy having to learn her dialogue, because there were pages of medical jargon that came right out of text books. You just had to memorize it by rote—half of it was in Latin.

At one point I was playing in a strange story that Irna created. There had only been one case ever, I think, in the annals of medical history, and she latched onto it: a case of hysterical pregnancy that was taken through to a Cesarean section. I was the unfortunate gynecologist who Lisa came to in her moment of need. Eileen Fulton was playing Lisa. She was wonderful; she helped me keep sane during those days.

We finally got to the big Friday tag—these were live days, too—and after this huge operation, after I'd opened her up, I turned to an assistant, and said—and this was the tag of the show—"We've made a terrible mistake!"

After you've said that line in front of millions of people, the next best step is to write it yourself, and see if you can try to bring something new to daytime.

Douglas Marland
Head Writer, As the World Turns
from a seminar at The Museum of Television & Radio
November 9, 1991

and marshals and outlaws just like hundreds of B Westerns, but how he used all those ingredients makes *Stagecoach* a better and more important film than *Six Shootin' Sheriff*. The auteur theorists showed us one way to make these distinctions with regard to movies.

They didn't do this, however, until movies had been around for over half a century. Thurber, on the other hand, was writing about the soap opera less than twenty years after its invention. That his essays did not lead to a more sophisticated understanding of the daytime serial is probably more the fault of his readers than of Thurber himself. Had they chosen to concentrate on Thurber's innovative invitations to focus on the people who made the soaps rather than on his characteristic humorous broadsides, the genre may have received—nearly fifty years ago—the attention it is finally getting today.

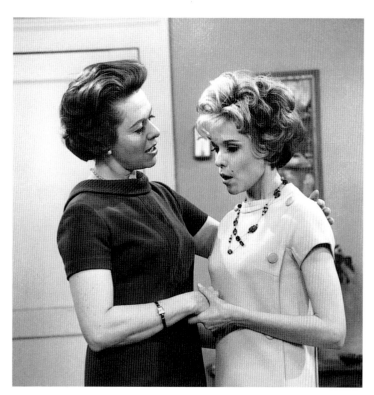

As the World Turns: *Nancy Hughes (Helen Wagner) and Lisa Miller (Eileen Fulton)*

Agnes Nixon with Douglas Marland in a story meeting for Loving

William J. Bell and Lee Phillip Bell

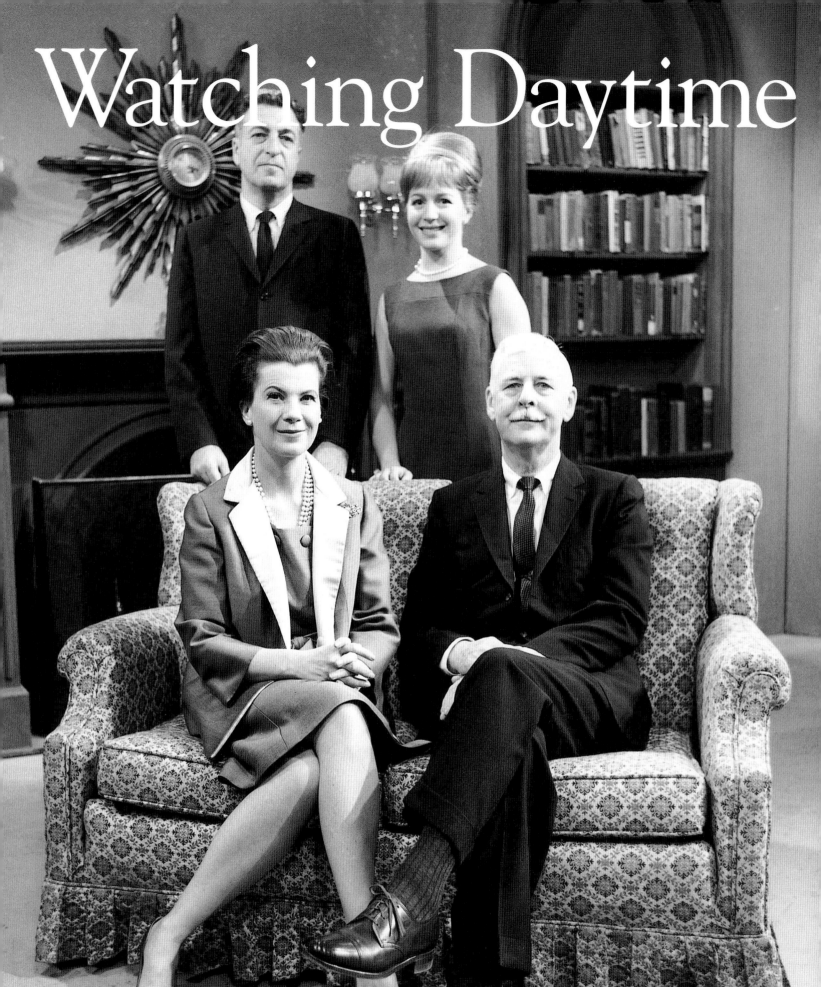

Watching Daytime

Soap Operas

The Power of Pleasure ◆ by Louise Spence

Most studies of daytime soap operas begin by remarking on the huge profitability of soaps or, more often, their huge popularity. Those that begin with popularity usually lament the discredited nature of the genre, how critics have not taken soaps seriously, have denied credibility to an entertainment form that has been loved by millions. They invariably list some of the anomalous people who watch soaps—anomalous because they are movie stars, athletes, college students, a supreme court judge, a governor, or an avant-garde artist, not housewives.[1] Yet, it is precisely those people who seem hardly worth mentioning that the shows are made for—the unexceptional women who are at home during the day and who have the responsibility for purchasing the health, beauty, food, and cleaning products that are advertised twenty-seven to thirty-five times an hour.

This study is based on my conversations with more than twenty-five such women since 1985.[2] It is not an attempt to construct a quantitatively typical viewer, or a quantifiably representative experience, but it represents a saturation of viewings, a polyphony of voices, and, like soap operas, is inherently incomplete. In order to illuminate the experience of watching and talking about soaps, it is often important to retain and savor the ambiguities and the variety of meanings.[3] It is also necessary to be sensitive to differences among viewers and within viewers, for in our self-identity, there is both diversity and contradiction, fulfillment and longing. Because of this, it may sometimes be difficult to recognize the deep ambivalence surrounding fantasy and pleasure. How women acknowledge the relationship between watching television and their household responsibilities, and how they feel their viewing experiences have a practical relevance to their material and social situation is politically and metaphorically complex.

It is important to recognize that people may be conflicted about many of their emotions; there is a tension between how we live (and this includes extracting enjoyment from our lives) and how we would like to live. We may even find that we really enjoy some things that we are opposed to for one reason or another. One well-educated woman that I spoke with mused, "What is interesting to me is why I continue to watch *The Bold and the Beautiful,* when I don't approve of the way they portray women. I think that the women on that show are basically—except for Stephanie—victims." Another woman said that her husband thinks it is foolish for someone who is so intelligent to watch so much television, but she told me that she is not ashamed. When they were traveling in Europe one summer, she didn't want to miss her soaps; "I have this friend who's really—she's a very intelligent person. In spite of what she might think of me [laughing], I asked her to tape it!" After a long discussion, she summarized by justi-

As the World Turns: (clockwise from top left), Doug Cassen (Nat Polen), Ellen Lowell (Patricia Bruder), Judge James T. Lowell (William Johnstone), and Claire Lowell (Barbara Berjer)

On the audience

I think the tendency in all soap operas is to play down to the audience, and I think that is a huge and a profound mistake. We play to an audience of professional people—policemen, firemen, doctors and nurses, and anyone who works at night and is home during the day. A couple of football players on the Dallas Cowboys tune in because they like to look at the clothes I wear, they think they're cool, the silk and cashmere.

It's fascinating what turns people on to a soap opera. So the football player watches because I've got a pretty costume that looks fancy, and then suddenly he finds he's involved in the story.

Charles Keating
"Carl Hutchins," Another World

fying her viewing, "I mean, when you think about it, it really *is* a waste of time. But on the other hand, it's also entertaining and [with emphasis] I want to be entertained a little bit!" And another woman excitedly volunteered to be interviewed, saying that "Eighteen years of watching *All My Children* should be good for something!"[4]

Although they seem to be denied the consolation of respectability and good taste, many of the women I spoke to seemed to feel that they had an intuition for the divine, where others find only coarseness. They also seemed confident that they deserved some pleasure. At the same time many of them,

especially the more middle-class, felt that watching soap operas was an activity of little worth.[5] Echoing the Frankfurt School's concern for the degradation of "free time," many seemed to distinguish between "real pleasures" and "mere diversion."[6] Candy Lampropoulos, for example, who was a social worker before she had her first child, said, "I was very involved with the soaps after I had the baby, and so when I first started making friends and stuff, I would try to get together before 1:00 or after 3:00. And I thought that that wasn't very good. I have relaxed about that." Hanni Lederer, a retired bookkeeper, mentioned that she loves classical music

The Bold and the Beautiful: *Sheila Carter (Kimberlin Brown, left) and Lauren Fenmore (Tracey E. Bregman)*

All My Children: *Phoebe Tyler (Ruth Warrick)*

said that she enjoyed speculating about the show with friends; however, at the end of the interview, when I asked her if she would like me to use her name if I quoted her, she immediately requested I use a pseudonym: "I'm still ashamed enough."

I don't wish to imply that soap opera viewers are riddled with guilt, or that all are ambivalent about their activity; that is certainly not the case.[8] Perhaps pleasure and displeasure are intertwined. Are these necessarily incompatible feelings? One begins to wonder if part of the experience isn't doing something that is disapproved of, or secret, or that part of the appeal is precisely because their husbands or established critics find soaps so unappealing. Some of the fans I interviewed seemed to be bragging about their independence (from "acceptable" behavior or household chores), their willingness to indulge themselves, and perhaps even their daring. Yet even these women didn't claim the activity was intellectually or morally uplifting. Although there are many prescriptions for valuable ways in which a homemaker can spend her free time (crafts, physical exercise, civic or charitable activities), watching soap operas has seldom been described to me as a serious transgression.

Charlotte Siegel, whose children are adults and living on their own, has household help to assist with her domestic

and had expected that when she stopped working she would play the piano more, an activity she clearly felt was more worthy. Instead she watches two-and-a-half hours of soap operas each day. One of those is a show that she says she really doesn't enjoy and feels that if she didn't watch it, she "could do something more constructive."[7]

Another woman, of working-class background, spoke tenderly of her memories of her mother and her grandmother watching soap operas. Yet later she called watching soap operas her only "flaw." A hairdresser, she also goes to school at night, and occasionally cuts some of her clients' hair after hours in her apartment. "I work six days a week, fifteen hours a day, that's my average week; I work very hard. And I feel like, God, I'm out there and doing so much and I still watch soap operas? You know, it's like I still can't get out of that housewife mentality." Another, a lawyer who had a more privileged upbringing, mentioned that she remembered the family maid listening to soaps on the radio, "I found out after a while that my mother had been watching *As the World Turns* for twenty-five years and had never mentioned it." When asked if it was embarrassing, she laughed and said, "Yes, it was the kind of thing, you know, people like us didn't watch soap operas!" She began to watch *General Hospital* with her own teenage daughter, "And then I branched out, it was like this whole new world." She is one of the women who

Days of Our Lives: *Stefano DiMera (Joseph Mascolo)*

chores. When I asked if she watched any soaps other than *General Hospital*, she laughed and told me how she was once convinced to watch *The Bold and the Beautiful*, but wouldn't allow herself to get committed, "I'm very involved in volunteer work for our synagogue, that's my, you know, my work now. I don't really do anything that's income producing. So I just couldn't do, I mean, I'm not ashamed of watching *General Hospital* but I could not—something stops me from getting involved with the other ones."

Many of the conversations seemed to reflect conflict about the suspect nature of pleasure, and there often seemed more a sense of routine than fierce abandon. One woman described her nighttime ritual almost as if she were proud of her "transgression." She watches her taped soap opera before she goes to sleep, sitting on the edge of the bed ("I don't want to lie down because sometimes it would put me right to sleep in the middle of it!"), but waiting until her husband goes to sleep, because, "I think it's psychological, I think he's interested in it to the extent that he doesn't want to admit that he's interested in it, and it irritates him so when I put it [on], 'You have all day to watch that' [she mimicked his angry voice], so I kind of wait, he falls asleep within ten seconds, and the thing goes on."

For almost all the women that I spoke to, watching soap operas is part of a pattern of weekday life, another activity in a task-oriented perception of time. While the regularity, constancy, and familiarity of soaps are surely part of the comfort, these same aspects promote a scheduled, ritualized viewing experience. The seriality itself encourages the entrenchment of habit. As Candy Lampropoulos put it, "I guess the feelings that I have definitely grow. I mean, time is important. If you watch every day—you get so invested."

Although soap operas are no longer transmitted live, there is still a sense of timeliness and immediacy associated with their daily broadcast. The episode happens once, on schedule, and is never repeated. (Even if one is able to time-shift by preserving an episode with a videotape recorder, one still has to be attentive to the scheduled urgency of the telecast to capture the event.) When an episode is preempted, it is in most cases lost forever.[9] The gap in the continuity of the story is generally minimized by the high redundancy of soaps, but the change in the viewer's routine and what seems to many like an arbitrary exercise of television's scheduling power seems to offend some viewers. The popular press often carries stories of the complaints.[10] Even those I interviewed who tape their shows seemed to have a regular, habitual time for viewing them. If we are torn between duty and desire, responsibility and romance, soaps offer us both together. We can be seduced by the familiar and can take comfort in the

On the audience

I think about the lady in Indiana, who only has one spare hour a day, and I wonder what keeps her watching, when she has so much to do. Maybe she's alone and maybe her family life isn't very good, and you try to give her something to relate to. So she can say, "That's like me." Whether the show is outrageous or naturalistic, I think there's something there that the audience connects with.

Carolyn Culliton
Associate Head Writer, *The City*

fact that, if everything is as it should be, soaps are reliable, recurring, faithfully present.

Although few of the women that I spoke to directly addressed the need for something of their own, many of their descriptions implied it. Marilyn Morales watches *All My Children* when she's at home during the day, but says that she doesn't worry too much if she misses a broadcast and would never think of videotaping it. When she does watch it, however, she sends her six-year-old son away. "I tell him that's my time, don't talk to me, that's my time, I'm watching it. Go play with Legos or watch the other TV. After 2:00 is your time." Charlotte told me, "It's *my* nighttime thing to do, when everything else is done for the day, and every bit of other television that I might want to see is over with, then it's time for [*General Hospital*] and that's when I watch it. . . . I look forward to it at night . . . it's a soporific . . . it's really for me." Maybe these small transgressions are a sort of makeshift inventiveness, one of our ways of "making do." Or as one woman who lives in a two-room apartment with her husband and three-year-old daughter put it, "Maybe even more important than what I'm watching is the fact that I've set time aside and I'm by myself and I'm doing something just with me."

One of ABC's promotions spoke to this need. A comic spot showed a bride, still in wedding gown, distracted by a mini-television, and ignoring her groom in their bedroom. This was intercut with scenes from one of ABC's soap operas with an upbeat chorus of women singing "My time for me / something to do / something to see / my time, don't talk to me / my time for me / watching my soaps on ABC." Numerous commercials also try to capitalize on this need. A Carefree pantyliners commercial, for example, showed several long shots of a woman in various outdoor activities (bounding down the steps of a brownstone, hailing a cab, relaxing in a park), each activity represented by a different style of dress;

then, in her bedroom, in a filtered close-shot, she directly addressed the camera and confided that Carefree is "something I do for me." "How often do you do something for yourself?" asks Mon Cheri chocolates.

Many of the women I spoke to mentioned performing chores while watching, and also spoke about how they felt soaps were particularly suited to distracted viewing. Candy, for instance, told me, "When we rent films, Senovia [her daughter] has to be asleep, I have to be settled down. I know that I have to give more concentration. Whereas when I start the soaps I can still wash the dishes, feed the cat, do all these things, and then I can be right into it." Hanni mentioned that after sitting silently and immobile during the two shows she likes the most, she sometimes straightens up or puts on makeup during the show that she least prefers.

Perhaps we have to consider both the satisfaction and the surrender in our pleasures and acknowledge the difficulty in accounting for the conflicts that arise between soaps and daily life. Though many women seem to enjoy child rearing and find it pleasurable and rewarding—or say they do—there is still a certain tension and sometimes ambivalence about the role, because the responsibilities associated with child rearing made them into housewives and contributed to their lack of leisure. Julie Pars Cadenhead, a college student in New York City who described herself as a feminist, looked back twelve years to when she was a young mother fresh from the Midwest: "Motherhood can be about isolation. Soap operas were a welcome friend—adult company. . . . This was not an act of escapism. I loved being home with my child and enjoyed my situation. The reality, however, was that my mobility was now limited, and I did not know any new mothers in my neighborhood." Another woman said that her three-year-old is "too demanding," so she tapes her shows and watches them after her daughter has gone to bed. Awilda Valles told me that when she watches her shows she wants complete concentration. Her brother watches some of the same shows, but he talks too much, so she insists that he watch in the other room, and she usually convinces him to take her infant daughter in with him.

As William Boddy has noted, early television producers worried about integrating television viewing into housewives' daily responsibilities. As with radio, the television industry was counting on sales of receivers to families for use in the home and commercial advertising to pay for the programs. With women as the target audience of the commercial appeals, success depended, as one Philco executive put it in 1944, upon "the degree to which housewives would drop their housework to watch television during the daytime."[11] A CBS monograph the following year noted that daytime radio

broadcasting had served as background activity to daily chores. While noting television's special demands, they nonetheless argued that daytime programs "can be constructed so that full attention will not be necessary for their enjoyment. Programs requiring full attention of eye and ear should be scheduled for evening hours when viewers feel entitled to entertainment and relaxation."[12]

The idea that work and leisure in the home are separate entities is probably false. The two activities flow together, repeating and reinforcing each other.[13] Empirical studies suggest that women do not watch television in their home the same way that men do, and that they are more distracted.[14] This should be seen in the context of household responsibilities. For most men, the home is a not a place of production; it is associated with leisure and generally with comfort and relaxation.

One woman told me that beside caring for the home and her child, she is responsible for much of the paperwork for the family business. When I asked her when she finds time to do it she laughed and said that after her child goes to bed she sometimes sits down, but if her husband is home, he gets angry, "It's like, 'Pay attention to me. . . .' So I do stuff late at night after they've both gone to sleep. Sometimes I'll be sitting here and I'll turn on [the tape of] One Life to Live and I'll do my work." Another, whose children are grown and away from home, and whose husband comes home from work later than she likes to eat, tapes The Bold and the Beautiful and Loving and watches them while she has her dinner. During our conversation, she also seemed quite knowledgeable about One Life to Live. When I asked her about it, she said that twice a month, when she pays her bills, she listens to that show. Marilyn, describing why she has trained her son to play

---

On a Bill Bell story line

One of the great story lines on Days was between Bill and Laura and Mickey, with the belief that Mike was Mickey and Laura's son when we, the audience, knew all along that he was really Bill and Laura's son. All the while the network was crying for the end of the story in three months, and Bill Bell said, "I'll end it when I see fit."

Eight and a half years later, it is finally "revealed" that Mike is really Bill's son, not Mickey's. That was a high watermark in storytelling because it proved to us that if something's working, you don't have to fix it. You must let stories find their own tempo.

Ken Corday
Executive Producer, Days of Our Lives

General Hospital: *Jason Quartermaine (Steve Burton), Brenda Barrett (Vanessa Marcil), A. J. Quartermaine (Sean Kanan), Robin Scorpio (Kimberly McCullough), Jagger Cates (Antonio Sabato, Jr.), and Karen Wexler (Cari Shayne)*

by himself for an hour while she watches her show, says "I'll get angry if I miss something important. Since I'm not really into it as much, I want to know what's going on when I'm watching it, while I'm watching it, so you don't want a little kid, 'Mommy this, Mommy that' [she imitated a child's voice]." However, if a story line she doesn't care about comes on, she'll "leave the volume up high and go into the kitchen or go do whatever else I have to do," and listen for something more interesting to come on.[15]

Watching soaps may be one of the ways we function in a world that does not always meet our needs. We are able to provide ourselves with our own space, an "elsewhere" focused on our own pleasure and will, an active site in which our own desires encroach upon the isolation and fragmentation of daily life.

On the audience response to design

People see the design. I think they watch closely. We used to get letters on Brooke's little teapot or water kettle in her kitchen on All My Children. People wanted to know where to get one. I'm sure it had been long out of commission, but we would write back and try to help them out. Wall coverings and furniture are always noted and people write in and ask, "How did you do that?"

Bill Mickley
Production Designer, As the World Turns

Love of Life: Caroline Aleata (Deborah Courtney), David Hart (Brian Farrell), Ben Harper (Christopher Reeve), and Betsy Crawford (Elizabeth Kemp)

Another World: *Alice Frame (Jacqueline Courtney)*

Aloneness and isolation, the state shared by almost all of the viewers I spoke to,[16] are pictured in frequent one-shots on the screen, yet at the same time the experience is constantly subverted as the characters talk things out, and as the stories tell of mutual caring and sacrificing for others. The plots always involve other people, the problems are interpersonal, and characters are constantly being assured by other characters that they are not alone.[17]

Most viewers who watch soap operas do so alone, experiencing a public spectacle that is private, but also capable of being shared. We might think of this as a dialogue between belonging and loneliness. *Soap Opera Digest* has run a classified section of viewers requesting pen pals and local contacts with people who watch a specific soap or admire a certain character or performer. *Daytime TV* has advertised "900" telephone numbers where you can call to join a party-line conversation or hear and leave a personal message for a soap opera performer. More recently, the Internet has offered both anonymity and communality as viewers converse about story lines and characters on electronic bulletin boards.[18] Luncheons

are held in larger metropolitan areas, where viewers can meet each other as well as two or three performers. Many fan activities are opportunities to demonstrate not only enthusiasm but loyalty. Diana Ortiz claims that as a teenager she belonged to about twenty-five fan clubs. Peggy Orr said that she often browses at a thrift shop not far from ABC's Manhattan studio, and once bought a blouse that had the wardrobe tag of "Nina" on *All My Children*. Lee Meltz told me that she had been shopping for a shower curtain and ran into the performer who plays Jeremy on the same show. They picked the same style curtain and Lee switched the two as they were checking out. She invited me to go into her bathroom and see "Jeremy's curtain" and gleefully reminded me that "hers" was in his bathroom.

Soap opera commercials also often try to forge an imagined solidarity among women. Correctol laxatives, for example, tells us that "women don't have time for irregularity but they are constipated three times as often as men." In an Always sanitary napkins commercial, a woman identified as Jane in a superimposed title speaks to the camera, extending her space into ours, in an extremely close and intimate shot, and asks, "Did you ever wonder . . . ?" In another commercial, a mother assures her daughter that "every woman on the planet has that not-so-fresh feeling one time or another" and suggests Massengill douche "for that pure, fresh, absolutely clean feeling." Other ads provoke an experience of community as they proffer good advice from one of our own. In one commercial "Judy Kennedy, mother and Citrus Hill Plus Calcium technician," offers us an accepted truth, "At fifteen, kids don't want to be mothered anymore," and she wisely suggests, "You have to pick your opportunities. Citrus Hill Plus Calcium is one of those opportunities." Cybill Shepherd, in a commercial for L'Oréal hair coloring, looks into the camera and asks us, "Do anything wonderful for yourself lately? You should! We *all* should . . . we're *worth* it!" She seems to be proposing that this fictive "we" not only needs improvement and deserves indulgence but also that the product can make us what we all agree we ought to be. These (and other) commercials are based less on competition among women than on a comradeship premised on the assumptions that we are not alone, and that we share the wish to observe the procedures that ensure a life of desirability and security. The commonness of "community" is emphasized, while the specifics of locality (another implication of the concept) are erased.[19]

In writing about reading literature—but I think we might substitute watching soap operas—Sigmund Freud suggested that part of the enjoyment comes from the release of our mental tensions and perhaps, "much that brings about this result consists in the writer's putting us into a position in which we can enjoy our own daydreams without reproach or shame."[20] Adults cherish their daydreams as their most intimate possessions and would often rather confess their wrongdoings than their fantasies.[21]

Our longings, like our soaps, are steeped in the insignificance of the everyday. Because our pleasures and discontent are often private, and because they are often rooted in and draw upon unexpressed or unrecognized feeling, they are sometimes difficult to acknowledge. They may also be too precious to share. Perhaps part of the power of pleasure lies in luxuriating in a personal space, an elsewhere not far from home where desire helps negotiate the constraints of the domestic role.

On Pine Valley

*P*ine Valley is the Peyton Place of the nineties. It's that small town just a train ride away from Philadelphia, Center City, and New York City that has never changed. We have no interest in really going urban or bizarre, because that doesn't serve the character of this particular show.

The show has always been invested in realistic storytelling with characters, not manipulating character for story. It's like the great movies of the forties. That, to me, is what daytime really is about. It's replaced all the Susan Hayward or Bette Davis movies that they don't make anymore.

If you listen to the fans, basically they're looking for family, friendship, romance, suspense. What is that? It's a forties movie!

Francesca James
Executive Producer, All My Children

All My Children: *Dr. Cliff Warner (Peter Bergman) and Nina Cortlandt (Taylor Miller)*

Another World: *Felicia Grant (Linda Dano)*

On the audience

When Soap Opera Weekly *came out, we were the first magazine that people could pick up and read about what was happening as they watched. Part of what we have done is to help create a very educated viewer: they are interested in what goes on behind the scenes; they know the names of the writers better than the media; they know who the producers are; they know who all the directors are; they follow as the talent moves from show to show.*

They can also sometimes learn in advance that somebody is leaving or somebody is coming. But we know we are in an industry based on surprise. We have to try to impart information without ruining the "tune in tomorrow" aspect of the business. It has been challenging.

Mimi Torchin
Editor in Chief, Soap Opera Weekly

Santa Barbara: *Eden Capwell (Marcy Walker) and Cruz Castillo (A Martinez)*

Different Soaps

for Different Folks

Conceptualizing the Soap Opera Audience ◆ by Jane Feuer

Who watches soap operas? Who is included in the audience for soap operas? These may appear to be the same question, but they are not. Although many different kinds of people in many identifiable demographic groups are known to watch soap operas, not all of them count—not with the advertisers, not with the networks, and not with some academic researchers. Some viewers count more than others (women). Some viewers care more than others (fans). Some viewers may care a lot, but aren't counted very much at all (college students, African-American men).

Soap opera audience research—the kind done by the networks and independent academic researchers—is one area where the concerns and opinions of women are taken very seriously. For advertisers, producers, and feminist researchers, women are the only group that counts, and not just any women, but eighteen- to forty-nine-year-old regular viewers who are assumed to be heterosexual. Why, if men view, do only women matter? Answering this question requires a look at the various theories about the soap opera audience.

Throughout the history of writing about soap operas there have been two competing notions of what I call the implied audience, the audience that is assumed to be watching based on an analysis of the structure and content of the programs. Many commentators have always assumed that the soap opera audience consisted of housewives, women who are not well educated and not very attentive to the nuances of drama. Other, and more recent, opinion holds that soap opera scripts are constructed in such a way as to allow for many different audiences to access the text in many different ways. (Robert C. Allen in *Speaking of Soap Operas,* is the leading proponent of this view.)

As the World Turns: *Steve Andropoulos (Frank Runyeon) and Betsy Stewart (Meg Ryan)*

Guiding Light: *Reva Shayne (Kim Zimmer)*

Days of Our Lives: *Marlena and Roman Brady (Deidre Hall and Wayne Northrop)*

Another World: *Rachel and Mac Cory (Victoria Wyndham and Douglass Watson)*

Ironically, the commentators who see the audience as housewives appear to have little else in common. They range from literary critics who refer to soaps as "gynocentric dramas" to my mother in Cincinnati, and to them soap opera viewing is assumed to be a trivial activity, a waste of time. No one ever questions what that means. If any nonproductive activity is a waste of time, then there really should be no difference between viewing *As the World Turns* and attending a production of *Twelfth Night.* The difference really lies in the value our society places on Shakespeare's plays as opposed to soap operas. All of which is to say that soap operas are a lowbrow form of drama.

Feminist film and television critics have also been interested in assuming that housewives are the audience that soaps want to address. The difference from the traditional view lies in the way the housewife is perceived. Feminist researchers took an interest in the genre during the eighties precisely because they wanted to redeem the housewife from a negative stereotype as someone who eats bonbons and watches soap operas. If in fact soap opera viewing could be demonstrated to be a productive activity, one that resembles consumption of the more socially valued arts, then the image of the housewife that accompanies it would also be enhanced. The earliest and best-known feminist work on soap opera did precisely this. In *Loving with a Vengeance,* Tania Modleski argued that the unique narrative structure of television soaps—the never-ending story line—created a position for the housewife/viewer that was like an all-knowing mother, one who sympathized equally with all her children. The pleasure women receive

The Bold and the Beautiful: *Brooke Logan (Katherine Kelly Lang) and Caroline Spencer (Joanna Johnson)*

On the college audience

Stephanie Braxton, the second Tara on All My Children, *had a cousin who taught graduate school at Ohio State University and wanted us to come talk to the graduate students about writing and acting. The graduate seminar was in the evening, and as we were walking with the professor he said, "We just have to go through the student-union lounge to get to my little room in the back." Then he said, "The light's on, I hope nobody's having a meeting." We walked in, and it was wall-to-wall students. So he asked, "Is something going on?" And someone said, "Man, this is* All My Children, *you couldn't have this without us!" In the end, the academics, who thought they were going to dissect the soaps amongst a small group of ten, learned something that night that they never expected to learn about the appeal of soaps.*

 Agnes Nixon
 Creator, All My Children, One Life to Live, Loving

from soap opera viewing thus might serve as a lesson to feminist artists trying to reach the same audience. Modleski went on to suggest that the constant interruptions of the soap opera narrative were directly related to the constant interruptions of women's work in the home.

 It is at this point that Modleski's interest in soap operas overlaps with that of advertisers and the companies that produce soaps. For reasons very different from hers (that is, capturing the audience rather than liberating it), network researchers are also interested in housewives' patterns of soap consumption, how many days a week they view, and what they like to see. They study these patterns via focus group interviews and audience tracking studies. The writers of soaps will be asked to adjust the pace of the story lines based on this research. If, for example, it is found that the desirable eighteen- to forty-nine-year-old female audience is not watching a particular soap frequently, the writers will increase the amount of retelling of the previous days' events. If it is found that a particular actor receives a high "Q" score (a measure either of popularity or notoriety) even during periods when he is not featured in a story line, that actor will be given a prominent place in the story. If it is found that the viewers prefer the sets and costumes of another soap, steps will also be taken to improve in this area.

Advertisers and networks, clearly, want to please women in order to sell them products. In this sense, women are a valued audience, but they are a commodity audience; any consideration of their pleasure is oriented solely toward consumption. Feminist researchers are more interested in why these women watch soaps; they focus upon the voids in women's lives that soap opera viewing fills. Louise Spence, for instance, interviewed one woman who would tape her soap operas and watch them in bed at night after her husband dozed off. This poignant anecdote would only be of interest to network researchers if they were worried that she might zip through the ads in this situation.

Until recently the so-called housewife audience was the only one studied by just about anyone. With the huge growth in soap viewership during the eighties, however, it became known that men also watch soaps, that young people watch soaps, that intellectuals watch soaps, that African-Americans watch soaps. (It was always known that women over forty-nine viewed, but everyone assumed that their loyalty to CBS—to the long-running *Guiding Light* and *As the World Turns*—could not be challenged. They didn't buy enough advertised products anyway, so they were not studied.) To take a look at the new patterns in soap opera research based on the emerging acceptance of multiple audiences, I interviewed Michael Kape, editor of *Soap Opera Now Online* and contributing editor of *Soap Opera Now*, Gloria Abernathy-Lear, whose dissertation centered on the black audience for soaps, and Sean Griffin, whose work looks at gay male viewers.

Working Women and the African-American Audience

As Michael Kape reminds us, "soap operas are a business first and an art form second." He notes that the broader scope of products being advertised today (automobiles, for example, and general interest products instead of women's products) represents a subtle shift toward catering to new audiences. But he cautions that the main new audience being accommodated is the working woman, because it is assumed that as more women enter the workforce, their interests will broaden (in other words, they will purchase a wider range of products and tolerate a greater range of story lines). Kape emphasizes

that although this working population, which generally videotapes soaps to watch at night, is now more important to soap producers, the most important demographic remains women between the ages of eighteen and forty-nine who are at home viewing during daytime hours.

African-American women form an increasingly crucial part of this daytime audience. When Gloria Abernathy-Lear of the University of Illinois at Chicago researched African-Americans' relationship to daytime serials for her 1992 Ph.D. dissertation at the University of Wisconsin, she found that among the many criticisms this audience had of daytime soaps was the fact that blacks on soaps were never shown as part of a larger African-American community. According to Michael Kape, African-Americans are now acknowledged by the networks as a very large audience segment to whom soaps must appeal.[1] In order to do so, says Kape, producers have broadened the scope of characters. He attributes the continuing ratings success of *The Young and the Restless* to its appeal to the African-American audience, for whom it has long been the number-one soap. Black characters are now integral to the fabric of the show.

The introduction of *Generations* by NBC in 1989 was an attempt to deal with the problem that soaps did not seem to have black core families. Michael Kape believes that *Generations* was a deliberate effort by NBC to reach the African-American community, which had made *The Young and the Restless* such a big success for CBS. When *Generations* was canceled, Kape wrote in *Soap Opera Now* that the serial was a victim of institutional racism within NBC and its affiliates, where it was given a bad time slot (opposite *The Young and the Restless*) and little support.

According to Gloria Abernathy-Lear, African-American viewers have always had an ambivalent relationship to television, and daytime soaps are not an exception. She reveals that "although African-Americans gained pleasure from watching daytime serials that were similar to those of mainstream viewers, distinctly African-American meanings and pleasures were identified in this study's viewing population."[2] Her audience, for example, was troubled by the love triangle on *All My Children*, wherein Dr. Angie Hubbard had to choose between the white core character Dr. Cliff Warner and a black competitor introduced merely to fulfill this story line. As one interviewee said, "I mean Angie needs to get real. Girlfriend, you are black! Let's hear you say it at least once."[3] Although the scripts set up Cliff as the better suitor, African-American women still preferred the black man for ethnic and cultural reasons. Examples like this demonstrate the usefulness of Robert Allen's method of studying soaps as texts open to various interpretations.

The Young and the Restless: *Nathan Hastings (Adam Lazarre-White) and Drucilla Winters (Victoria Rowell)*

Another World: *Angela Rivera (Randy Brown), Thomas Rivera (Diego Serrano), and Maggie Cory (Robyn Griggs)*

All My Children: *Jeremy Hunter (Jean LeClerc) and Erica Kane (Susan Lucci)*

The Fan and the Gay Male Audience

Although they may not be counted as a commodity audience, demographic groups other than women in the age range of eighteen to forty-nine may be interested in soap opera as an art form. The common word for those viewers who are overly invested emotionally in soap operas is fans, and according to Michael Kape, the level of affective investment differentiates the fan from the ordinary viewer. (Very few soap fans are as extreme as, say, the one who stalked soap star Andrea Evans and forced her to leave *One Life to Live.*) Kape makes a distinction between fans who merely have an emotional investment and the readers of *Soap Opera Now,* whom he sees as better educated and more discriminating. But not everyone agrees with this distinction. Many academics believe that the audience/fan distinction has been too sharply drawn, and they now feel that viewers may be deeply emotionally involved in soaps and, at the same time, may be critical of them.

If fans have been given bad press, perhaps too sharply setting them off from other viewers, then one group of viewers presents a particularly interesting case: gay men. Gay men are known to be more devoted fans of soap operas than straight men. Since many gay fans are not forthcoming about their sexual identities, this is an impossible audience to study statistically. Yet Michael Kape believes that the networks are aware of their presence, and that they will do more to cultivate this audience in the future. According to Sean Griffin of the University of Southern California, who has researched among gay male fans of *All My Children*, the show's producers are aware of this audience, or hoped to increase its size by creating the openly gay male character, Michael Delaney.

Network recognition of the gay male fans is only part of the reason why this alternative group may be of interest to students of soap operas. Gay male viewers, like African-American women viewers, raise the question whether different audiences receive different messages from the same programs; that is, whether or not they constitute interpretive communities that differ from the assumed eighteen- to forty-nine-year-old housewife audience. The experts I interviewed disagree about whether gay men create different meanings from soaps than other audiences. Michael Kape does not believe that gay men respond differently from other groups. He says that if you look at the origins of soap opera as a form that relies heavily on emotional response, you will discover that "people are people," that sexuality ultimately does not affect responses to powerful soap opera dramatics. Sean Griffin, on the other hand, says that it does. His interviews with gay male fans of soaps from the Internet news group "rec.arts.tv.soaps.abc" led him to the conclusion that gay men had a fundamentally different response from other viewers to the introduction, for example, of the gay character Michael Delaney (played by Chris Bruno) on *All My Children*. According to Griffin, however, the responses of gay men are

not uniform, and some conform to those of women and straight men. Some gay men, for instance, agree with some straight viewers that actor Chris Bruno is perfectly believable; other gay men find that the actor, who has declared that he is straight, is uncomfortable in the role. (There are straight fans who share this view too.) Griffin says that "Gay men seem more often to do a 'double reading'. While they remain completely engrossed in the story lines and characters, they also see the whole thing through the eyes of 'camp'."

Griffin's research found that the gay culture's investment in the diva phenomenon (as explored in *The Queen's Throat: Opera, Homosexuality, and The Mystery of Desire* by Wayne Koestenbaum) factors into the pleasure of some gay male fans. Griffin makes the comparison of certain gay men who are staunch defenders of Erica Kane with those who are tired of her snotty egotism. Griffin also finds that gay men generally have a greater sense of whimsy or irony with regards to soaps, because they know that they are not the networks' intended audience. He also believes that the ability to read the small clues or social signs that help gay men identify one another in an often hostile society may help them in reading where soap story lines are going (in other words, which two characters are being set up for a romance, or that a character has been limping although others ignore it).

Lastly, gay men obviously like looking at handsome male actors. Here, it is hard to differentiate between how straight women and gay men appreciate the show. In the online discussions of soap opera Web sites on the Internet, Tad Martin was usually spoken for by the female fans, while Pierce Riley (at least when played by Jim Fitzpatrick) was championed by gay men. When asked why this research is important, Griffin replied, "Well, my main interest (other than I am a gay male myself who loves soaps!) is how gay male fans challenge the often rigid ideas about how who the viewers of soaps are and how they read these things."

If this is true, then the title of this article, "Different Soaps for Different Folks," is a lot more complex than it seems. It is not so much a question of say, *Generations* being targeted at black viewers and *The Bold and the Beautiful* at whites. The issue is really that different audiences seem to make different meanings out of the same soaps.

Generations: *Henry and Ruth Marshall (Taurean Blaque and Joan Pringle)*

All My Children: *Dixie Cooney (Cady McClain) and Tad Martin (Michael E. Knight)*

Taking

Issue

Social Themes in the Soaps ◆ by Laura Stempel Mumford

From their earliest origins in radio, soap operas in the United States have taken the social world as their subject, depicting their fictional communities primarily in terms of the social relations—the elaborate romantic and kinship networks—that bind characters together. That focus, along with the structure of soap operas and the viewing habits such a structure encourages, have enabled the genre to examine a wide range of social issues in far greater detail than any other form of fictional television allows. Although its prime purpose remains entertainment, daytime soap opera has become an ideal forum for educating its core audience of women about social problems.

Since the genre's central interest is personal life, issues that have to do with family, romance, and the like tend to predominate. These issues are usually dealt with in personal rather than political terms. A wide range of social questions make an appearance, but characters are more likely to become entangled in a story line about the ethics of abortion than in one about, say, welfare or the environment. And even the abortion story line is more likely to be cast in terms of conflicts among individual characters than within the larger debate over public policy. The practice of organizing U.S. soaps around reasonably well-educated middle- and upper-class families (versus the lower-middle- and working-class communities of British serials such as *Coronation Street* and *EastEnders)* also means that certain kinds of issues, such as unemployment or illiteracy, are usually treated via relatively short-lived "problem" stories rather than being integrated into characters' ongoing daily lives.

Soap operas began to build major stories around contemporary social issues in the late sixties. CBS's *Love Is a Many*

General Hospital: *Simone and Tom Hardy (Stephanie Williams and David Wallace)*

Splendored Thing, premiering in 1967, attempted daytime's first interracial romance; *One Life to Live* (1968) started out with a unique mix of upper- and working-class characters, and featured Jews, Poles, and, eventually, African-Americans among its core families; and *All My Children* (1970) even incorporated the Vietnam War into its early story lines. Over the years, soap writers have increasingly stressed the connections between the problems characters face and those of the world beyond the show's fictional borders. Stories about alcoholism and addiction, for example, have been soap opera staples for decades, but they now often include references to actual treatment programs, with characters attending generic 12-step programs and even going to real clinics—from *One Life to Live's* use of New York's Odyssey House in 1970 as the site for Cathy Craig's drug rehabilitation through Erica Kane's 1996 sojourn at the Betty Ford Clinic on *All My Children.*

This does not mean that soap opera story lines are always either consistent or accurate in their details. Pregnancies can last longer than nine months, while complex murder trials may take only a few days; characters often experience miraculous recoveries from even the most realistically depicted illnesses. To some extent, the use of real-world reference points is simply a reflection of an overall increase in naturalism among daytime soaps, including a greater use of outdoor locations and the setting of more serials in real rather than fictional places. Social realism is inevitably subordinated to the demands of drama, and may also be limited by real or feared responses from networks and viewers. But when a woman seeking an abortion confronts pro-life demonstrators, or a rape victim attends a support group for sexual-assault survivors, the character's fictional experiences become linked directly to the larger social world. And when, as in both of the examples just cited from the life of *All My Children's* Julia Santos in 1994, the encounters are the focus of lengthy scenes, rather than providing color or background for other

The Bold and the Beautiful: *Valerie (Michele Lamar Richards), Eric Forrester (John McCook), Margo Lynley (Lauren Koslow), Bill Spencer (Jim Storm), Caroline Spencer (Joanna Johnson), Ridge Forrester (Ronn Moss), Stephanie Forrester (Susan Flannery), Clarke Garrison (Dan McVicar), and Kristen Forrester (Teri Ann Linn)*

One Life to Live: Max Holden (James DePaiva) and Luna Moody (Susan Batten)

events, that social world inevitably resonates across the entire program.

The fact that U.S. daytime soaps focus on personal life does, however, limit the genre's capacity to engage social questions. While soaps have been more attentive than most prime-time series to issues like domestic violence (*All My Children*'s Leora Sanders, 1981), religious conflict (*Days of*

On changing attitudes toward women

*I*n our breakdown meeting last week, one of the writers had written something that comes up in drama all of the time: a man and a woman are in love, and the man grabs the woman into a passionate embrace; she fights it, and then gives in. Well, what we're trying to reinforce now, for the sake of women and to help change the society at large that still passively accepts rape, is that no means no. So that old, somewhat romantic picture the writer came in with needed to change, and we accomplished it by writing the scene differently.

  Michael Laibson
  Executive Producer, Guiding Light

One Life to Live: Karen Wolek (Judith Light)

One Life to Live: *Cathy Craig (Amy Levitt) attends a group therapy session at the Odyssey House in New York City*

On Erica's History

*I*t was groundbreaking what Agnes did in 1994—to go back a
year before the program actually started to show the climatic
horror in the relationship between Erica and her father: she was
raped by his best friend when she was fourteen.

Agnes often writes story lines before they're in the newspapers. I felt such a sense of responsibility in playing this story line
that I started doing research into the lives of women who had
been raped and were in counseling. That was a very groundbreaking story for Agnes, as a storyteller, and for me, as an
actress, to move the character forward.

Susan Lucci
From All My Children *seminar at*
The Museum of Television & Radio,
November 24, 1995

Our Lives's Robin Jacobs and Michael Horton, 1986), or
breast cancer (*General Hospital*'s Monica Quartermaine,
1994), their focus remains consistent with the ideology that
dominates television in the United States. Soaps may be
broadly liberal in their openness to cross-cultural or interracial romance, but they are equally conservative in their basic
acceptance of the existing fabric of family and community
life. Political movements that question prevailing norms, as
feminism does, rarely appear, and politics operate on an
almost entirely local scale. Individual characters may hold
elected office—a U.S. senator on *Another World* or *Capitol*, a
city councilman on *General Hospital*—but everyone's behavior is presented as arising from exclusively personal motives.

Yet soap opera structure and audience members' viewing
practices enable this genre to incorporate controversial social
issues that prime-time series often evade. The cast of characters on any given soap is large, ever-changing, and connected
through an intricate network of relationships that are repeat-
edly disrupted by newcomers, making it easy to bring on a figure specifically in order to explore a social question. Characters
move back and forth between "front burner" and "back burn-

er" status, allowing writers to attach a social problem to one individual, work it through, and then eliminate either the problem or the character. They can take the risk of bringing disruptive or threatening ideas prominently into a program without worrying about being stuck with a character marked permanently by their "problem," as they might be on a prime-time series with a limited cast.

Equally important is the fact that as serials, soaps need not resolve any questions in a single episode—or even in a week, a month, or a year of episodes. When prime-time series examine contemporary social questions, it tends to be in individual episodes devoted to the problem, such as special sitcom installments dealing with illiteracy, drug abuse, or teen pregnancy. Some dramatic series take such issues as a major subject, but even a show like NBC's *Law & Order*, which draws many of its weekly plots from current headlines, is controlled by the need for episodic closure. Despite the importation of serial-style cliff-hangers into prime time, most series still require that story line threads be tied up in thirty or sixty minutes, which demands a tidier conclusion than serious social problems admit.

The soap opera form's open-ended structure also gives writers the freedom to follow a story down as many fictional byways as they desire. Despite recent innovations such as location-shooting, soaps are in stylistic and performance terms far less realistic than gritty prime-time crime dramas, yet the daytime programs' elongated story line development lends a different sort of realism by letting writers follow the progress of a particular disease or examine an extremely complicated social issue over time. This also allows for greater emotional realism, since there is room for changes to resonate in individuals and the community, and to explore new social questions over a long period. *One Life to Live*, for example, has tracked Victoria Lord's multiple personality disorder for more than twenty-five years, through dramatic shifts in her professional and personal relationships and major changes in

public attitudes toward her illness. Initially, her condition was explained as the result of her father's insistence on treating her like a son, and later, in 1989, by the earlier traumatic birth of her illegitimate daughter, Megan. In keeping with the show's repeated linking of this story line to contemporary social issues, Viki's 1995 relapse brought a new explanation of its origins: she was sexually abused by her father during adolescence.

While few people would call soap opera characterization subtle, the genre's dependence on long-term and often quite gradual shifts in behavior or relationships leaves room for a more subtle presentation of the meanings and effects of a social issue. Key here is the fact that story lines always explore a variety of character reactions to any development, and deal constantly with the consequences of people's actions, rather than focusing, as conventional episodic television usually does, primarily on individual dramatic events. Every event on a soap is explicitly located within the context of the show's fictional community, so that despite their obsession with the personal realm, social-problem stories necessarily pay close attention to the implications for the entire community of, say, homophobia, rather than presenting it as important mainly to isolated individuals with no particular relation to the world around them.

Finally, the genre's structure encourages viewers to develop certain ways of watching, and the daytime audience's unique viewing practices help to explain the special power of issue-oriented story lines. Regular viewers have a rich, complex relationship to their favorite programs and possess a dense historical knowledge of the relationships among the characters. Whether they watch in real time or on videotape, the

All My Children: *Leora Sanders (Lizbeth MacKay) and Joe Martin (Ray MacDonnell)*

daily broadcast of soaps permits viewers to make the shows part of their regular domestic routine, and that repetition works to build an intimate connection with the individual characters.

Soap operas have been very successful in presenting story lines that bring issues of health and personal safety to the attention of their target female audience. The days of soap characters suffering from illnesses that existed only in the imaginations of their creators are largely over. Instead, writers try to make on-screen diseases conform at least in general terms to their nonfictional counterparts. (In 1992, when Viki

Lord's daughter Megan died from lupus—a disease that disproportionately affects women but is rarely fatal in the short-run—*One Life to Live* writers also gave the condition to another character, Marty Saybrooke, who continues to live with it.) Shows now routinely incorporate specific health questions into dialogue—a casual 1996 conversation between *The Young and the Restless's* Nikki Newman and her daughter Victoria included a reminder that women should get regular Pap tests—while information about safe-sex practices is commonly presented before a first sexual encounter. Climactic episodes in issue-oriented story lines often end with an epi-

One Life to Live: *Victoria Lord (Erika Slezak) as "Princess" (left) and as "Niki" (right)*

On creating Viki/Niki

I had read The Three Faces of Eve *by Dr. Thigpen, which is a real case, and it fascinated me. I've always been very interested in psychiatry. Then I had heard a story about a movie star who was so sure his first child was going to be a boy that he had "Jr." embroidered on his infant pajamas.*

It turned out that the baby was a girl, and I do think she grew up feeling she had displeased her father, while trying to be perfect for him. I thought of this situation in terms of the father, and how his daughter became his girl Friday.

I thought about trying to live up to this yardstick with such constraints, and that led me to Victoria named for Victor. The stories just sprang out from there.

> Agnes Nixon
> Creator, All My Children, One Life to Live, Loving

On playing Viki

*W*hen I took the part of Viki in 1973, she was already a very established character with an unbelievable history in just three short years. I had never followed another actor in a part—I always had a chance to start from scratch—so this was a challenge.*

Viki already had the split personality and had been married, and not married, and almost married many times. And as the years went by she got busier and crazier and better and funnier. It has been an extraordinary experience.

> Erika Slezak
> From One Life to Live *seminar at*
> The Museum of Television & Radio
> July 8, 1993

One Life to Live: *Carla Gray (Ellen Holly) and Ed Hall (Al Freeman, Jr.)*

logue in which an actor steps out of character to recommend a toll-free number or to read material about the subject of the story, especially when the topic is a life-threatening one such as domestic violence or AIDS.

Still, despite such events as the high-profile Soap Summits held in 1994 and 1996, in which industry professionals and family-planning advocates met to discuss the responsibilities of producers to viewers, soaps continue to focus mainly on conventional melodramatic complications in the romantic and family lives of their characters. A few examples of story lines about social identity illustrate both soaps' unusual ability to examine complex issues and their essential commitment to the social status quo.

Questions of Identity: Race

One of *One Life to Live*'s early story lines concerned Carla Gray, a black woman passing as white who was romantically involved with both a white and a black man. Those relationships were depicted explicitly in terms of the three characters' racial identities, and Carla was also shown attempting to forge a new class identity by turning her back on her mother Sadie, a cleaning woman. This mother-daughter conflict over race and class was underlined by Sadie's insistence on calling her daughter by her given name, Clara, rather than the supposedly more sophisticated-sounding Carla.

Like most soap opera attempts to tackle inflammatory subjects such as racism, Carla's story focused narrowly on the personal, ignoring the institutional connections between, say, bigotry and poverty in favor of a story about the risks of interracial romance. For many years, such relationships were largely taboo on soaps, and mixed-race couples remain practically nonexistent even on current prime-time series. Since the eighties, however, *General Hospital, All My Children, One Life to Live*, and *As the World Turns* have all introduced black-white pairings. Yet once the community's initial objections are overcome, questions about racial difference are largely abandoned. One exception came in 1987 on *General Hospital*, when Simone Ravelle, a black doctor, faced criticism for her impending marriage to Tom Hardy, a white doctor. Controversy over their relationship erupted again in 1990, when Simone's brief affair with another black doctor led to a paternity mystery that was standard soap fare in every way but one: Simone's one-time lover argued for custody of her son on the grounds that a black child deserved two black parents, directly invoking public debates about racial identity. (The argument was rendered moot when Tom was proven to be the boy's biological father.)

African-American characters now have major story lines on many shows, and often occupy important slots within the show's social hierarchy. Yet apart from love affairs, they remain isolated from the dominant white community, as if romance is the only route to real integration. Despite the fact that *The Young and the Restless*'s Neil Winters holds a high-ranking position at Newman Enterprises, for instance, he and his African-American wife, brother, and sister-in-law rarely seem to interact with the other characters outside of work. A vivid exception to this segregation was NBC's *Generations* (1989–91), the first soap to include African-Americans among its core families from the very first episode. Interestingly, although the cast was not in fact predominantly black, it was widely perceived as a "black" program.

Questions of Identity: Sexuality

Many soaps have also featured highly publicized stories about AIDS and HIV, and have even joined in an annual "Day of Compassion" intended to educate audience members about the epidemic. *General Hospital*'s story of teen lovers Stone Cates, who died of AIDS in 1995, and Robin Scorpio, who discovered that she was HIV-positive shortly before Stone's death, was especially powerful in demonstrating its long-term consequences. The choice to make Robin, a regular character for more than a decade, HIV-positive personalized the issue for viewers who had grown attached to her through the years, as well as serving the didactic purpose of stressing the risks of unprotected sex. But such story lines have also been wildly inaccurate in terms of the populations they portray: none have significantly involved on-screen gay characters with HIV (although *General Hospital* did feature occasional appearances by a gay actor with AIDS playing a gay man with AIDS—a television first—and when the actor died, his character's death was included on the program). Instead, most have focused on white, heterosexual women (the shows' target audience) who contracted the virus from sexual contact with an infected male drug abuser; and only on *The Young and the Restless* has the depiction even involved African-Americans, the heterosexual group most affected by HIV/AIDS.

In 1995, *All My Children* broke dramatic new ground by introducing a long-term gay character, high school history teacher Michael Delaney, who was deliberately integrated into the community of Pine Valley several months before his sexual identity was revealed. Linked to one of the town's major kinship networks through his sister Laurel Dillon and to the larger community through his friendships with several important characters, Michael disclosed his sexual preference first to his friend Dixie Martin, and then to his students during a lesson on the Holocaust. A bitter controversy over his fitness to teach followed, leading to his suspension. This was followed by a sensational appearance on a local television talk show, during which Laurel was accidentally shot and killed by Jason Sheffield, an alcoholic maniac obsessed with Dixie and convinced that Michael had corrupted his (Jason's) younger gay brother Kevin as well.

This story represented an enormous departure from soap tradition because it encouraged viewers to become attached to Michael before revealing that he was gay. Earlier soap opera presentations of gay and lesbian characters (such as *All My Children*'s own 1983 lesbian story line and *One Life to Live*'s 1992 gay teen plot) tended to be short-term, problem-centered stories. But this one not only had a clear social agenda—the active promotion of tolerance and acceptance—but also suggested that gay characters might exist permanently throughout the soap opera world. Michael's persecution inspired Kevin to come out (which his teenage friends accepted without much difficulty), and revealed the presence of at least two additional adult gay male characters, including a doctor whom Michael later dated.

Yet *All My Children* stopped well short of confronting central aspects of homophobia, and of asking some obvious questions about the community's acceptance of anyone who departs significantly from the status quo. The story presented Michael as both flawless (a marvelous and charismatic teacher) and flawlessly masculine (an athlete without a single

---

On the AIDS story line

When we decided to do the AIDS story, we knew it had to be Stone because Stone was the most believable, the most viable. He was important to us, but he could die. It was he who could affect someone so central to the core—Robin—that it would shock everybody, and it was he whom we could take through the awful process. He was sufficiently important to us and important to Robin, so that it worked.

Two-thirds of the way into the story, the network simply asked, "Do we have to go through with it, does Robin have to have AIDS?" And I said, "If she doesn't, it's a sensational stunt and it means nothing."

I was scared about the audience response to it. It was not a surprise to me that they found it hard to take. I have to tell you, by the time we were halfway into it, I hated to get up in the morning. I was so grief-stricken, I was so upset. Then I started getting these letters from people who were grateful for the story. So as far as I was concerned, that story was a smashing success.

Claire Labine
Creator, Ryan's Hope
former Head Writer, General Hospital

Generations

On the AIDS story line

*O*ur AIDS story line was a collaboration of many people. When I came on the show, there were certain stories that I wanted to tell, but the characters needed to be in the right place. When Claire Labine and I got together, we talked about this. We wanted to do a love story, a heterosexual love story dealing with safe sex and AIDS. We felt it was easy to dismiss by saying, "Oh, it's that gay disease, or, oh, it's that drug addicts' disease." Unfortunately, statistics tell us now that the heterosexual teenage community is the largest at risk.

As Claire became more intimate with the characters, Robin and Stone's love story evolved. One day in the middle of a conversation, Claire turned to me with a glint of delight in her eye that only she possesses and whispered, "It's Robin and Stone," and I knew she had it . . . and we had our story. Stone's background and Robin's intelligence and strength, the timing, their youth, all made it right. From the start we wanted to do a love story about two people who thought they were informed about safe sex, and weren't.

Wendy Riche
Executive Producer, General Hospital

stereotypically gay trait). It separated the homophobia plot from any hint of actual sexual activity on his part, and it characterized nearly all who opposed him as irrational homophobes and hypocrites. The program thus oversimplified the challenges such a figure might pose to the close-knit community of Pine Valley. Where, for instance, do gay couples fit into its elaborate kinship network, and how would Michael's supporters feel about a gay man or a lesbian who conformed more closely to popular stereotypes? By making Kevin a similar teenage paragon of athletic prowess and popularity, the story also implied, perhaps unintentionally, that gay men can be accepted only if they achieved a high level of asexual perfection.

Despite such shortcomings, however, story lines like this demonstrate the soap opera's ability to integrate viewers' real-world concerns into their fictional worlds. They may remain fixated on personal life at the cost of deeper political insight and shy away from certain overt challenges to tradition, but daytime soaps over the last four decades have become more directly connected to the larger social world, bolder in their willingness to tackle controversial issues, and more detailed and realistic in their depiction of complex problems. The genre's unique structure, its fundamental emphasis on social relations, and its audience's special relationship to characters and events encourage a degree of social engagement that prime-time series rarely exhibit. Viewers can expect the treatment of such issues to continue their evolution in the years to come.

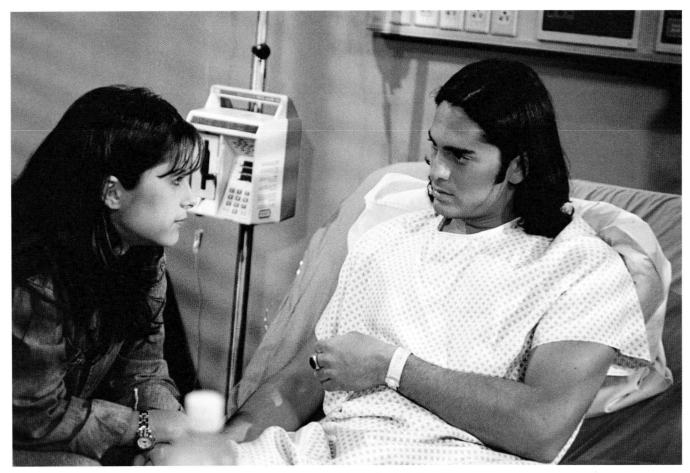

General Hospital: *Stone Cates (Michael Sutton) and Robin Scorpio (Kimberly McCullough)*

All My Children: *Michael Delaney (Chris Bruno) and Tim Dillon (Tommy Michaels)*

Tunes In

An International Perspective ◆ by Robert C. Allen

We in the United States see the characteristics of daytime serials as central to our notion of what constitutes a soap opera, and with good reason: they and their radio predecessors have been defining features of American commercial broadcasting since 1930, when a former schoolteacher from Dayton, Ohio, Irna Phillips, wrote *Painted Dreams* for Chicago radio station WGN. And we have been absorbed by the lives and loves of Mother Moynihan and all her figurative children ever since. But the insularity of the U.S. television market obscures the remarkable diversity and vitality of the soap opera form to be found in the rest of the television universe. Except on specialized cable services and broadcast channels dedicated to foreign language programming in large U.S. cities, we never get a glimpse of the extraordinary diversity of television serials made in dozens of other countries and watched in hundreds of countries around the world.

Most Americans would be surprised to learn that Brazil, not the United States, is the world's most prolific producer and important exporter of soap operas. Brazilian *telenovelas* can draw 90 percent of the viewing audience on a given night in a country where more homes have televisions than refrigerators. These stories are seen by many more people around the world than are U.S. daytime soaps.[1] Similarly, most Americans have no idea of the remarkable cultural resonance that foreign-produced soap operas have in their own and other cultures. Soaps dominate the prime-time television schedules of nearly all Latin American countries. Mexican soap operas have been the most popular television programs of the year in countries as diverse as Korea, Turkey, and Russia. Viewers of the Chinese soap *Ke Wang (Yearnings)* in the People's Republic of China might well have constituted the largest national audience—550 million people—for any television

program ever when it was shown there in 1991. In India, the soap form is used to dramatize religious epics, and these serialized stories attract hundreds of millions of devoted followers.

Such is the size and scope of the international soap opera scene that comprehensive discussion of it would require several books, not a single essay. All I can accomplish here is the briefest of overviews, pointing out some of the most important formal and institutional differences and similarities between U.S. daytime soap operas and those produced in other cultures, and suggesting something of the power of the soap opera form in the global television economy.

The area of the world where the soap opera exerts its strongest influence is undoubtedly Latin and South America. The Spanish term for soap opera, *telenovela,* suggests both this form's essential link to U.S. soap operas and its key structural difference. Shared by all of the programming forms that I'm grouping under the term soap opera—whether made or watched in Beijing, Rio, Melbourne, Moscow, or Manhattan— is the organization of their narratives as serials. The term *telenovela* links the Latin American soap opera to the late eighteenth- and nineteenth-century tradition of serialized novel publishing. Most novelists during that time—Dickens perhaps most prominent among them—wrote for audiences who would read their novels as a series of weekly magazine installments spread out over a period of months. Writing proceeded as the installments were being read, and weekly sales of the magazines in which they were published were used to gauge audience response to characters and plotlines. Novelists whose works were published in serial form learned that one way to maximize sales was to heighten reader anticipation between episodes by concluding each episode with an unresolved plot development, the cliff-hanger, which subsequently became a defining feature of other serial forms: the movie serial, radio soap opera, and television soap.

EastEnders from Great Britain

Brazil's O Rei do Gado *(The Cattle King): Antonio Fagundes, Leonardo Bríco, and Vera Fischer*

By establishing a connection between itself and the literary novel, the *telenovela* implicitly announces that it shares with it an eventual conclusion, even if that conclusion is not accomplished until dozens or even hundreds of chapters or episodes have been read or viewed. It is the presence or absence of a conclusion—what narrative theorists call clo-

sure—that divides the international soap opera genre into two fundamentally different types. Latin American, Indian, Japanese, Chinese, and many other non-U.S. serials are written, produced, and watched with the presumption that their stories will be told over a finite number of episodes (sometimes several hundred), by the last of which the central narrative question that initiated the story will be answered and through which the fates of the central characters will be fixed. In a sense, the narrative logic of what we might call closed serials works backwards from the moment of resolution in the final episode, with each antecedent episode bringing the story one step closer to resolution or, at the very least, narrowing down narrative possibilities and closing off some avenues of plot development.

Thus, anticipation intensifies with each episode of the closed serial as viewers both eagerly await the final installment of the story and the revelations and plot twists it is bound to contain, and dread the finality that episode brings both to the story and to the viewer's engagement with its world and its characters. The most popular television pro-

Great Britain's Coronation Street: *Archie Crabtree (John Stratton) and Hilda Ogden (Jean Alexander)*

grams of the post-Soviet era in Russia have been dubbed eighties versions of Latin American *telenovelas*. One of the most spectacularly successful of them, *Los Ricos También Lloran* (*The Rich Also Cry*), was given credit by one Russian commentator for doing more to extend the lifespan of the average Russian than any government health measure: old people, he said, simply refused to die until they discovered

On directing

My job as a director is to tell the story. It's true of all of our jobs here—as actor, director, producer, or as writer. But particularly as a director, you really can't lose sight of the fact that you're not here to make pretty pictures unless that shot is telling the story the best possible way. If it's not, it's just so much garbage getting in the way of telling the story.

Gary Tomlin
Director, One Life to Live

how the serial would finally end. After the final episode of the Indian epic *Ramayan* was broadcast, one columnist referred to the country's suffering "national withdrawal symptoms," and a newspaper headline complained that "Without *Ramayan* Sunday Mornings Seem Empty."[2]

Closure is definitely not a feature of U.S. daytime soap operas, some of whose stories have been told for decades without any sign of concluding. British and Australian viewers also know their soaps as never-ending narratives. Viewers of the British soap *Coronation Street* have been following the residents of this working-class community since 1960. These stories, what we might call open soaps, are the only form of continuous narrative that presumes its own immortality. This absence of closure effects every aspect of soap opera writing, production, and viewing, producing a very different kind of pleasure for viewers, as well as a very different narrative structure than stories that build to some sort of resolution.

This lack of closure in the open serial means that no one sits down to watch an episode of *All My Children* or the British soap *EastEnders* or the Australian serial *Neighbours*

Los Ricos También Lloran (The Rich Also Cry), *from Mexico: Mariana Villareal (Veronica Castro) and Luis de la Parra (Rogelio Guerra)*

with the expectation that it will be the last or, even if they knew it would be the last, that it would provide justification for all the hours spent watching previous episodes. It also means that nothing that any character does nor any event that occurs in the world of the open serial will bring the over-all narrative one step closer to ultimate resolution.

If, then, there is no point of final resolution toward which the narrative of open soap operas is headed, why do so many people around the world watch them? There are all sorts of reasons, but one of them has to do with the viewer's ability to get to know a community of characters over a long period. Our interest is secured by and diffused among this entire community rather than concentrated on the fate of any one particular character. The longer we watch, the more we become a part of the history of that community and the more intricate its fabric appears to us.[3]

Japan's Hoshi no Kinka (Heaven's Coins): Takumi Nagai (Yutaka Takenouchi), Shuichi Nagai (Takao Osawa), and Aya Kuramoto (Noriko Sakai)

Thus, open and closed soap operas work in significantly different ways to attract and hold an audience's attention, and on one level they hold out the promise of quite different kinds of viewing pleasure. But, whether closure comes after several hundred episodes (the outer limits of the *telenovela*'s run) or is still not in sight after more than 12,000 (the number of *Guiding Light* episodes on television alone), soaps' seriality binds them together as a distinctive type of television narrative wherever they are produced and shown around the world.

Soap operas also share important connections between the distinctive ways they engage their audiences and the kinds of things they tend to be about. A complaint heard about soap operas wherever they are produced or watched in the world (made principally by those who do not watch them) is that we never see anything happen on soap operas, that all people do is talk and emote. This is, I would argue, in part a fundamental misunderstanding of the way soap operas, particularly open soap operas, work: what happens is not nearly so important as the effect of an action on relationships. But however widely this criticism misses its mark, it does point to a common feature among soap operas: soaps are about talk, and, as a consequence, much of what we see on soap operas around the world is people talking. These conversations activate, expand, reinforce, and alter the network of interpersonal relationships so important to our experience of watching soaps. The content of soap talk obviously varies between soaps, across cultures, and in relation to the audience sought.

The centrality of talk to the soap opera form is also a function of the economics of international soap opera production. With few exceptions, in comparison to other forms of dramatic programming, soaps are made on very small budgets per episode. Furthermore, the quantity of programming they represent demands that they be shot quickly and simply. Thus, although there are notable exceptions, most soaps generally eschew extended exterior shooting, elaborate interior sets, special effects, or complicated postproduction editing.[4] The emblematic soap opera image is the close-up of a human face: talking or reacting to talk. Talk, in other words, is cheap.

One nearly universal characteristic of soap operas is that soap talk on the screen seems to provoke talk about soaps among people who watch them. The gaps between episodes, which often end by raising more plot questions than they answer, leave a space that viewers almost inevitably fill with their own talk about what has, will, and should happen next.

Scholars in England have examined the important role that talk about soaps plays in structuring social interaction among office workers and between mothers and daughters. Asian teenagers in London talk about Australian soaps with their parents as a way of negotiating intercultural and generational differences.[5] Anthropologist Lisa Rofel has studied the talking space provided between the episodes of China's most popular soap opera, *Ke Wang* (*Yearnings*) in 1991. Although made with the blessing of the Chinese government and praised by officials of the office of propaganda, *Yearnings*'s treatment of the conflict between traditional and modern social values and the role of women in Chinese society sparked debates in homes, factories, and cafés that neither the government nor the soap's own political agenda could contain.[6]

Talk about soap operas, soap opera actors, indeed, the very popularity of soaps, has been the subject of public discourse in many countries. Although some U.S. soap actors have large and loyal followings, soap opera stars in other countries frequently find themselves objects of both massive public adulation and press scrutiny. Around the world, the press seems fascinated with the relationship between a prominent soap actor's role and his or her off-screen life, particularly if some dissonance can be found between the two. British tabloid newspapers chronicle the real-life tragedies, embarrassments, and peccadilloes of the stars of *EastEnders* and *Coronation Street* in front-page stories with headlines most other papers would reserve for national catastrophes.

Public talk about soap operas frequently seizes upon those occasions where the fictional world of the soap opera and the presumably nonfictional (real) world on the other side of the screen bump up against each other. Sometimes this overlapping of fiction and reality is purposive. Writers of the hugely successful 1993 Venezuelan soap opera about politics and political corruption, *Por Estas Calles* (*In These Streets*), updated episodes almost daily to keep the show current with the latest developments in the run-up to national elections. Although the producers claimed that any similarity to real political figures and controversies was coincidental, viewers saw the characters and situations as thinly veiled commentary on political graft and greed. So did the ruling party's minister of the interior, who threatened more than once to take the show off the air.[7]

It is not difficult to understand why soap operas, more than any other form of fictional programming, are associated with the blurring of the relationship between fiction and reality. Open serials and those closed serials with contemporary settings operate as parallel fictional universes, recognizable as possible worlds, removed from our own but running alongside it. Their characters, whom we get to know in closed serials over the course of several months, and in open serials over the course of many years, have faces, mannerisms, qualities, and personalities nearly as familiar as those of our coworkers and neighbors. Little wonder, then, that soap operas around the world engender fierce loyalty among viewers or that viewers are fascinated by the duality between actor and character that all soap operas produce.

Finally, although some soap operas seem deeply rooted in the particularities of the culture within which they are produced, many soap operas have a remarkable ability to speak both to their own culture and to be integrated into the cultures of viewers in countries on the other side of the world. Brazilian soaps are among the most widely distributed television programs in the world, having been seen in more than a hundred countries. Mexican soaps have attracted huge followings in nearly sixty countries, including Turkey, Korea, and Russia, as well as in their core market of Latin America.

On the power of soaps

There is a great need in human beings for other people's stories. You can follow a story for six weeks on a soap and learn a little something about different kinds of relationships, about life. I think young people tune in, and always have, because they are generally optimistic about life, and looking forward to romance and happy endings, which is just what soaps dwell on.

Harding Lemay
former Head Writer, Another World

Soaps have become an important cultural export for Australia, whose *Neighbours* has been sold to more than twenty-five countries and battles *Coronation Street* nearly every week at the top of the British ratings chart. Although latecomers to the international scene, U.S. daytime soaps are now seen throughout Europe and are carried by satellite programming services in Asia.

That soap operas are distributed globally is in large measure a function of sweeping changes that have occurred in television markets around the world in the last fifteen years, the combined effect being the significantly increased demand for low-cost programming of all types. Many western European countries have expanded the number of privately owned television channels, and in eastern Europe and the former Soviet Union commercial television has been introduced. At the same time, cable and satellite services have opened up whole new channels of programming around the world. Working on the precept that it is always cheaper to buy programming made by someone else than to make your own, programmers of these new television services have looked more and more to imported programs to fill all these new channels. Having made back their relatively low production costs in their domestic markets, soap operas can be offered on the international market for a fraction of the cost of producing original programs.

The economics of global television distribution alone, however, do not explain the popularity of Mexican soap operas in Russia or Japanese soap operas in Belgium. It is dangerous to generalize about the transcultural appeal of an entire genre of television programming: some soaps work well in some cultures but not in others, even though they may share a common language and cultural tradition. *Coronation Street* is popular in Canada but has not found an audience in Australia or the U.S. *Neighbours* tops the ratings in Britain but flopped when test marketed in Los Angeles and New York. But scholars and marketers have suggested a few reasons why the soap opera form seems to travel well, although these apply differentially to individual programs.

Many soap operas are about themes that resonate with audiences around the world: romance, family, love, happiness, personal struggle, and so forth. Even though these stories may be grounded in the specific context of the culture of their production, they do not require an audience's knowledge of that culture to empathize with the plight of the story's protagonist.

Furthermore, the narrative structure of soap operas, with their attenuated plots and gaps between episodes that invite viewer involvement, makes them especially open to different cultural readings. In other words, they can be appropriated by

On Bold vs. Y&R in the international market

*T*he international market is very unpredictable. Even though The Young and the Restless *and* The Bold and the Beautiful *are very similar in tone and style, and American audiences see them back to back and occasionally with characters crossing over, the international audience doesn't really know the relationship between the two. Interestingly enough, almost consistently, when one show is a huge success, the other show does rather poorly. For example,* Bold and Beautiful *became an undisputed hit in Italy and* Young and Restless *had been on there for years and was always struggling along and never developed a solid audience.*

Then there is France. Bold *hit a couple of real bumps on the way—we went on the second channel, maybe in the wrong time slot—and it went off the air for a little while;* Young and Restless *went on to become a huge success. In other markets like Turkey,* Young and Restless *is a huge success and* Bold and Beautiful *is not, but the reverse is true in Holland. We have yet to find a market where both shows are a home run; however, we really don't have too many markets where both shows fail, either.*

> Bill Bell, Jr.
> President, Bell-Phillip Television Productions, Inc.

The Bold and the Beautiful

Neighbours, *from Australia: Max and Maria Ramsay (Francis Bell and Dasha Blahova)*

viewers in different cultures in different ways. Researchers attempting to explain the extraordinary popularity of the Japanese soap opera *Oshin* in Belgium, for example, noted that many viewers saw parallels between the early-twentieth-century setting of the beginning of the serial and the Belgium of their grandparents' era. In Iran, on the other hand, where *Oshin* was also one of the most popular programs of the eighties, a majority of viewers surveyed saw similarities between the show and the contemporary situation in their own country. Anthropologist Daniel Miller has examined the process by which *The Young and the Restless* is not merely "consumed" in Trinidad, but actively refashioned by its viewers there and

made to speak to the current economic and social conditions of that island culture.[8]

Soap operas are an important part of the everyday life of literally hundreds of millions of television viewers around the world. The serial is one of the most diverse and dynamic forms of television in the world today and one of the most compelling ways to tell a story ever devised. Although it is difficult for us in the United States to observe, soap operas have also gone global in the last decade, enabling some countries—Brazil and Mexico chief among them—to become important exporters of television culture. As the world turns, so does the soap.

The Classic

Soap Operas

One way to explore the history of soap operas is to trace the lineages of several important shows through their most significant creators. Creating a radio or television series is a collaborative process, and the most talented people usually work their way up to decision-making roles. Those who assist the originators of one series often strike out and establish their own body of work. The chart of this journey within this genre very much resembles a generational family tree.

The diagram reproduced on pages 122–23 juxtaposes the dominant creators in radio with the creators of television soaps that were being broadcast as of September 1996. (It includes Roy Winsor, whose shows are no longer on the air, but whose *Search for Tomorrow* was the first significant television soap.) Moreover, each of the creators listed has at least one series that has been on for twenty years or more.

The diagram visualizes two very important stories:

- Irna Phillips was the only creator of radio soap opera to successfully create television serials.
- Through the fall of 1996 every extant soap but one can trace its creative roots back to Irna Phillips. (The exception is *General Hospital*, which was created by Doris and Frank Hursley, who made dramas and comedies on radio, but no soap operas.)

Although there is no direct cause and effect, it is intriguing to note that soaps that cannot trace their roots to Phillips are no longer on the air (for example, *Search for Tomorrow*, *The Secret Storm*, *The Edge of Night*, or *Santa Barbara*, created by the Hursley's daughter Bridget and her husband Jerome Dobson).

This chart is not a comprehensive history of series by any means; head writers are listed only if they went on to establish their own programs. (For example, James Lipton was the head writer in between Irna Phillips and Agnes Nixon on *Another World*, but he is not listed because he did not start his own series.) It is not as if there were no other important creators of radio and television serials, for there were Carlton Morse of *One Man's Family*, Jane Cruisinberry of *The Story of Mary Marlin* and Claire Labine and Paul Avila Mayer of *Ryan's Hope*, just to name a few. But that is another story.

The point here is that when the lineage of soap operas is plotted, the story becomes that of Irna Phillips—how she established numerous, important soaps on radio, then took her vision to television, which found the fullest expression in *As the World Turns*. On each of her long-running television serials, she worked with two young writers who were to become her protégés, Agnes Nixon and William J. Bell. Ted Corday, a director of many of Phillips's radio serials, was a key collaborator in the development of *As the World Turns* and then established another of the longest-running television soaps, *Days of Our Lives*, with Irna.

Much research needs to be done to determine how a soap evolves over the years. How much of Irna Phillips remains in *As the World Turns*? Who were the dominant writers and producers who also left their mark on the serial, and how did their work affect Phillips's original vision? How did Nixon and Bell's pioneering efforts affect the writing on Irna Phillips's original series? The hope is that this effort will inspire others to continue the study of this complex genre.

The write-ups beginning on page 124 of the series in the exhibition were prepared by Alisa Levien, based on the scholarship of Chris Schemering's *The Soap Opera Encyclopedia* and Robert LaGuardia's *Soap Opera World*, as well as on original research by the author and the Museum's curatorial department. The series are described in chronological order based on their premieres.

All My Children: *Erica Kane (Susan Lucci)*

RADIO

THE HUMMERTS

STOLEN HUSBAND
1931
Created and written by **Robert Hardy Andrews**
Produced by Frank and Anne Hummert

BETTY AND BOB
1932–1940
Written by **R. H. Andrews**
Produced by Hummerts

JUST PLAIN BILL
1933–1955
Written by **R. H. Andrews**
Produced by Hummerts

MA PERKINS
1933–1960
Created and written by **R. H. Andrews**
Produced by Hummerts
Directed by **Roy Winsor**

THE ROMANCE OF HELEN TRENT
1933–1960
Produced by Hummerts

MARY NOBLE, BACKSTAGE WIFE
1935–1959
Produced by Hummerts

LORENZO JONES
1937–1955
Produced and directed by Frank Hummert

OUR GAL SUNDAY
1937–1959
Produced by Hummerts

THE COUPLE NEXT DOOR
1937–1960
Produced by Hummerts

YOUNG WIDDER BROWN
1938–1956
Produced by Hummerts

STELLA DALLAS
1938–1955
Produced by Hummerts

VALIANT LADY
1938–48; 1951–52
Created by Hummerts
[on television from 1953–57]

FRONT PAGE FARRELL
1941–1954
Produced by Hummerts

IRNA PHILLIPS

PAINTED DREAMS
1930–36; 1940
Created, written by, and starring Irna Phillips
(Phillips leaves over dispute, 1932)

TODAY'S CHILDREN
1932–1938
Created, written by, and starring Phillips

THE ROAD OF LIFE
1937–1959
Created and written by Phillips
[on television from 1954–55]

THE GUIDING LIGHT
1937–1956
Created and written by Phillips
Directed by Ted Corday (late forties, early fifties)
[on television from 1952–present]

THE WOMAN IN WHITE
1938–1948
Created and written by Phillips
Agnes Nixon meets Phillips;
writes dialogue

THE RIGHT TO HAPPINESS
1939–1960
Created and written by Phillips
(spin-off of **The Guiding Light**)

THE BRIGHTER DAY
1948–1956
Written by Phillips
Directed by Ted Corday
(spin-off of **Joyce Jordan, M.D.**)
[on television from 1954–62]

ELAINE STERNE CARRINGTON

PEPPER YOUNG'S FAMILY
1936–1959
Earlier known as **Red Adams** (1932–33),
Red Davis (1933–35), and
Forever Young (1935–36)

Created and written by Carrington
Produced by Betty Corday (daytime producer
for Benton & Bowles, 1953–57)

WHEN A GIRL MARRIES
1939–1957
Created and written by Carrington
*[went to television as **Follow Your Heart**
from 1953–54]*

ROSEMARY
1944–1955
Created and written by Carrington
Produced by Betty Corday (daytime producer
for Benton & Bowles, 1953–57)

ONE LIFE TO LIVE
1968–PRESENT
Created by Agnes Nixon

ROY WINSOR

SEARCH FOR TOMORROW
1951–1986
Created by **Roy Winsor**
1951   Nixon writes for first 13 weeks
1956–63   Frank and Doris Hursley
        head writers

LOVE OF LIFE
1951–1980
Created by **Roy Winsor** and John Hess

THE SECRET STORM
1954–1974
Created by **Roy Winsor**

THE HURSLEYS

GENERAL HOSPITAL
1963–PRESENT
Created by Frank and Doris Hursley

TELEVISION

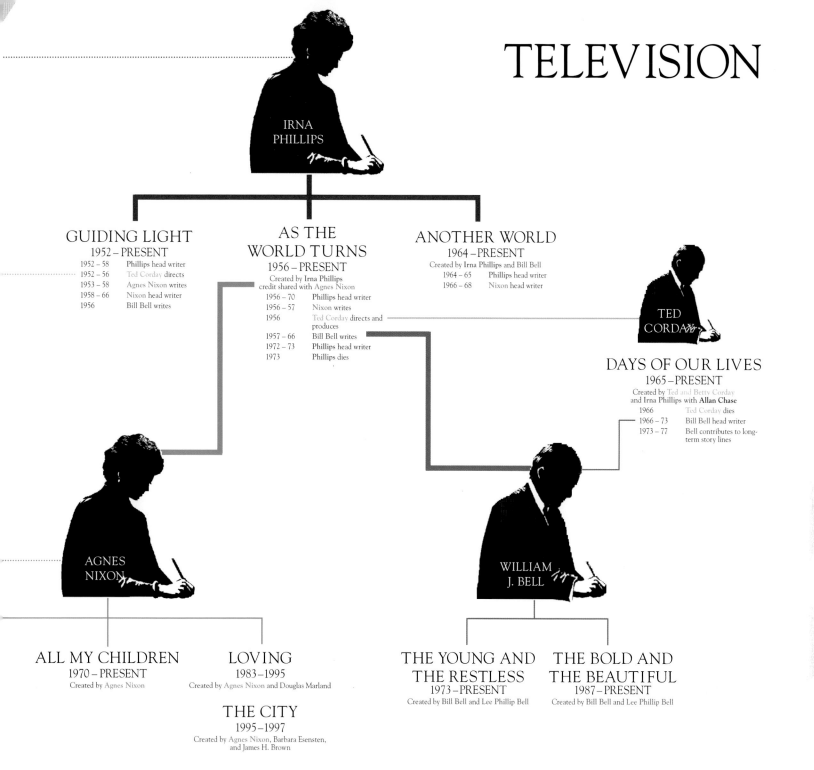

IRNA PHILLIPS

GUIDING LIGHT
1952 – PRESENT
1952 – 58	Phillips head writer
1952 – 56	Ted Corday directs
1953 – 58	Agnes Nixon writes
1958 – 66	Nixon head writer
1956	Bill Bell writes

AS THE WORLD TURNS
1956 – PRESENT
Created by Irna Phillips
credit shared with Agnes Nixon
1956 – 70	Phillips head writer
1956 – 57	Nixon writes
1956	Ted Corday directs and produces
1957 – 66	Bill Bell writes
1972 – 73	Phillips head writer
1973	Phillips dies

ANOTHER WORLD
1964 – PRESENT
Created by Irna Phillips and Bill Bell
1964 – 65	Phillips head writer
1966 – 68	Nixon head writer

TED CORDAY

DAYS OF OUR LIVES
1965 – PRESENT
Created by Ted and Betty Corday
and Irna Phillips with **Allan Chase**
1966	Ted Corday dies
1966 – 73	Bill Bell head writer
1973 – 77	Bell contributes to long-term story lines

AGNES NIXON

ALL MY CHILDREN
1970 – PRESENT
Created by Agnes Nixon

LOVING
1983 – 1995
Created by Agnes Nixon and Douglas Marland

THE CITY
1995 – 1997
Created by Agnes Nixon, Barbara Esensten, and James H. Brown

WILLIAM J. BELL

THE YOUNG AND THE RESTLESS
1973 – PRESENT
Created by Bill Bell and Lee Phillip Bell

THE BOLD AND THE BEAUTIFUL
1987 – PRESENT
Created by Bill Bell and Lee Phillip Bell

The Legacy of Irna Phillips

Many conflicting sources have tried to establish specific years for changes within soaps over their sixty-five-year history. For radio dates, this chart (designed by Jack CK Chen) follows Frank Buxton and Bill Owen's *The Big Broadcast*, John Dunning's *Tune in Yesterday*, and Vincent Terrace's *Radio's Golden Years*; for television the dates reflect the scholarship of Christopher Schemering from his *Soap Opera Encyclopedia* and Robert LaGuardia from *Soap World*.

* In 1977 *The Guiding Light* officially changed its name to *Guiding Light*.

SEARCH FOR TOMORROW

From the earliest days of television, serial veterans tried to transfer the popular soap opera format from radio to the new broadcast medium. There were early attempts as far back as 1948, but Roy Winsor, a producer and director whose radio credits include *Ma Perkins* and *Vic and Sade,* was the first to succeed. Debuting on September 3, 1951, his creation, *Search for Tomorrow,* was an immediate ratings hit despite production values only marginally more sophisticated than those on radio. The reason was simple: Winsor was the first serial creator to recognize that both the audience and the medium had changed profoundly. In an America freed from the depression and world war, soap audiences no longer wanted or needed the palliative of romantic fantasy. Instead, they craved a fictional world that reflected their own struggles and concerns. Television was tailor-made for the intimacy and realism such storytelling required. In fact, the new medium demanded it. Winsor took advantage of this fact. Borrowing elements familiar to radio audiences—the single heroine and simple theme—he created a naturalistic style of domestic drama that was as resonant with fifties audiences as the depression-era romantic fantasies had been earlier. Assisting Winsor in his endeavor were Agnes Nixon, who penned the first thirteen weeks, and Irving Vendig, who wrote the show for the next five years.

Search for Tomorrow might not have been the success it was without actress Mary Stuart and the character she so completely inhabited, Joanne Tate. Jo, as she was fondly known by audiences for over thirty-five years, was a direct descendant of the serial heroines of radio. She cared about other people's problems, providing wise counsel to neighbors and friends, while facing her own heartaches with quiet dignity and resolve. But she was also the first of a long line of heroines unique to television soap opera, struggling more with issues of marriage, children, and family than those of romantic fulfillment. Her conceptual heirs continue to populate soap opera today, though in diminishing numbers.

The first two decades of *Search for Tomorrow* focused exclusively on Jo, her family, and her friends. Widowed six weeks after the show debuted, Jo had to contend not only with her own grief, but also with the interference of her mother-in-law, who sued for custody of Jo's young daughter, then kidnapped the girl when she lost. Later stories involved Jo's romances with Arthur Tate, Sam Reynolds, and Tony Vincente and her constant battles to save Motor Haven Lodge, the motel and restaurant she owned, from various opportunists. Even when stories did not center around Jo, the characters involved would turn to her for advice. Throughout her own ordeals, Jo could rely on the love and encouragement of next door neighbors and best friends Stu and Marge Bergman. Their support, always offered with a joke or a smile, provided much needed comic relief from all of the turmoil.

By the early seventies, competitive pressures from newer, more successful soap operas and younger audiences combined to shift the focus from Jo onto other characters. First Jo's teenage daughter, Patti, and Patti's best friend, Janet Bergman (daughter of Stu and Marge) took center stage, then other more recent arrivals. When ratings didn't improve, the show tried a variety of different styles to attract a larger audience. Husband and wife head writers Ralph Ellis and Eugenie Hunt added a dose of feminism to the show with law student Kathy Parker choosing abortion when a baby would have interfered with her career. Other head writers tried a multigenerational approach with stories focusing on teenage Liza Walton (Janet's daughter), young marrieds Scott and Kathy Phillips, and a new romantic triangle for Jo.

But with every change, *Search for Tomorrow* only moved further from its roots in domestic drama—where a single complication can provide years of compelling story—and seemed less interested in Jo, still the show's most beloved

On the ending of Search

Jo had a dream of how things ought to be. She said, "You know, I wish Patty would be happy, I wish so-and-so would be happy, I wish this would happen, I wish that would . . ." and that's what they did. They wrapped up everything. Those shows were the hardest to fit the moments, because they were so complicated. I felt like a spider weaving a web because I had so many people to relate to, and it all had to work. Well, we got through, somehow, down to the last two lines, just me and Larry Haines. I heard his voice break, and I thought, "Oh, Larry, don't lose it now, because we'll never get it back. If either one of us loses it, at this moment . . ." He got it under control and said the line, and I said mine, and we were off.

Mary Stuart
"Jo Tate"

Search for Tomorrow: *Jo Tate (Mary Stuart)*

character. Audiences no longer recognized their soap. Neither the popularity of Liza's pairing with dashing Travis Sentell, nor the show's move from CBS to NBC in March of 1982, nor the publicity-generating airing of a live episode on August 4, 1983, could stop the ratings decline. On December 26, 1986, *Search for Tomorrow* broadcast its final episode. Fittingly, Jo spoke the final words. As she stared at the stars, her longtime friend Stu asked her, "What is it, Jo? What are you searching for?" "Tomorrow," she responded. "And I can't wait."

Love of Life: Bruce Sterling (Ronald Tomme) and Vanessa Dale (Audrey Peters)

LOVE OF LIFE

Roy Winsor's second television soap opera, *Love of Life*, debuted on September 24, 1951, just three weeks after his *Search for Tomorrow*. It also borrowed its simplicity of theme—good outlasts evil—and its focus on a single heroine from its radio forebears, even employing an opening epigraph to make the point: "*Love of Life:* The story of Vanessa Dale in her courageous struggle for human dignity." But despite the similarities, this television serial was more sophisticated than its antecedents, including *Search for Tomorrow*. Sexuality, though not explicit, was acknowledged as a part of life in stories about divorce, adultery, and infertility. In contrast to her untouchable radio counterparts, whose chaste quests for romance remained unconsummated, virginal Vanessa eventually married. Even *Love of Life's* initial good-versus-evil theme was not as simplistic as it sounded. Stories remained focused on home and heart, but the never-ending standoff between Vanessa and her immoral sister Margaret also reflected the deeper societal anxieties of the cold-war world in which the moral threat of Communism appeared equally unrelenting. *Love of Life* reassured viewers with its continual reaffirmation of the quiet rewards of a life lived according to core American values.

For its first five years, *Love of Life* focused almost exclusively on the story of Vanessa (Van) and Margaret (Meg) Dale. While Van struggled to live a proper life, Meg flaunted her indiscretions, marrying for money, ignoring her young son, and engaging in one affair after another with men of questionable character. Van moved from their childhood home of Barrowsville to New York City in order to keep an eye on her unpredictable sister, but returned frequently to keep their mother apprised of Meg's latest adventures. Van also found time for romance. She fell in love with and married lawyer Paul Raven, who defended her sister on a murder charge.

With Meg's departure in the midfifties, *Love of Life* followed the lead of more successful soaps such as *Guiding Light* and *As the World Turns* and dropped its simple, morality-play format in favor of an expanded canvas of characters and sto-

ries. Van, now widowed, moved to suburban Rosehill, New York, where she fell in love with teacher Bruce Sterling and became involved in the lives of other townspeople. While Van herself remained above reproach, she had to deal with the infidelities and jealousies of her new husband and the meddling of his selfish family. By the late sixties, with CBS in control, and Winsor no longer guiding his creation, ratings pressures from newer, more contemporary soap operas began to drive the storytelling. As the show increasingly borrowed themes and stories—drugs, campus unrest, love triangles involving pregnancy—from its more modern competition, it lost its own moral center completely. The changes demoralized longtime viewers. The divorce of flawless heroine Vanessa during this period, and the outrage it caused, reflected both the changing mores of much of American society and the traditional values still held by *Love of Life's* core audience. The ratings, always among the weakest in CBS's blockbuster lineup, began to fall precipitously.

In 1973, producer Jean Arley and writers Claire Labine and Paul Avila Mayer revitalized the show briefly. They were able to satisfy longtime viewers by bringing Meg back into the story and returning the show to its earlier theme of good versus evil, while mixing in a good dose of young love and lavish production values to entice newer viewers. The resurgence, however, was short-lived. The series of writers who replaced Labine and Mayer were unable to finesse the disparity between the show's traditional core audience of older housewives and the newer, younger soap viewers whose interests were defining the genre in the seventies. By the end of the decade, when *General Hospital's* phenomenal success had solidified daytime's demographic shift, *Love of Life* was not satisfying either group. On February 1, 1980, after close to twenty-nine years on the air, the soap aired its final episode. Rather than end any of its story lines, the show left them dangling in the hope it would be picked up by another network. When it wasn't, the long-standing moral battle between sisters Van and Meg was left forever unresolved.

GUIDING LIGHT

The *Guiding Light* that Irna Phillips brought to television on June 30, 1952, was very different from the show that she premiered on radio on January 25, 1937. Originally conceived as the story of the Reverend Dr. John Ruthledge of the Little Church of Five Points, his family, and his troubled parishioners, early episodes had a strong religious tone with sermons sometimes consuming the entire fifteen-minute broadcast. Family togetherness and the belief that faith brings happiness were strong underlying themes. But the spiritual nature of the serial did not preordain a timidity of subject matter. While the rest of radio soapdom dealt with romantic wish-fulfillment, *Guiding Light*'s story lines involved labor unions, isolationism and antiwar sentiment preceding World War II, incest, sadomasochism, justifiable homicide, adultery, and illegitimate pregnancy. Ruthledge, the first in the long line of professional men and women who would populate Phillips's soaps, would argue mankind's inherent decency in the face of trying circumstances with Ellis Smith, also known as Mr. Nobody from Nowhere, a cynical man who only saw the inhumanity in others.

By the time *Guiding Light* premiered on television in 1952, the serial had undergone a complete metamorphosis. The Bauers, a family of German immigrant parents and their American-born children, had supplanted Ruthledge and his congregation as the central characters of the program. While faith remained a strong theme, it was now played out in the daily tests faced by family members; whether it was the melodramatic plights of daughter Meta, who bore a son out of wedlock and then murdered his abusive father, or the more ordinary problems faced by young marrieds Bill and Bert Bauer. Meta's stepdaughter, Kathy Roberts, took center stage during the four years *Guiding Light* was broadcast on both radio and television (1952–56) and for several years thereafter. Her death in 1958 demonstrated another aspect of the Phillips philosophy: the writer responded to the outpouring of viewers' grief-stricken letters with the homily, "We cannot, any of us, live with life alone . . . ."

Throughout the fifties and early sixties, *Guiding Light* thrived under the confident leadership first of Phillips and then of her protégé, Agnes Nixon, who introduced daytime's first significant black character, nurse Martha Frazier, and wrote one of the earliest social-issue story lines, in which Bert's life was saved by a Pap smear. After Nixon's departure, however, the show began to falter. It failed to adjust to the contemporary spirit of the newer soaps, especially those written by Nixon and fellow Phillips's protégé Bill Bell. The soap was in serious trouble by the time Bridget and Jerome Dobson took over head-writing responsibilities in 1975 and began revitalizing the show. They introduced two new families, the Spauldings and the Marlers, and constructed story lines around villain Roger Thorpe. They also updated the title by officially shortening it to *Guiding Light*.

Douglas Marland continued the reconstruction when he took over the show in the spring of 1980, following his role in the resurrection of *General Hospital*. With the additions of the poor Reardon family and the wealthy Chamberlains, *Guiding Light* was once again competitive, climbing to number three in the Nielsens despite being programmed opposite ratings powerhouse *General Hospital*. The show also won critical acclaim and Emmy gold for its imaginative fantasy sequences, in which movie fan Nola Reardon played out her longings and frustrations by imagining herself in scenes from her favorite films.

On breast cancer

We had a story about breast cancer that Tina Sloan portrayed. In a television movie of the week, that would happen in two hours, from start to finish. We did it in real time: the character discovered a lump, agonized for weeks whether or not she had the courage to tell anybody about it, then finally had the courage to tell a doctor, who talked about self-examination. We actually did a mammography on camera, and then dealt with the issues of whether to do a radical mastectomy or what the various options were. The character went through all of these decisions. It is really a stunning victory for daytime. We can tell real stories that matter to people.

Roy Steinberg
Producer, Guiding Light

Guiding Light: *Papa Bauer (Theo Goetz) and Bert Bauer (Charita Bauer)*

The eighties saw several changes, as the new head writers decided to write out several members of the Bauer family. Within a short time, Hope, Michael, and Hillary Bauer were written out of the story or killed off. The biggest blow to the family was the offscreen death in 1985 of the irreplaceable Charita Bauer, who had played matriarch Bert Bauer for over thirty-five years. The nineties have seen the great romance of Reva and Josh and the further intrigues of Roger, while Bert's grandchildren Rick and Michelle link today's *Guiding Light* to the show's rich history.

The Secret Storm: *Valerie Hill Ames (Lori March) and Amy Ames (Jada Rowland)*

THE SECRET STORM

Perhaps no daytime drama demonstrated Roy Winsor's belief that good soap opera was simply a matter of delineating a solid theme and adhering to it than his third creation, *The Secret Storm*. Retaining the simple thematic format of his first two television serials (*Search for Tomorrow* and *Love of Life*), but adding the familial structure that had proved so successful on *Guiding Light*, Winsor devised the story of a family, the Ameses, who were so devastated by tragedy that each of its members retreated into his or her own secret world of despair. Even the father, who possessed the stoic dignity of characters like Jo (*Search for Tomorrow*) and Van (*Love of Life*), succumbed to his overwhelming grief. Raw and immediate in a way never seen on daytime television before, the show became an instant success. Its psychological theme of inner conflict and hidden desire was as resonant with audiences as the domestic, romantic, and moral themes of Winsor's earlier soaps. Only when the show abandoned that original concept, and the Ames family with it, did *Secret Storm* lose its audience. For fifteen years, however, under the guidance of Winsor and director Gloria Monty, a theater veteran new to television and the serial format, it was one of the most compelling and progressive shows on daytime television.

The Secret Storm began on February 1, 1954, with a car accident that would deprive the Ames family of wife and mother. The use of an immediate tragic climax to open the program was new and shocking to daytime viewers. It was also highly effective. The audience was able to witness every consequence this catastrophic event had on a typical, loving family. Peter, the father, became depressed and started drinking. His attempts to raise his three children and find new love were thwarted by his sister-in-law, Pauline. Teenage son Jerry, overcome with anger and grief, tried to kill the man responsible for his mother's death and was sent to reform school. Meanwhile his sister Susan tried to replace their mother by exerting a tight control on the rest of the family. Even the youngest Ames, nine-year-old Amy, was uncompromisingly portrayed as lost, despondent over her mother's death. Despite the dark tone of the stories, the realism of the situation and the emotions riveted the audience.

For fifteen long years, viewers stayed tuned in large numbers as the Ames family struggled to move beyond their original tragedy—with little success. Peter eventually remarried, and his new wife, Valerie, provided some relief from the stormy emotions, but as the children grew older their prob-

lems only worsened. Amy, all grown-up by the early sixties, remained haunted by the loss of her mother. Insecure and impetuous, she soon dominated the story line with her romantic troubles. She bore a child out of wedlock, married and divorced several times, and was abandoned by her paraplegic husband. But the greatest tragedy to befall the Ames family during the decade was the 1969 departure of Winsor and Monty following CBS's acquisition of *The Secret Storm* from its sponsor American Home Products. New writers killed off Peter and wrote out Jerry, Susan, and Valerie, obliterating the show's continuity and theme. Provocative story lines about a priest renouncing his vows for love and then being drawn back to the church, or Amy's artificial insemination by a doctor who was in love with her, did nothing to appease the audience's devotion to the Ames family. It was their story the audience wanted to see and their disappearance from the show that ultimately sealed its fate.

In 1968 *The Secret Storm*'s audience enjoyed the most unusual celebrity cameo in daytime history. When Christina Crawford, who played the character of Joan Kane, became seriously ill, her mother, the legendary Joan Crawford, offered to fill in for her. The former movie star was forty years too old when she played the part, but the network was still thrilled to have her star power on the soap.

CBS canceled *The Secret Storm* in the final weeks of 1973. As story lines were wrapped up at an accelerated pace, audience outrage encouraged American Home Products to find a new home for the serial. Unable to convince ABC or NBC to pick up the show, the agency negotiated an unusual syndication deal with stations across the country, but the arrangement fell through at the last moment. On February 8, 1974, after twenty years and one week, *The Secret Storm* broadcast its final episode. Although most of the Ames family had been relegated to the back burner years ago, that last installment brought the clan their long-sought happiness; Amy's husband returned and rose from his wheelchair, and three generations of the family were reunited in the final scenes.

AS THE WORLD TURNS

When *As the World Turns* debuted on April 2, 1956, there was no other show like it: it was the first half-hour serial. Irna Phillips's creation was historically significant in its length and revolutionary in its style, pacing, and structure. These innovations were not unrelated. Recognizing that the camera took up its own time and place on-screen, Phillips wanted the extra fifteen minutes not to tell more story, but to use the camera to explore every nuance of her characters. This introspection not only slowed down the tempo of the show, it was a deliberate attempt to simulate the passing of internal time, the gradual process of realization, understanding, and maturation that accompanies experience. Viewers were not carried along by melodramatic plots, but were persuaded that they were observing life lived at its real pace. This was Phillips's second insight: audiences wanted not just to follow a plot, but to become immersed in the moment-to-moment emotions of the characters. Daytime drama, as she saw it, unfolded in terms of time and character, not story. The conversations over cups of coffee, recaps of previous events, pregnant pauses, and long close-ups preceding fade-out that were introduced on *As the World Turns* are all clichés now, but at the time they were the strikingly original building blocks of Phillips's new, visual style of soap-opera storytelling. After an initial hesitancy, audiences embraced the show in its second year and sent it to the top of the ratings, where it would remain, virtually unchallenged, for an unprecedented two decades.

As the World Turns was also innovative in terms of its structure. Its basic organization—two families, one wealthy and troubled (the Lowells), one middle-class but more stable (the Hughes)—proved to be extremely dynamic. Almost every soap opera that followed would build from this same foundation, though none exploited its potential as completely as *As the World Turns* itself. Starting with the story of the illicit affair between free spirit Edith Hughes and the unhappily married Jim Lowell, the show used the construction to illuminate the complexity of human emotions. When the couple's secret was exposed, for example, its aftershocks reverberated throughout both families as each person reacted to the news differently. The variety of responses provided a Rashoman-like view of the human condition, heartbreaking in its opposing and seemingly irreconcilable perspectives.

Not everything in daytime television had changed, however. Phillips had hoped to challenge soap opera orthodoxy by allowing Jim and Edith's affair to end happily in marriage, but various forces led Phillips to kill Jim off. Following his death, the story shifted to younger members of the Hughes and Lowell families. Jim's daughter Ellen gave birth to a son out of wedlock, put him up for adoption, then fought to reclaim him. Eventually she fell in love with and married the boy's adoptive father. Ellen's best friend, Penny Hughes, became involved with Jeff Baker in daytime's first major young-love story. Their six-year relationship, beset by familial and personal problems, turned the actors Rosemary Prinz and Mark Rydell into daytime's first supercouple. Eileen Fulton's portrayal of Lisa Miller also created a furor among viewers as she gallivanted around town, shirking her responsibilities as wife to Bob Hughes and mother to their young son, Tom. For several years during the sixties, when these three stories were peaking, the show averaged more than a fifty share of the audience. The show's popularity even spawned a prime-time spin-off, *Our Private World,* in 1965 with Fulton as its star.

By the early seventies, *As the World Turns*'s ratings were beginning to slide. Phillips, who had left the show in 1970, returned two years later to clean up some of the problems, but only alienated the audience by writing out or killing off most of the characters involved in the most problematic story line. She even came close to destroying her last great creation, the ultraliberated Kim Reynolds, a heroine patterned after the soap legend herself, by pairing her in an adulterous relationship with her brother-in-law Bob that angered viewers. Audience defections continued, ultimately costing Phillips her job. Ironically, the couple's reunion a decade later would prove extremely popular, and their illegitimate baby, lost to miscarriage as penance for their affair, would be brought back to life.

As the World Turns remained at the top of the ratings until 1978 when the popularity of the more youth-oriented ABC soaps knocked it from the top spot. Two years later, Procter & Gamble enlisted Bridget and Jerome Dobson, who had successfully written for *Guiding Light,* to try to update its sister show. They refocused the story on younger members of the core families: Bob and Lisa's son, Tom, was paired with independent-minded cop Margo Montgomery, and Ellen's granddaughter, Betsy Stewart, was matched up with brooding Steve Andropoulos. They also revitalized longtime villain John Dixon, putting him at the center of several important plots involving marital rape and faked death.

It was Douglas Marland, however, who would bring the show some of its greatest post-Irna Phillips glory. The writer continually tapped into the serial's rich history for story ideas, rewarding longtime viewers and newcomers alike with emotionally satisfying resurrections of past relationships and surprising revelations of long-buried secrets. Restoring the Hughes family to the heart of the show, he brought back Chris and Nancy, who had been banished to the near-oblivion of recurring status, to provide guidance for their children and grandchildren. In addition, he introduced a new clan, the Snyders, as a foil for the Hughes. The new family's ordeals would become equally important to the success of the soap during the nine years Marland wrote *As the World Turns*.

Against this strong familial backdrop, Marland also told a series of topical stories, dealing with such controversial issues as homosexuality, AIDS, incest, euthanasia, and abortion, among others. In each case he emphasized the importance of forgiveness, understanding, and love in healing wounds and overcoming differences. His untimely death in 1993 saddened his fans and left others to carry on Irna Phillips's vision.

As the World Turns (clockwise from top left): *Kim Hughes (Kathryn Hayes), Bob Hughes (Don Hastings), Tom Hughes (Gregg Marx), Margo Montgomery Hughes (Hillary Bailey Smith), Andy Dixon (Scott DeFreitas), Frannie Hughes (Julianne Moore); (seated) Chris Hughes (Don McLaughlin) and Nancy Hughes (Helen Wagner)*

On "Bob Hughes"

*B*ob is a very straight character—dedicated to his profession and family. So when Kim came on and seduced Bob—her sister's husband—the audience was very shocked. She and her sister were both pregnant by me. Some people didn't like that at all, but others stood by him. If the writers had Bob kill somebody, there are a lot of people out there who would make excuses for him. They would say, "Oh, well, so the gun went off." But if it were Larry Bryggman [playing John Dixon], the audience wouldn't be so understanding. Larry once said to me, "You can say anything and they love you, and no matter what I do, they think I'm a rat!"

Don Hastings
"Bob Hughes," As the World Turns

The Edge of Night: *Nancy and Mike Karr (Ann Flood and Forrest Compton)*

THE EDGE OF NIGHT

Although initially hesitant about the viability of the half-hour soap opera format, Procter & Gamble grew excited about the idea as the April 2, 1956, premiere of *As the World Turns* approached. The idea, in fact, became so appealing, that they decided to launch a second thirty-minute show the same day. The company had wanted to do a mystery serial for some time, and tried to acquire the rights to *Perry Mason,* a successful radio drama it had sponsored for its entire twelve-year run. When that attempt failed, P&G did the next best thing: it hired *Perry Mason* writer Irving Vendig to create an original series and engaged John Larkin, the voice of Perry Mason, to play the lead. The result was *The Edge of Night.* With its focus on crime melodrama, the serial was unlike anything seen on daytime television before. The formula worked: *The Edge of Night* attracted an audience of action-enthusiasts with its dramatically staged live shoot-outs without scaring away the housewives who traditionally watched at that hour. Premiering in the 4:30 P.M. time slot to reflect its ominous title and theme, the serial had an audience of nine million viewers—half of them men—and a place near the top of the daytime ratings after its first year.

The Edge of Night strayed from the typical serial format in a number of ways. With its emphasis on mystery rather than domestic story lines, the show forsook the family structure of traditional soap operas. Instead, the program focused on a few core characters—originally Assistant District Attorney Mike Karr and his wife, Sara Lane—and introduced a new group of secondary characters with each new story. The story lines would last a year or two, but *Edge of Night* never had the luxury of the decade-long romantic or domestic situations that drove the story forward on other soaps. Still, the show did develop romances for most of the continuing characters and the intricacy of the never-ending series of murders and sensational trials proved equally capable of holding an audience.

From the beginning, *Edge of Night*'s prime crime fighter was Mike Karr, played originally by John Larkin, but longest by Forrest Compton. He was later joined by Police Chief Bill Marceau and, in private practice, by law partner Adam Drake. Mike's first wife, Sara, was killed in a car accident early in the show's run, but the audience outcry at her death demonstrated that even an atypical serial like *Edge of Night* generated a strong attachment between viewers and the continuing characters. To fill the void left by the tragedy,

reporter Nancy Pollack moved to Monticello. Her 1962 wedding to Mike cemented one of the longest-lasting marriages in daytime history. Equally popular was the pairing of virile Adam with spirited Nicole Travis. Their battle of the sexes and obvious love fueled the serial's ratings for several years.

All of the elements—romance and mystery, labyrinthine plotting and witty banter—came together under the guidance of producer Erwin Nicholson, who joined the show in 1966, and veteran mystery writer Henry Slesar, whose imagination and creativity would spawn most of the show's more memorable story lines. A master of the intricately woven, twist-laden, surprise-ending mystery, Slesar's fifteen-year stint as writer on *The Edge of Night* was the longest in soap opera history. His stories were imbued with the irreverent spirit of the *Thin Man* movies, and his plots were peopled with offbeat and unforgettable characters. Many of them, including Raven Alexander and Brandy Henderson, would become mainstays of the show.

In 1972, despite the show's unflagging success, Procter & Gamble asked CBS to shift *The Edge of Night* to an earlier time slot in order to create a block of the sponsor's popular soap operas in the middle of the network's faltering lineup. Unfortunately, the move cost the show much of the youth and male audience who were only at home in the late afternoon. CBS canceled the series three years later. Although ABC picked up the serial and returned it to an "edge of night" time slot at 4:00 P.M., the show never regained its position in the ratings. *The Edge of Night* struggled on for another decade on its new network, but eventually fell victim to affiliate defections. On December 28, 1984, after twenty-eight years and dozens of compelling mysteries, the serial broadcast its final episode. *The Edge of Night*'s earlier success, however, remains a testimony to the versatility and flexibility of the soap opera format, and its intricately woven crime melodramas provided the standard for the murder mystery story lines still told on many daytime dramas.

GENERAL HOSPITAL

The story of *General Hospital* is the tale of a soap that spans two very distinct eras. Created by former *Search for Tomorrow* writers Frank and Doris Hursley, *General Hospital* was one of two hospital-based dramas to premiere on April 1, 1963 (the other was *The Doctors)*. Predating the feminist movement by several years, it nevertheless spoke to an audience that was widening its attention beyond the home by shifting soap opera's ritual conversations about life and relationships from the kitchen to the workplace and from family to coworkers. It was a very different *General Hospital,* however, that would transform the serial format fifteen years later. With the show on the verge of cancellation, former *Secret Storm* director Gloria Monty instituted a variety of technical and story innovations that not only revived the soap, but also reformed the genre itself.

When *General Hospital* premiered, the show focused on the friendship of seventh-floor coworkers Steve Hardy and Jessie Brewer and on their complicated love lives. The self-sacrificing Nurse Jessie suffered for years at the hands of her faithless and much younger husband, Dr. Phil Brewer. Although she divorced him and married again (more than once), she always returned to Brewer and his emotional abuse. Only his murder finally freed her. Dr. Hardy, meanwhile, faced his own romantic heartbreak in the form of an on-again, off-again relationship with Audrey March. Their story ended more happily when the couple remarried and Hardy adopted her son, Tom.

As Jessie and Steve's stories wound down, *General Hospital* lost its focus. Neither new head writers, including the Hursleys' daughter Bridget and her husband Jerome Dobson, nor a new star, Denise Alexander, who had been lured away from *Days of Our Lives* at great expense, could help the struggling show. By 1977, with its ratings in precipitous decline, *General Hospital* was about to be canceled. With nothing left to lose, ABC executive Jackie Smith hired producer Gloria Monty and head writer Douglas Marland in one last attempt to save the show. She gave them six months and almost complete artistic freedom to turn the show's ratings around. What she got instead was an outright resurrection.

It was Marland's genius to recognize the need to maintain a connection with the past for the audience. His stories were not cut from new cloth but intricately woven from story-line threads left dangling by previous writers. He put young lovers Laura Vining and Scotty Baldwin center stage, adding levels of confusion and ambivalence to their relationship that excited audiences. He introduced the scheming Bobbie Spencer as Laura's rival for Scotty and Bobbie's brother Luke as her accomplice. And, building on their romance from years earlier, he threw Rick Webber and Monica Quartermaine back together, to the consternation of their new spouses, Lesley and Alan. Even Steve and Jessie remained part of the story, if only as peripheral characters.

While Marland revamped the stories, Monty transformed the look of the show and with it the soap opera genre. She sped up the pace, shortened scenes, and emphasized action over dialogue. Synthesizing trends—youth, lush production values—that had been changing daytime since the early seventies, and employing techniques borrowed from prime-time television, Monty created a new visual language for the serial format. It was a language perfectly suited to the youth-oriented romances that Marland was telling. The ratings soared.

The show, however, would achieve its greatest success several years later with the Luke and Laura romance. Pat Falken Smith, the new head writer, created one of the most controversial story lines in daytime history when the newly married

On the Luke and Laura story line

*U*nlike today, the producer used to let actors know where the story was going. Gloria Monty believed that an actor could arc a character better by having some knowledge about what tomorrow is about. So I knew about three months before that Luke was going to be enamored of Laura. We were going to do sort of a rich man/poor man situation: he was from the bad side, she was from the good side. I had no idea it was going into the rape, or that this would be the centerpiece of the story line. It wasn't until afterwards that I heard there was quite a furor, and I lived with that controversy for a long time.

From that point on, we played his regret and his total devastation. That's a story nobody wants to tell—that the rapist's life is as devastated as the person he rapes. His great love and regret and guilt are what caught the audience so off guard. There were two victims there, even though he was the perpetrator.

The character of Luke Spencer was designed to commit horrendous acts and recover from them.

Anthony Geary
"Luke Spencer"

*The Quartermaines: (clockwise from left) Edward (David Lewis),
Alan (Stuart Damon), Monica (Leslie Charleson), and Lila (Anna Lee)*

Laura's fascination with the older and more worldly Luke culminated in his rape of her on the floor of his disco. Once the writers decided to take the story in a different direction, making Luke and Laura lovers, the rape was looked back on as a seduction, causing an uproar among many viewers that remains a topic of debate to this day. What is incontrovertible is that the ratings continued to soar, and Luke and Laura's wedding, which aired on November 16 and 17, 1981, was the most-watched event in the history of daytime, even attracting a guest appearance by Elizabeth Taylor.

By then, however, *General Hospital* was already a show in trouble. As it turned from the complicated sexual fantasies of the early Luke and Laura story line to the comic-book fantasies of mad scientists bent on global domination of their

later years, the audience remained large, but the demographics changed. Viewers grew younger and more fickle in their viewing habits. When Genie Francis, who played Laura, left the show, so did millions of fans. Attempts to hold on to the audience focused more and more on action-adventure and less on complex characterizations and psychological drama.

In the early nineties, under the guidance of head writer Claire Labine, the soap revolved around a series of social-issue story lines involving organ transplants as well as a groundbreaking AIDS story line. The latter story involved the central character of Stone, who died, and his lover, Robin Scorpio, whose continuing presence on the show as a young woman living with HIV keeps the issue prevelant.

Dr. Matt Powers (James Pritchett) with nursing staff

THE DOCTORS

In addition to *General Hospital*, the other daytime medical program to premiere on April 1, 1963, was Colgate-Palmolive's *The Doctors*. Although it would become NBC's first successful foray into daytime television and the serial format, it was not originally a soap opera. Created, produced, and written by longtime *Ma Perkins* scenarist Orin Tovrov, the show began as an anthology series with a new story each day featuring one of four regular characters. By July 9, when James Pritchett joined the cast as Dr. Matt Powers, a character who would be at the center of the serialized version of the show, stories had expanded into weeklong arcs, but retained narrative closure. It wasn't until March 2, 1964, nearly a year after its debut, that *The Doctors* abandoned its episodic roots entirely and converted to open-ended storytelling with a regular cast of characters. It was now a fully realized soap opera.

While retaining its focus on strong, well-researched, medically oriented story lines, the show in its new format began exploring the personal lives of the hospital staff in greater depth. Beginning with star-crossed doctors Matt Powers and Maggie Fielding, *The Doctors* continued through the opposites-attract romance of brash surgeon Nick Bellini and sophisticated physician Althea Davis, and the transforming love affair of shy nurse Carolee Simpson and womanizing doctor Steve Aldrich. The show created a series of strong, adult love stories that kept the audience transfixed and put the soap near the top of the ratings. The formula was not only a Nielsen success, but also a critical one: in 1972, *The Doctors* won the first Emmy ever awarded for Outstanding Achievement in Daytime Drama. It would repeat the win two years later, with actress Elizabeth Hubbard (Althea Davis) also picking up a statuette for Best Actress.

Even as it picked up its second Emmy for Best Daytime Drama, *The Doctors* was a show in trouble. An exclusive medical focus proved too limiting for the soap opera format, and audience interest tapered off. Between 1974 and 1976, both *The Doctors* and the similarly conceived *General Hospital* lost nearly a third of their viewers as the hospital settings grew claustrophobic and story lines became repetitive. *General Hospital* would eventually reinvent itself as an action-adventure soap, but *The Doctors*'s attempts to resuscitate itself—with new writers, new characters, and new attention-grabbing plots, involving kidnappings, fires, and hurricanes—all failed. Even the youth-oriented story lines of Douglas Marland were only marginally successful before he was quickly hired away by rival *General Hospital*.

As the ratings dwindled, NBC affiliates dropped the show. By 1982, *The Doctors* was on the verge of cancellation. In one final effort to attract an audience, the show featured a series of radical, irreverent stories that included such daytime firsts as grave robbing, kinky sex, and a Fountain-of-Youth drug. None of it worked. On December 31, 1982, *The Doctors* aired its final episode, ending, as it had started, with the love story of Matt and Maggie Powers. Their final New Year's toast, "Every end brings a new beginning," was a tribute to a twenty-year-old romance, and the enduring appeal of soap opera storytelling.

ANOTHER WORLD

Despite the strength of *The Doctors*, NBC, still lagging far behind CBS in the daytime ratings, commissioned a second soap opera in an effort to become competitive. This time the network turned to Irna Phillips, who was not only already responsible for two of the most successful soap operas on television, but had also created several very popular serials for the network when it had dominated daytime radio in the thirties and forties. With assistance from William J. Bell, she presented them with *Another World*. Although the soap legend originally envisioned her new serial as a companion series to *As the World Turns* (thus the wry title), she abandoned the family drama and slice-of-life storytelling that had brought her success in the past. Instead, from *Another World's* May 4, 1964, premiere, she focused on melodrama in an attempt to garner attention . . . and quick ratings success.

The experiment failed. Phillips, who cowrote the show with her protégé Bell, was uncomfortable with the constant stream of tragedy, illegitimate pregnancy, illegal abortion, murder, and highly charged trials. The sensationalism of the storytelling clearly did not play to her interests and the strengths she had shown in writing about the day-to-day lives of average Americans. She had no time to explore the nuances of her new family, the Matthews, or the conflicts between the two branches of the clan, one rich and one middle-class. The show floundered in the ratings, and, after two years, its creator left.

On comedy

For a while, Another World was known for its comedy. We were actually credited at one time for being the first soap to incorporate comedy, and that goes back to Gretchen Oehler.

Gretchen was the wonderful actress who played this wacky maid Vivien Gorrow, from 1978–84, to Iris Cory Bancroft, then played by Beverlee McKinsey. She was a theater-trained actress and—I don't think it was intentional—she developed this comedic style on the show.

The writers picked up on it, and soon the madcap antics of this very prim and proper Iris and her wacky maid, who was tripping over things and getting phone messages wrong, became hysterical. The audience loved it.

R. Scott Collishaw
Producer

The show continued to struggle until Procter & Gamble brought in another Irna Phillips's protégé, Agnes Nixon. She quickly killed off several characters created by interim writers and refocused the story on the Matthews family. She continued the show's melodramatic storytelling style, but created characters and characterizations that worked within that format. Within months the show soared to second place in the ratings as audiences became entranced by Missy Palmer's trial for murder, her continuing romance with Bill Matthews, and the volatile relationship of new district attorney Walter Curtin and socialite Lenore Moore. But above all else, viewers tuned in to see what would happen next to the naive Alice Matthews, the arrogant and smoldering Steve Frame, and the scheming Rachel Davis. Their triangle was one of the most compelling in *Another World's* history, ultimately keeping the audience watching for more than seven years.

Audiences were not the only ones to notice the success Nixon was having with *Another World*. After less than two years, she was hired away by ABC to create a new soap opera. Again the show struggled in the ratings and again Procter & Gamble found a brilliant new head writer to take over the floundering show: Harding Lemay, a playwright with no television experience. Lemay, one of thirteen children, brought a unique understanding of both familial relationships and emotionally charged drama to daytime. The combination proved potent, particularly in his reworking of the still vital Steve/Alice/Rachel triangle. Rachel, under Lemay's sure hand, was no longer a one-dimensional villainess. As her motivations emerged, viewers began to understand her and see her in a more sympathetic light. Lemay also created a family for Steve in order to bring together the two sides of his personality (one coarsely sexual, the other intellectual). He, like Alice and Rachel, became a full human being trapped between his desires and a world unable to fulfill them in anything but a destructive way. The psychological replaced the melodramatic as the motivation for story. No more sensational murder trials, illegitimate babies, nor other gimmicks to propel plot. Lemay focused instead on the drama of typical relationships. Once again, the show rose to the top of the ratings. Its success allowed producer Paul Rauch to expand the show to an hour on January 6, 1975. It became the first daytime soap to broadcast at that length.

New characters were introduced, like the dignified Mac Cory, who was paired with the now-reformed Rachel, and his

Rachel Cory (Victoria Wyndham) and Carl Hutchins (Charles Keating)

scheming daughter, Iris Carrington, who wanted daddy all to herself. A parade of highly accomplished theater actors filled additional roles. On March 5, 1979, *Another World* became the first and only soap to expand to ninety minutes. Lemay, exhausted after eight years of writing the show, left soon after.

It became evident, however, that ninety minutes daily ate up story much too quickly, so Procter & Gamble cut *Another World* back to sixty minutes in August of 1980, thus making room for the show's second spin-off, *Texas* (the first, *Somerset*, aired from 1970 to 1976). The death in 1989 of actor Douglass Watson, who portrayed Mac Cory, left his widow Rachel as the show's only connection to the eras of Nixon and Lemay. In the nineties the show has remained true to its legacy of strong, theatrical acting, with the likes of Charles Keating (villain Carl Hutchins) and Linda Dano (romance novelist Felicia Gallant), both of whom have received the Emmy Award for outstanding acting.

Tom and Alice Horton (Macdonald Carey and Frances Reid), Marlena Brady (Deidre Hall)

On the creation of Days of Our Lives

I *wasn't there firsthand; I was maybe all of fourteen years old. But my mother and father and Irna, and oftentimes Bill Bell (who would come with Irna from Chicago), would meet in New York, perhaps three or four times a year, to discuss story ideas for* As the World Turns *or* Guiding Light.

At one point, I guess it was in the early sixties, they were all sitting around, and my father said to Irna, "You know, all the soap operas are very urban; they could take place in one very large building with a penthouse and a basement, the rank of income going from basement to penthouse."

There wasn't a rural, or even suburban, feel to any of the soap operas then. It was about doctors, lawyers, and the housewives that waited at home for them. So their concept was to launch a show that took place in the Midwest, about a rural kind of country doctor and his wife and their grown children, now in their twenties, and how they deal with their childrens' lives.

Salem, Middle USA, anywhere.

Ken Corday
Executive Producer

DAYS OF OUR LIVES

When *Days of Our Lives* premiered November 8, 1965, on NBC, it was not a revolutionary show. Firmly connected to soap opera history through creators Ted Corday, who also produced, and Irna Phillips (with credit given to Allan Chase), its characters were deeply rooted in the traditions of the genre and the heartland of America. It was not the show one would expect to lead daytime television into the sexual revolution, but following the untimely death of Corday in 1966, that is exactly where the new creative team—head writer William J. Bell (who had previously written *Guiding Light* and *As the World Turns)* and producers Betty Corday and H. Wesley Kenney—took it. Combining the romantic fantasies of the Hummert radio soaps and the familial drama of Phillips's shows with a more contemporary attitude about sex, Bell created a sexual and psychological melodrama perfectly suited to the changing times.

Bell's modern storytelling style could not have succeeded without the comforting presence of the Hortons, a soap family whose background and values (remnants of *Days*'s conventional beginnings) were not that different from the audience's. Through the experiences of patriarch Tom (played by Hollywood leading man Macdonald Carey), his wife Alice (Frances Reid), and their five grown children, viewers encountered sexual situations that were shocking, titillating, and new to daytime television. Among the most memorable: daughter Marie unwittingly fell in love with her own brother, then fled to a convent; granddaughter Julie Olson competed with former friend Susan Hunter for the attentions of David Martin and a string of other suitors before losing her true love, Doug Williams, to her own mother, Addie; and the rivalry between brothers Bill and Mickey for the heart of Dr. Laura Spencer caused years of anguish for the trio as rape, mistaken paternity, involuntary manslaughter, and amnesia continued to reshape their relationships.

When Bell left the show in 1973 to create *The Young and the Restless,* he continued to contribute long-term story material for several years, but handed the day-to-day writing responsibilities to his longtime assistant, Pat Falken Smith. Under her guidance, *Days of Our Lives* gained critical success and recognition, landing stars Bill and Susan Seaforth Hayes on the cover of the January 12, 1976, issue of *Time* magazine (which called the soap daytime's "most daring drama") and

earning twelve Emmy nominations for Best Show and Best Writing in seven years. Falken Smith's romantic sensibility and penchant for strong heroines also kept the show near the top of the Nielsens.

Falken Smith's 1977 departure in a contract dispute heralded one of the worst periods in *Days of Our Lives*'s history. Following a severe ratings slump, the show tried to revamp by writing out fourteen characters in six months, including fan favorites Bill and Laura Horton. The purge, dubbed the St. Valentine's Day Massacre by cast members, only alienated viewers further. It took five years, and the return of Falken Smith, to turn the show around again. During the head writer's brief return, she brought intrigue and romance back to the show in the form of sexy cop Roman Brady who was assigned to protect psychiatrist Marlena Evans from the Salem Strangler, a serial killer preying on young women. The cop and the "doc" soon fell in love, propelling their portrayers, Wayne Northrop and Deidre Hall, to the top of the fan polls.

The success of the Roman and Marlena story line provided a template for *Days of Our Lives*'s third decade. Following the formula that had made that pairing popular, the show stamped out a procession of fan-pleasing supercouples that included such favorites as Bo and Hope, Kimberly and Shane, Patch and Kayla, and Jack and Jennifer. But the shift from complex, psychologically motivated triangles to ultraromantic love stories was not the only change in the soap's focus. International espionage replaced sexual quandaries as the greatest obstacles to love, and Roman's family, the Bradys, replaced the Hortons at the center of the show.

Although it had built a strong and loyal fan base, *Days* struggled in the ratings for most of the eighties and early nineties until writer Jim Reilly brought his strange mix of Gothic story and contemporary appeal to Salem. Critics (and audiences) laughed at outrageous plots involving heroines buried alive, trapped in pits, and possessed by the devil, but they watched. At the same time, and with far less fanfare, Reilly also created never-ending triangles reminiscent of the soap's early years. Although Carrie, Austin, and Sami's plight lacks the sexual and psychological underpinnings of past story lines, their adventures are a real audience pleaser.

DARK SHADOWS

ABC's attempts to find a show to complement *General Hospital* on its schedule spawned a series of experimental soaps targeted at a new and younger daytime audience. Only *Dark Shadows,* born more of the Gothic romance novel than the broadcast serial, survived long enough to be considered a success. Created by Dan Curtis and developed by Art Wallace, the show became a camp classic, known as much for its falling sets, forgotten lines, and unscripted guest appearances by crew members as for its suspenseful tales of vampires, witches, and other supernatural beings. *Dark Shadows* never garnered high ratings, but its popularity among teenagers established ABC as a legitimate contender in daytime, and foreshadowed the network's eventual dominance of the youthful soap opera audience.

Dark Shadows debuted on June 27, 1966, as the story of the Collins family and their new governess, Victoria Winters. The April 1967 arrival of vampire Barnabas Collins, however, marked the true beginning of the story. Although introduced as a standard villain, albeit one with fangs, Barnabas's portrayer, Jonathan Frid, quickly imbued the character with a sense of pathos that made him a fan favorite. Picking up on his performance, the writers, particularly Gordon Russell, began adding psychological layers of guilt, moral ambivalence, and wry self-hatred that only increased the bloodsucker's popularity. Barnabas became the vampire who wanted to be mortal, and his quest became the unresolved dilemma at the heart of the show. Backstage, the literary character of Russell's scripts earned him the head writer's job on the show.

As the soap's focus shifted more and more to Barnabas, additional characters were added to fill out his story, including Dr. Julia Hoffman, who fell in love with the vampire as she tried to cure him, and Angelique, the witch whose spell had doomed Barnabas two hundred years earlier. Their history, retold in a six-month flashback, allowed many of the actors to portray their characters' ancestors.

But *Dark Shadows* began to exhaust its store of supernatural plots. The introduction of popular new mystery man Quentin Collins relieved some of the story pressure, but it was only a matter of time until the constraints of the soap's concept sapped its creativity. *Dark Shadows*'s final episode aired April 2, 1971, just shy of its fifth anniversary, but it did not tie up the story lines. When viewers complained that stories had been left dangling, head writer Sam Hall felt compelled to write an article in *TV Guide* resolving Barnabas's fate, allowing the vampire to find happiness with Julia. But the serial's story did not entirely end there either. *Dark Shadows*'s popularity continues to inspire a loyalty that has spawned books, videotapes, fan clubs, annual conventions, and a short-lived, prime-time revival series in 1991, more than a quarter century after the original was taken off the air.

Dark Shadows: *Barnabas Collins (Jonathan Frid) and Maggie Evans (Kathryn Leigh Scott)*

*The Buchanans (clockwise from left), Cord Roberts (John Loprieno), Clint (Clint Ritchie), Bo (Robert S. Woods),
and Asa (Philip Carey)*

ONE LIFE TO LIVE

One Life to Live premiered on July 15, 1968, against a backdrop of student protests, civil rights marches, war, and assassination, a world very much reflected in the heightened social consciousness of the show. While other daytime serials had dealt with societal upheaval peripherally, this Agnes Nixon creation was the first to explore issues of race, illicit drugs, and sexual freedom not only in a dramatic context but also in a socially relevant one. Like her mentor Irna Phillips, Nixon understood that soap operas were an ideal vehicle for education as well as entertainment. But she would take this insight one step further, making it an explicit rather than an implicit feature of the genre.

To tell her issue-oriented stories, Nixon constructed a community of characters in the town of Llanview whose diversity went far beyond the economic and educational differences on other shows. Her families displayed a proud ethnicity unheard of in the WASP world of daytime television. The Irish Catholic Rileys, Polish Woleks, African-American Grays, and Jewish Siegels were as important to the drama in the early years as the central family, the very white, very Protestant Lords. *One Life to Live* used this structure to great effect in telling the breakthrough story of Carla Gray. Carla was introduced as a Caucasian, but the revelation that the popular character was merely passing for white forced the audience to face their own feelings and prejudices about race.

In addition to presenting the first black characters whose lives reflected the reality of the African-American experience, *One Life to Live* examined the experiences of drug-addicted Cathy Craig by taping her recovery at Odyssey House, a real-life rehabilitation center in New York City. Real-life addicts shared their own experiences on camera. Years later, the same Cathy Craig wrote an article on venereal disease that was offered free to viewers who requested a copy from the show.

The double-life theme, used so successfully in the Carla Gray story, became a recurring motif on the show. Victoria Lord's sexual awakening was explored in a split-personality story line that saw the character's repressed sensuality expressed in her alter ego, Niki Smith. Pimp Marco Dane was transformed (at least temporarily) when he assumed the identity of his dead brother, Mario. And, most famously, housewife Karen Wolek lived with the shame of her secret life as a prostitute. Indeed, *One Life to Live* reached one of its high

points with this story in the late seventies. Under the guidance of head writer Gordon Russell, several years of parallel storytelling culminated in March of 1979 with Karen's courtroom admission of her life as a "common whore." Many critics still consider her testimony the single most powerful moment in daytime history.

As the new decade began, *One Life to Live* proved that it was not immune to the split personality of its characters. Inspired by the success of *Dallas* at night and *General Hospital* in the daytime, the show introduced a new family, the oil-rich Buchanans, and shifted its stories from psychological examinations of the human condition to faster-paced, youth-centered plots. In many instances, broadly drawn caricatures replaced the nuanced characters of the past. This trend reached its peak in the second half of the eighties with a series of bizarre story lines centering around time travel to the Old West and the search for a lost fortune in the buried city Eterna.

In recent years, *One Life to Live* has begun to return to its roots with stories focusing on issues such as teenage homosexuality, AIDS, and gang rape, as well as the introduction of a Hispanic family and neighborhood. At its core, however, the one consistent element throughout the show's nearly thirty-year history has been Victoria Lord and her relationships with her father, the late Victor Lord, and her longtime nemesis, her stepmother Dorian Lord.

On the collaborative process

One Life to Live *made me fully aware that soap opera is truly an ensemble effort. The best writing in the world will be dull and boring without a talented producer, good directors, and the best actors to make it come alive. It's also vital to have excellent set and costume designers, camera and sound crews, the entire production staff. I think they're the hardest working people in all of show business. Every day is opening night, 260 days a year. Truly, in this case, the whole is greater than the sum of its parts.*

Agnes Nixon
Creator
From a seminar at The Museum of
Television & Radio, January 27, 1988

ALL MY CHILDREN

Following the success of *One Life to Live*, ABC asked Agnes Nixon to create a second soap opera for them. Instead of writing a new one, she dusted off a previous effort, which Procter & Gamble had been interested in about five years earlier, but for which they were unable to secure the time slot on the network they wanted. The show was *All My Children*, and this time, the timing was right. Nixon lured soap expatriate Rosemary Prinz, beloved for years as *As the World Turns's* Penny Hughes, back to daytime television for a six-month guest appearance intended to entice longtime serial viewers to sample the show. But it was changing demographic realities that helped ensure the soap's success. The baby boom generation was growing up. As its oldest members entered their teens and early twenties, they were looking for television that addressed their concerns and interests, which the domestic dramas their mothers loved did not do. *All My Children*, however, with its focus on young love and topical issues such as the Vietnam War, abortion, and the environment, did speak to them. From its January 5, 1970, debut, the show attracted college students in unusually high numbers, expanding the soap opera audience and changing the emphasis of the genre for the next quarter century.

The structure of *All My Children* was Irna Phillips-traditional. The Tyler family of Pine Valley was WASPy, wealthy, and dysfunctional, while the Martins were middle-class, moral, and upwardly mobile. The story lines were primarily romantic. What made the show unique was its celebration of young love and young lovers above all else. Chuck Tyler and Phil Brent were teenagers when their rivalry for Tara Martin shattered their friendship and pitted their families against one another. This conflict drove the story for many years. A decade later, high school sweethearts Greg Nelson and Jenny Gardner found themselves at the center of the romantic intrigue as they fought parental interference to be together. They were followed by other young couples who first fell in love while in school, including Jesse Hubbard and Angie Baxter, Charlie Brent and Julie Chandler, David Rampal and Melanie Cortlandt, and Brian Bodine and Hayley Vaughan.

But young love was not *All My Children*'s only appeal. Through the years, a succession of flamboyant, broadly drawn troublemakers settled in Pine Valley. Many of the most destructive and enduring of these villains, from Phoebe Tyler and her obsession with social propriety to Opal Gardner and her dreams of easy fortune, were meddling mothers who put their own needs ahead of their children's. Despite being more caricatures than characters, they provided welcome, and often comic, relief to the earnestness of *All My Children*'s young lovers and the stability of its tentpole characters.

None of these characters, however, has wreaked as much havoc as beautiful, spoiled, and vindictive Erica Kane. Played with vampy good humor by Susan Lucci, Erica is an Agnes Nixon staple, the lost daddy's girl who wants nothing more than her father's love. She has remained sympathetic even as she has seduced, manipulated, and discarded a series of husbands and lovers over the years in an attempt to fill the void left by her father's absence and neglect. Though Erica has matured as she has dealt with abortion, rape, substance abuse, and motherhood, she remains compulsively destructive, not only harming the people in her life, but her own happiness.

In addition to featuring tender young love stories and flamboyant characters, *All My Children* continued Nixon's long-standing tradition of social-issue storytelling. Through the years, the show has presented plots about Vietnam War protest, legal abortion (Erica had television's first legal abor-

On the series

I just happen to have the original All My Children *bible here. Every writer must have a different way of doing this, but I happen to start with a concept, and the concept or theme for this was the brotherhood of man. I stated it in a few words on the first page of the presentation, and it reads: "The great and the least, the weak and the strong, in joy and sorrow, in hope and fear, in tragedy and triumph, you are all my children."*

Agnes Nixon
Creator
From a seminar at The Museum of Television & Radio, *January 28, 1988*

Jenny Gardner (Kim Delaney) and Greg Nelson (Laurence Lau)

tion in 1973), cocaine addiction, domestic violence, AIDS, alcoholism, and more. It is this juxtaposition of seemingly disparate elements—sympathetic heroines and outrageous caricatures, issue-oriented stories and youthful romances—that give the soap its unique character. And it is *All My Children*'s continuity in the characters and writing (Nixon has overseen the story for the show's entire run) that ensures the audience's continuing loyalty.

THE YOUNG AND THE RESTLESS

Early television soap operas, reflecting their radio roots, were written for the ear. Dialogue and story were primary; sets and action secondary. Even when shows such as *As the World Turns* began embracing the visual aspects of the medium, the focus was on character exploration, not aesthetics. All of that changed on March 26, 1973, when *The Young and the Restless,* created by William J. Bell and his wife Lee Phillip Bell, premiered as the first truly visual soap opera. As the show progressed, it assumed a look that broke with the visual conventions of the genre. Shadowy, sensuous lighting, intriguing camera angles, and Hollywood production values supplied a lavish romanticism that not only appealed to its female viewers but also influenced the way other soaps were

photographed. By eroticizing the genre—embodied in an attractive, young cast rapturously presented, which Bell had first explored on *Days of Our Lives—The Young and the Restless* propelled the soap opera into a new era.

But the series did not rely on style alone. Building from the typical soap opera structure of two intertwining families—the troubled rich family, the Brooks, and a struggling middle-class one, the Fosters—the Bells created a world steeped in romance and fantasy: a sheltered young pianist, Leslie Brooks, was transformed by the power of love; a poor hairdresser, Jill Foster, fulfilled her dreams of wealth and glamour when she fell in love with her millionaire boss, Phillip Chancellor. Moreover, the stories in this world have

Christine "Cricket" Blair (Lauralee Bell) and Danny Romalotti (Michael Damien)

deep emotional and psychological undertones. Leslie, for instance, separated from Eliot by her sister's manipulations, became a manic-depressive and had to be hospitalized; Phillip's wife, Kay, drove off a cliff with her husband in order to keep him away from his pregnant mistress.

When *The Young and the Restless* first began, story lines were both traditional and revolutionary. The slow pace of story for heightened dramatic effect and the use of only a handful of characters was a throwback to the earliest days of soap opera, but the frank sexuality was new. The show banished forever the twin beds and shy sensuality that had been a mainstay of the genre. It brought daytime television directly into the middle of the sexual revolution and the cult of youth that defined the seventies. The explicitness of the dialogue, which included conversations about premarital intercourse, the carnal needs of an engaged man, impotence, and the trauma of rape, far exceeded anything seen on daytime before, including the sexual dilemmas Bell had favored on *Days of Our Lives*.

In the early eighties *The Young and the Restless* succeeded in doing what no other soap has done before or since: it shifted its focus away from its original core families to an entirely new set of characters. As the actors who had populated Genoa City abandoned the show in the late seventies, the Bells slowly began introducing the wealthy Abbotts and the poor, but spirited Williamses. By the time the last of the Brooks and Fosters (except Jill) had left town, the two new families were firmly established. The overlap of the two groups of characters allowed the audience to get to know and like the newcomers before their favorites disappeared, while the ongoing feud of Jill and Kay maintained some continuity for viewers. With the arrival of Victor Newman, an enigmatic stranger popular with women, the show's revived tableau was complete. It was an amazingly seamless transition, but not surprising for a show that over its entire history has achieved a remarkable consistency in story, style, and character due to the vision of its creator.

Victor's relationship with ex-stripper Nikki Reed has been a dominant force in the show since the early eighties. Although the couple has been divorced for years, the lingering feelings between them and the romantic problems of their now-grown children ensure that they will remain a part of each other's life and keep the audience hoping for a reunion. Combined with a series of social-issue story lines covering everything from AIDS and date rape to the plight of the elderly, as well as featuring a group of popular young African-American characters, and several long-term romantic and professional relationships, Victor and Nikki's love story has kept viewers enthralled for many years.

On taking the show to an hour

Once assured that Y&R was a runaway hit, CBS inevitably wanted to talk to me about an hour. I'll spare you the gruesome details, but after months of enormous pressure from the network and the affiliates, I somehow found myself committed to doing the hour show. What ultimately happened was that our ratings went down and it took us three years to become number one again.

How could this have happened? One reason was that when we went to an hour, we had a number of cast defections. The issue of performing in a one-hour show had not been part of their contracts. And some of our leading actors understandably felt their popularity on Restless would open the door to fame and fortune in nighttime or films. Obviously we had to recast prime characters in our two core families, the Brooks and the Fosters. It was then that I decided if one more actor from these families decided to leave the show, I'd have to do something radical.

A short time later, Jamie Lyn Bauer, who played Lauralee Brooks and was one of the very few original cast members remaining, came to me and said she was physically exhausted, which she was, and that she wasn't going to renew her contract when it was up in August. This was February.

There was no other answer. I had to replace what had been the core of our show since its inception. Two complete families. About eleven actors in all. But replace them with what?

As I studied the remaining cast, I realized I had two characters—Paul Williams, played by Doug Davidson, and Jack Abbott, played by Terry Lester—both of whom had a relatively insignificant presence on the show. They didn't have families. Hell, they didn't even have bedrooms. But these became the two characters I would build our two new families around. I remember the head of daytime for CBS advising me "with the strongest possible conviction" that I was making a grave mistake by replacing these families. There was a great risk, no question, but my conviction was that it could be even more disastrous if I didn't.

I immediately began to establish new families while interweaving the old. We made this transformation without losing so much as a share point. In fact, our ratings and our share points kept building, with our two new families emerging as the dominant characters on the show.

This is where Victor Newman came into the picture.

William J. Bell
Creator

RYAN'S HOPE

Ryan's Hope debuted on July 7, 1975, as a throwback to an earlier soap opera era. Rejecting the youthful characters, sexual situations, and pretty faces that pervaded the genre following the success of *All My Children* and *The Young and the Restless*, creators Claire Labine and Paul Avila Mayer (who had helped revive *Where the Heart Is* and *Love of Life)* brought to life a series revolving around a single Irish-American family, complete with all the characters and storytelling possibilities implicit in that tradition.

Drawing on an Irish heritage in both their familes, Labine and Mayer's work tapped into the same essence that had made Irna Phillips's work so sucessful: in fact, no daytime serial has focused so intensely on familial relationships since the heyday of *As the World Turns*. Where Mayer and Labine departed from tradition was in using a real setting, New York City, a single core family, and a Roman Catholic, not Protestant, morality. Moreover, they rejuvenated decades-old family themes with fresh, strong writing and a contemporary attitude. Within a year of its debut, *Ryan's Hope* was ABC's second most popular soap.

The interfamilial conflicts of the Ryan clan were largely responsible for that success. In long conversations, deeply personal confessions, and petty squabbles, the opposing values and aspirations of parent and child, the long-held resentments and jealousies of brothers and sisters, and the inevitable betrayals and accommodations of husband and wife were explored in detail. Even tragedy, such as the accident that left oldest son Frank fighting for his life, provided an opportunity for poignant scenes of bonding and recrimination.

Ryan's Hope also had success with a series of memorable romances: Frank Ryan and Jillian Coleridge, separated for nearly a decade by the machinations of his wife, Delia, and a series of misunderstandings; strong-willed Mary Ryan and equally stubborn reporter Jack Fenelli, whose marriage ended tragically in a mob hit; and Siobhan Ryan and mobster Joe Novack, whom even death could not separate. But the show was soon overshadowed by many of the very trends that it

had rejected. As *General Hospital* shot to the top of the ratings, *Ryan's Hope* became an anomaly on ABC's schedule, an old-fashioned soap opera in a block of youth-oriented, fast-paced dramas. The show tried to compete by airing a series of stories borrowed from the plots of famous movies, but the attempt misfired.

And then began a pattern that would mark the final years of *Ryan's Hope*: ABC, unhappy with the show's ratings, brought in a new head writer who shifted the focus away from the Ryans, eroding the audience further. Then the network reinstated Labine and Mayer, who reinvigorated the core family

On the creation of Ryan's Hope

*P*aul Mayer and I had been head writing Where the Heart Is *when it was cancelled. We sent some of our scripts and outlines around, and ABC said, "Come in and talk to us. How would you like to develop a new serial called* City Hospital?" *And we said, "*City Hospital? *Let us think about that." In the fall of 1973, CBS signed us to write* Love of Life. *The day after, we did a development deal with ABC for a new serial. We had gone to them and said, "What would you think about a show about an Irish-American family that runs a bar across the street from a city hospital, in which one of their sons is an intern?" And they said, "Swell."*

We did that because on Where the Heart Is, *we had had a prolonged sequence with two characters who were having an affair. He was a respected college professor, so they were meeting on the other side of town in a small Irish bar called O'Neill's Red Hand.*

We had so much fun with that bar and that whole sequence that we thought, "We want to write about an Irish bar." Well surely, you're going to have a politician coming out of that, and, surely, he's going to be in trouble all the time. We thought it enormous fun to make the heroine the adulterous party in the triangle. And then Delia, his incredibly ditzy, over-the-top, wonderful, enchanting, neurotic wife, who was going to slowly drive the family crazy.

It all just evolved; we knew who these people were so well, and soon the Ryans were the ones who were telling the stories. We didn't have a lot to do with it.

Claire Labine
Creator

Johnny and Maeve Ryan (Bernard Barrow and Helen Gallagher)

and reemphasized the strong moral world they lived in. But the ratings didn't go up fast enough for ABC, so they brought in yet another new writer, and so on. The result, from the audience's point-of-view, was incoherent and inconsistent.

The low ratings made cancellation inevitable. On January 13, 1989, the final episode aired. It was a bittersweet ending for a show of unique grace, dignity, and heart, qualities that helped to bring *Ryan's Hope* an unprecedented six Emmys for writing.

(*Clockwise from top left*), Tom Hartman (Greg Mullavey), Martha Shumway (Dodie Goodman), Mary Hartman (Louise Lasser), Raymond Larkin (Victor Kilian), Cathy Shumway (Debralee Scott), George Shumway (Philip Bruns), and Heather Hartman (Claudia Lamb)

MARY HARTMAN, MARY HARTMAN

As upset about the waxy yellow buildup on her kitchen floor as about the high school football coach who drowned in a bowl of her chicken soup, Mary Hartman was no more typical of the soap opera heroine than *Mary Hartman, Mary Hartman* was representative of the soap opera genre itself. Created by legendary prime-time television producer Norman Lear, and developed by a group of writers that included veterans of daytime serial and nighttime comedy, the show was more satire than soap, using the genre to make fun of everything from country music and television talk shows to serial killers and impotence. But its main target was the mundane nature of small-town life, where values taught by television, particularly the consumerism played out in commercials, were replacing traditional American values and beliefs.

Rejected by the networks, *Mary Hartman* survived in the wilderness of late-night syndication from January 1976 to mid-1978 with an odd mix of naive characters and outrageous situations, tired fifties-style soap opera, and wicked satire (its skewering of the confessional function served by talk shows and our need to reveal ourselves publicly when we are at our lowest was years ahead of its time). It was Mary who brought all of these elements together. Whether it was her grandfather's shenanigans as the Fernwood Flasher or the electrocution-by-television of eight-year-old evangelist Jimmy Joe Jeeter, it was Mary's bewildered responses that made it all seem wildly possible and completely improbable. And it was her nervous breakdown during cross-examination by a panel of experts determined to understand the "typical American housewife" on *The David Susskind Show* that gave the serial the emotional center that kept audiences returning. The result was comic genius or offensive parody, depending on the reviewer.

After 325 episodes, star Louise Lasser left. *Mary Hartman* brought a new cast of characters to the forefront of the story and later changed its title to *Forever Fernwood*, but its satirical sensibility remained the same. The comic highlight of the revamped format was the chemical vat accident that left Mary's father with a new face—Tab Hunter's—and an ecstatic wife. But the show had run its course and after three seasons (including the summer talk show spoof, *Fernwood 2-Night)*, the residents of Fernwood, Ohio, fell victim to the commercial realities they had so brazenly parodied.

LOVING/THE CITY

The series *Loving* debuted on June 27, 1983, on ABC amid great anticipation and high hopes. Created by two of the best writers in daytime history, Agnes Nixon (creator of *One Life to Live* and *All My Children*) and Douglas Marland (former head writer of *General Hospital* and later *As the World Turns*), it was introduced on June 26, 1983, as a two-hour prime-time feature starring Lloyd Bridges and Geraldine Page and directed by Michael Lindsay-Hogg (*Brideshead Revisited*). After the serial began, critic Chris Schemering wrote that the new half-hour daytime series "effectively integrated social problems with romance, domestic drama, and wit. . . ."

The series focused on four families with diverse ethnic backgrounds à la *One Life to Live:* the Aldens, Forbes, Donovans, and Vocheks. They lived and worked in Corinth, a university town on the East Coast, and much of the initial action centered on campus life and young love. Early story lines, written by Marland, were critical successes that explored the delayed-stress syndrome that plagued Vietnam veteran Mike Donovan or drew early attention to the AIDS crisis through nurse Noreen Vochek's research work. Other important story lines explored a range of personal and social issues, including Shana Sloane's struggle over whether to abort her fetus, which had a genetic defect; the problem of adult literacy, as Lotty Bates, in prison for attempted robbery, learned to read; and the trauma of childhood abuse, as incest survivor Lily Slater faced the pain of her past.

Unfortunately, the show never captured an audience, and the ratings remained low. Agnes Nixon had assumed that the series would be hammocked between her two other creations: *All My Children* would move to 12:30 P.M. E.S.T., *One Life to Live* would remain at 2:00 P.M., and the half-hour *Loving* would run in between. But in this case, this standard practice for programming a new series did not come to pass, which some ABC daytime executives have regretted in hindsight.

Loving: *The Donovans, Noreen (Marilyn McIntyre), Rose (Terri Keane), Douglas (Bryan Cranston), and Mike (James Kiberd)*

The City: *Jacob Johnson (Darnell Williams) and Angie Hubbard (Debbi Morgan)*

Moreover, within the first two years, Douglas Marland left the show and shortly after became head writer on *As the World Turns.*

By the midnineties ABC was nearly ready to cancel *Loving,* but they instead assigned head writers James Harmon Brown and Barbara Esensten the task of creating a new serial from the existing series by moving some of Corinth's characters to a new location. In its final story line (ironically, one of its best) a serial killer stalked the residents of Corinth, creating suspense about which characters would survive the transition. The primary targets were the last remaining members of the original cast: the Alden family and popular heroine Stacey Donovan.

Almost a dozen characters from *Loving* moved to the new soap, set in New York City and called *The City,* and the show debuted on November 13, 1995. In what is clearly a trend of the nineties, they all found homes and set up workplaces in the same SoHo loft building, creating a surrogate family based on proximity rather than blood. Production values, particularly the camera work, were updated to reflect the fashions of nighttime television, including rapid cuts, snappy visual transitions, and jerky camera movements. While some

viewers and critics have hailed these innovations as the future of the soap opera genre, others found that the visual gimmicks, combined with ultra-short scenes, interfere with the most basic soap opera relationship: the one between audience and characters. The final episode of *The City* aired on March 28, 1997.

On fictional locations

I'm from the Midwest, and it used to drive me crazy when cities like Springfield and Bay City, which are in the Midwest, sounded like New York. If you say it's the Midwest, you must write about the Midwest. I think it is important to understand the customs of the area. You've got to know where Chicago is because everybody in the Midwest knows where it is. Taking cabs and living in lofts are details of New York life that do not belong in a Midwestern setting. I think the audience says, "That's not true," and they don't want to watch as much.

Carolyn Culliton
Associate Head Writer, The City

SANTA BARBARA

Only the second daytime drama to debut in the hour format (the first was *Texas* in 1980), *Santa Barbara* was a product of the post-*General Hospital* soap world. Here, the romantic fantasies of youthful viewers had replaced the domestic interests of housewives as the focus for story lines. Shows abandoned their "guidebook for living" morality in favor of a more contemporary attitude. Bridget and Jerome Dobson, the daughter and son-in-law of *General Hospital* creators Frank and Doris Hursley, had successfully updated the venerable serials *Guiding Light* and *As the World Turns* when NBC commissioned them to create their own show. The result, which debuted on July 30, 1984, was a classically structured soap opera with a perverse soul. It was also one of the most irreverent, humorous, outrageous, and intelligently written television serials ever produced.

Although the show set out to tell the story of four families—the Lockridges, Capwells, Perkins, and Andrades—*Santa Barbara*, from the beginning, focused primarily on the wealthy, and extremely dysfunctional, Capwells. The most troubled of them all was oldest son Mason. Resigned to the fact that he would never get the approval of his father that he desperately wanted, the Shakespeare-quoting attorney

drowned his sorrow in alcohol, sought redemption in the arms of former-nun Mary Duvall, and eventually found true love with Julia Wainwright, a fellow lawyer whose demons mirrored his own. The unrelenting melancholy of his story was relieved by the more traditional, Romeo-and-Juliet pairing of perpetual victim Eden Capwell and Hispanic detective Cruz Castillo. The romance of their relationship, with oceanside horseback rides, a champagne proposal, and an extravagant wedding—all shot on location—helped define the lavish visual look of the show.

Santa Barbara's stories enjoyed some of the best-written soap opera since the heyday of *Ryan's Hope*. Dialogue was alternately sharp and biting, poetic and philosophical, emotional and heartbreaking. Situations were inventive. Characters made love in ambulances, smuggled themselves into the country in coffins, and were killed by falling signs. A series of spoofs, satires, and allegories provided a new way to explore characters' inner feelings, as in the annual Christmas visits of Nick (also known as Santa Claus) or Greg Richardson's trip to the "Capwell Zone," where he learned to come to terms with his newly discovered paternity and the alien family he was now part of. At times, perhaps because of the show's lack of a moral compass, the outrageousness misfired. A prime example was the revelation that the doctor who had examined Eden after her sexual assault was her rapist. But at other times, it perfectly captured the nuances and imperfections of the human condition, such as the strain that the reappearance of old-flame Robert Barr put on Eden and Cruz's relationship. Through it all, *Santa Barbara* earned a well-deserved reputation as a show willing to take any risk, try any gimmick.

Unfortunately, the storytelling was never able to match the wit and wisdom of the dialogue. While many critics loved the serial, and it developed a strong cult following, *Santa Barbara* never managed to make an impact on the wider, more traditional soap opera audience. To do so, the show would have had to sacrifice many of the elements that made it unique. Instead, it aired its final episode on January 15, 1993.

On Santa Barbara

I was writing for Santa Barbara *and directing* Another World *in 1989–90, which was kind of fun because they were back-to-back on NBC.*

Santa Barbara wasn't really a soap opera, and that's the reason it's not still on the air. It was just a crazy, fun, wild show that we did a lot of crazy stuff on.

It was much more like an episodic show. We won Best Show three years in a row, and the next year it was off the air. Everybody said, "How can that happen?" We always had these great shows to submit for the Emmys and the show was so quirky; everybody in the business loved it.

But the audience wasn't compelled to watch it from day to day, the way that Bill or Agnes compels you.

We'd take a two-week period, tell a story, drop it, and move on to something else. People were in and out and the show didn't have any history for the audience to invest in.

Gary Tomlin
Director, One Life To Live

(*Clockwise from left*) *Augusta Lockridge (Louise Sorel), Laken Lockridge (Julie Ronnie), and Minx Lockridge (Dame Judith Anderson)*

The Bold and the Beautiful: *A fashion show*

THE BOLD AND THE BEAUTIFUL

William J. and Lee Phillip Bell's second soap opera, *The Bold and the Beautiful,* which debuted on March 23, 1987, defined what it meant to launch a new soap successfully in the eighties: craft a compelling story with a seductive glamour that would have the potential of luring both an American and an international audience. While a consciousness of the international audience was groundbreaking for the genre, the show's debut was ironically tied to the early soaps by being a half-hour series in the world of hour-long soaps.

Lush production values and beautiful people (also signature elements of its sister show *The Young and the Restless)* are critical elements of *The Bold and the Beautiful*'s identity. The fashion industry setting in Los Angeles, with its focus on models and evening wear, at times becomes a character in its own right; viewers are treated to elaborate fashion shows as part of the story lines.

Originally built around the Forrester and Logan families, *The Bold and the Beautiful* started as a clone of *The Young and the Restless* in a new setting. Not only was the rich family/poor family contrast at the center of the show identical to that of the earlier Bell show, but many of its initial stories were similar: Caroline Spencer's rape mirrored Chris Brooks's of years earlier, Ridge and Thorne Forrester's brotherly rivalry over Caroline mimicked Snapper and Greg Foster's over Chris, and Mr. Logan's desertion of his family was reminiscent of Mr. Foster's abandonment of his. The soap also copied the pattern of its sister show in its use of social-issue story lines, exploring such topics as cancer, incest, diabetes, and homelessness.

Over the years, however, *The Bold and the Beautiful* has gained an identity of its own through its lighter tone, epitomized by the broadly comic Sally Spectra, and a brighter mood, a reflection perhaps of its Southern California locale. It has also found success with the story of Ridge and his many loves. From Caroline Spencer to Taylor Hayes, the Forrester scion has wooed and wed some of Los Angeles's most eligible ladies. But, so far, he has not managed to get Brooke Logan, the one woman who has loved him through it all, to the altar. Other lovers may constantly keep them apart, but the seeming inevitability of their eventual marriage keeps viewers hoping and watching.

The formula has proved immensely popular, not only in the United States, but in the rest of the world: *The Bold and the Beautiful* is the most-watched American soap opera. An impressive 250 million viewers in more than ninety countries tune in daily. Its stars frequently appear on the covers of popular magazines from France to Greece as well as in Asia, and they are mobbed wherever they go overseas. The show's success reflects the new global market for American daytime serials, where the five-day-a-week format is frequently the most popular on television and the soap opera is afforded the respect that is usually reserved for prime time in the United States.

On The Bold and the Beautiful *internationally*

I am definitely aware of our international audience when I develop story lines. Romance—the focus of our show—is the international language. Everyone can relate to it, everyone is very drawn in by it.

I stay clear of long, drawn-out trials because I think that international viewers may get bored with endless details of how the American legal system works (the O.J. trial notwithstanding). Also, I don't think comedy translates very well to different cultures, so if we stick to romance and love triangles and love stories, we maintain a broad, universal appeal.

Bradley Bell
Executive Producer/Head Writer

GENERATIONS

Although it lasted less than two years, *Generations* was notable as the first soap to feature an African-American core family. Created by Sally Sussman, who had previously written for *The Young and the Restless,* and debuting on March 27, 1989, the show's multigenerational structure ingeniously reflected the changing relationship of blacks and whites in American society. Here the grandchildren of a wealthy socialite and her former maid not only attended college together but also considered each other close friends. *Generations*'s existence was a testament to the societal changes that made it possible, but it also acknowledged the growing importance of the African-American audience to the continuing success of the soap opera format.

The Marshalls were not the first black characters on daytime television or even the first black family. They were, however, the first to play a central role in virtually all of a soap's story lines. They were not the peripheral or token characters of years past; they were a fully realized pillar of the show's structure. This reality was reflected in a series of issue-oriented story lines that dealt with aspects of the African-American experience—sickle-cell anemia, the effects of both subtle and blatant racism—and integrated ones in which race was not a factor. Despite the progress they embodied, however, the Marshalls, like the show's white core family, the Whitmores, were actually familiar staples of daytime drama. For like their Caucasian predecessors, they were successful, professional, and apparently Protestant.

Unfortunately, the show did not lead a revolution. Whether for reasons of lingering racism, as some admirers have maintained, or lackluster storytelling, as its critics charged, *Generations* never found a large audience: it was canceled on January 25, 1991, after less than two years. Only one soap, time-slot competitor *The Young and the Restless,* integrated its cast in the wake of *Generations*'s premiere. Ironically, that soap found far greater success with the format than *Generations* ever did. Perhaps its compartmentalization of story lines was more comfortable for a soap opera audience that for the most part remained, like the rest of America, segregated.

Generations: *Jason Craig (Tony Addabbo), Sam Whitmore (Kelly Rutherford), and Adam Marshall (Kristoff St. John)*

Notes

SERIAL SEDUCTION: LIVING IN OTHER WORLDS

1. George Santayana, *Reason and Religion*, vol. 3 of *The Life of Reason* (New York: Scribners, 1905), 6.

2. Michael Kammen, *The Lively Arts: Gilbert Seldes and the Transformation of Cultural Criticism in the U.S.* (New York: Oxford University Press, 1996), 226.

3. Edgar Johnson, *Charles Dickens: His Tragedy and Triumph* (New York: Penguin Books, 1986), 196.

4. Michael Lund, *America's Continuing Story: An Introduction to Serial Fiction 1850–1900* (Detroit: Wayne State University Press, 1993). Lund examines the social nature of reading and quotes from a 1858 *Harper's* issue on how a serial story should be read: "as it is written, from month to month—sitting if you please, with a friendly circle who began with you, who know all the people in the book—who follow their fortunes as we hang upon the careers of real persons—who speculate, and wonder, and plan—who sympathize, and regret, and condemn; and who justly take a deeper interest in many of the characters than in many acquaintances, because they know them better—not to say because they are better worth knowing."

5. Robert C. Harvey, *The Art of the Funnies: An Aesthetic History* (Jackson: University of Mississippi, 1994), 63.

6. Kalton C. Lahue, *Continued Next Week: A History of the Moving Picture Serial* (Norman: University of Oklahoma Press, 1964).

7. Susan Smulyan, *Selling Radio: The Commercialization of American Broadcasting 1920–1934* (Washington, D.C.: Smithsonian Institution Press, 1994), 87.

8. *The Woman's Magazine of the Air* 2, no. 1 (February 15, 1931).

9. Robert C. Allen, *Speaking of Soap Operas* (Chapel Hill: University of North Carolina Press, 1985), 111. Although, as Allen points out, "soap opera" began as a derogatory term, it is interesting to note that soap was a crucial item during the war years. A by-product of soap was glycerine, a necessary element in the making of explosives. Because soap was in demand, there was no decrease in the advertising budgets of the major manufacturers.

10. Dr. John Ruthledge, *The Guiding Light* (Chicago: Guiding Light Publishing Co., 1938), 134.

11. Raymond William Stedman, *The Serials: Suspense and Drama by Installment* (Norman: University of Oklahoma Press, 1977), 235.

12. Ibid., 282–83.

13. Allen, 8.

14. Sylvester "Pat" Weaver, "Memo about NBC Matinee," 1955, vol. 4 of "Collected Writings," unpublished manuscript, 2.

15. David P. Lewis, quoted in "A Unique Twist to The Tele Soap Opera Given By Caples' Man Lewis," *The Televiser* (November–December 1946), 33.

16. Paddy Chayefsky, *Television Plays* (New York: Simon & Schuster, 1955), 178.

17. Robert LaGuardia, *Soap World* (New York: Arbor House, 1983), 174.

18. Irna Phillips, interview, "Every Woman's Life Is a Soap Opera!" *McCall's* (March 1965).

19. Agnes Nixon, "Coming of Age in Sudsville," *Television Quarterly* (Winter 1972), 62.

20. Agnes Nixon, interview, "Agnes Nixon's Children," *Women's Wear Daily* (April 17, 1990), 40.

21. *New York Times*, July 7, 1968; August 2, 1970; and May 28, 1972.

22. LaGuardia, 181.

23. Georgia Dullea, "As Gloria Monty's World Turns," *New York Times*, July 11, 1986, p. 26.

THE ARCHITECTS OF THE AFTERNOON

1. Robert C. Allen, *Speaking of Soap Operas* (Chapel Hill: The University of North Carolina Press, 1985), 177.

2. John Dunning, *Tune In Yesterday: The Ultimate Encyclopedia of Old-Time Radio, 1925–1976* (Englewood Cliffs, N.J.: Prentice Hall, 1976), 55.

3. Raymond William Stedman, *The Serials: Suspense and Drama by Installment*, 2nd ed. (Norman: University of Oklahoma Press, 1977), 297.

4. Muriel G. Cantor and Suzanne Pingree, *The Soap Opera* (Beverly Hills, Calif.: Sage, 1983), 44.

5. J. Fred MacDonald, *Don't Touch That Dial!: Radio Programming in American Life from 1920 to 1960* (Chicago: Nelson-Hall, 1979), 251.

6. Stedman, 389.

7. Cantor and Pingree, 44.

8. Stedman, 282–83.

9. Ibid., 283.

10. James Thurber, "Ivorytown, Rinsoville, Anacinburg, and Crisco Corners," *The New Yorker* (May 29, 1948).

11. Carol Traynor Williams, *"It's Time for My Story,": Soap Opera Sources, Structure, and Response* (Westport, Conn.: Praeger, 1992), 21.

12. *Agnes Nixon on Fifty Years of Soaps: An All-Star Celebration*, CBS Television, (October 27, 1994).

13. James Thurber, "O Pioneers!," *The New Yorker* (May 15, 1948).

WATCHING DAYTIME SOAP OPERAS: THE POWER OF PLEASURE

1. See, for instance, Ruth Rosen's "Soap Operas: Search for Yesterday," *Watching Television*, ed. Todd Gitlin (New York: Pantheon, 1986), 44–45.

2. This essay is part of a larger work, a much broader study of watching daytime soap operas. In it, I use ethnographic methods to investigate the pleasures and displeasures of watching and talking about soaps. The discussions ranged from informal conversations to slightly more formal audiotaped interviews in the viewer's home. I have conformed to the interviewees' wishes and used names where they requested and concealed names where they preferred. I would like to express my appreciation to the viewers who have given me so much of their time and their feelings. When it comes to acknowledging my debts, I am moved by how much this seems to be a collective inquiry. Parts of this essay were presented at the Columbia Seminar on Cinema and Interdisciplinary Interpretation, N.Y.C., in 1992.

3. Wide-ranging agreement among respondents is not necessarily evidence of a similarity of interpretation; it may indicate the prevalence of a conventional belief. See Paul Messaris, "Biases of Self-Reported 'Functions' and 'Gratifications' of Mass Media Use," *Et cetera* 34, no. 3 (September 1977), 326.

4. Watching soap operas doesn't seem to have the prestige that writing about them does!

5. This, however, is not unique to the already middle class. One young woman on public assistance mentioned that her mother was so disturbed at how much she had been watching that she had sent her for counseling.

6. Fredric Jameson points out that this differentiation is based on a false dichotomy. See his essay "Pleasure: A Political Issue" in the Formations Editorial Collective's *Formations of Pleasure* (London: Routledge & Kegan Paul, 1983), 3.

7. Some of the informants in Janice Radway's study of romance readers cited the social legitimacy of reading, yet seemed to need to apologize for reading romances. Even to them, romances were understood to be a deprecated and devalued genre. (*Reading the Romance: Women, Patriarchy and Popular Literature.* [Chapel Hill: University of North Carolina Press, 1984].) We might ask, however, if these feelings undercut their pleasures, as Charlotte Brunsdon argues ("Women Watching Television," *MedieKultur* 4 [1986]: 109), or does it add to them?

8. None of the women I spoke to, for example, expressed any doubt in the validity of my project.

9. Unless the preemption has been scheduled in advance and carried by all the affiliates, the episode that would have been broadcast is not shown at all.

10. See, for instance, "Fans of Soap Operas Protest Iran Hearings," *New York Times* (December 11, 1986).

11. James C. Carmine, quoted in Boddy's "'The Shining Centre of the Home': Ontologies of Television in the 'Golden Age'," in *Television in Transition: Papers from the First International Television Studies Conference*, eds. Phillip Drummond and Richard Paterson (London: BFI, 1986), 132.

12. *Television Audience Research*, quoted in Boddy, p. 132.

13. Michel De Certeau, *The Practice of Everyday Life* (Berkeley and Los Angeles: University of California Press, 1984), 29. A 1947–48 study of American housewives and their leisure time somewhat arbitrarily included sewing as housework and knitting as leisure. It also considered listening to the radio, knitting, and crocheting as discrete activities. "Leisure Time of the American Housewife," by J. Roy Leevy in *Sociology and Social Research* 35, no. 2, (November–December 1950).

14. See, for instance, Ann Gray's "Behind closed doors: video recorders in the home," in *Boxed-In: Women and Television,* eds. Helen Baehr and Gillian Dyer (London: Pandora, 1986); Dorothy Hobson's "Housewives: isolation as oppression," in *Women Take Issue: Aspects of Women's Subordination,* Women's Studies Group, Centre for Contemporary Cultural Studies, University of Birmingham (London: Hutchinson, 1978); and David Morley's *Family Television: Cultural Power and Domestic Leisure* (London: Comedia, 1986). See also Rick Altman's "Television/Sound" in *Studies in Entertainment: Critical Approaches to Mass Culture,* ed. Tania Modleski (Bloomington: Indiana University Press, 1986).

15. While some argue that the audio track and narrative structures of today's nighttime television are also based on an assumption of distracted viewing (see Rick Altman, loc. cit., for example) the typical U.S. network daytime schedule (the hours when children are at school) is made up of game shows, talk shows, courtroom trials, news, and soap operas, all dialogue-centered genres that are composed of short segments which can be easily missed without losing much understanding. They are genres that can be experienced in bits and pieces.

16. This was also reported as the typical state of the daytime viewer in Madeleine Edmondson and David Rounds's *The Soaps: Daytime Serials of Radio and TV* (New York: Stein and Day, 1973), 184. Robert E. Short, of Procter & Gamble Productions, was also of the opinion that the majority of the audience are women, who watch alone in the home. See "The Television Executive's View of Daytime Serials: An Interview with Mr. Robert E. Short," in Mary Cassata and Thomas Skill's *Life on Daytime Television: Tuning-In American Serial Drama* (Norwood, N.J.: Ablex, 1983), 175.

17. This is developed further in Tania Modleski's *Loving With a Vengeance: Mass-Produced Fantasies for Women* (Hamden, Conn.: Archon Books, 1982); Carole Lopate's "Daytime Television: You'll Never Want to Leave Home," *Radical America* 11, no. 1 (January–February 1977); and my "Life's Little Problems . . . and Pleasures: An Investigation into the Narrative Structure of *The Young and the Restless*," *Quarterly Review of Film Studies* 9, no. 4 (fall 1984).

18. C. Lee Harrington and Denise D. Bielby discuss "fan gossip" on the net in *Soap Fans: Pursuing Pleasure and Making Meaning in Everyday Life* (Philadelphia: Temple University Press, 1995).

19. See Raymond Williams's discussion of the history of the word "community" in *Keywords: A Vocabulary of Culture and Society* (New York: Oxford University Press, 1983), 75–76. Williams points out that unlike other terms for social units, "community" never seems to be used unfavorably.

20. "The Relation of the Poet to Day-Dreaming," (1908) in *On*

Creativity and the Unconscious (New York: Harper and Row, 1958), 54.

21. Ibid., 46.

Different Soaps for Different Folks: Conceptualizing the Soap Opera Audience

1. As of the early 1990s, according to Gloria Abernathy-Lear, A. C. Nielsen and several African-American media sources estimate that during the last decade (the 1980s) African-Americans have constituted 17 to 37 percent of the total daytime serial audience. Additionally, A. C. Nielsen reports that African-Americans' daytime serial viewing is 55 percent higher than that of the general daytime serial audience. See Gloria Abernathy-Lear, "African-Americans' Criticisms Concerning African-American Representations in Daytime Serials," *Journalism Quarterly* 71, no. 4, 838.

2. Ibid., 831.

3. Ibid., 832.

Taking Issue: Social Themes in the Soaps

1. Thanks to JoAnn Castagna for helpful suggestions and the kind of obsessive speculative exchange every soap viewer needs.

As the World Tunes In: An International Perspective

1. On the popularity of soap operas in Brazil, see, among many other works, Alma Guillermoprieto, "Obsessed in Rio," *The New Yorker* (August 16, 1993).

2. For a discussion of the impact of *Los Ricos También Lloran* on Russian culture, see Kate Baldwin, "Montezuma's Revenge: Reading *Los Ricos También Lloran* in Russia." The popular reception of *Ramayan* is examined by Philip Lutgendorf in "All in the (Raghu) Family: A Video Epic in Cultural Context." Both essays are in *To Be Continued . . . Soap Operas Around the World*, ed. Robert C. Allen (London and New York: Routledge, 1995), 285–300.

3. Examples of even the most central of soap opera characters (called "tentpole" characters in U.S. daytime parlance) being eliminated or shelved are legion—from Luke and Laura's abrupt departure from *General Hospital* in the 1980s to Angie and Dennis Watts's emigration and murder, respectively, in the British soap opera *EastEnders*. Nor is it unusual for a character to "leave town" for a few months only to return played by a different actor.

4. Among them would be some Brazilian *telenovelas* that achieve almost cinematic production values and the extensive use of standing exterior sets in British soap operas.

5. See Dorothy Hobson, "Soap Operas at Work," in *Remote Control: Television, Audiences, and Cultural Power*, eds. Ellen Seiter, Hans Borchers, Gabriele Kreutzner, and Eva-Maria Warth (London: Routledge, 1989); and *Crossroads: The Drama of a Soap Opera* (London: Metheun, 1982). For British-Asian families' views on Australian soaps, see Marie Gillespie, "Technology and Tradition: Audio-Visual Culture Among South-Asian Families in West London," *Cultural Studies* 3 (1989).

6. See Lisa Rofel's "The Melodrama of National Identity in Post-Tianamen China," in *To Be Continued . . . Soap Operas Around The World*, 301–20; and Min Wang and Arvind Singhal, "*Ke Wang*: A Chinese Television Soap Opera With a Message," *Gazette* 49 (1992):177–92.

7. David Marcus, "How a Soap Opera Shatters Taboos—and Politicians," *IPI Report* (September 1993), 2–3.

8. One of the first and most influential studies of the cross-cultural appeal of television serials was conducted by Elihu Katz and Tamar Liebes on the extraordinary international appeal of *Dallas* in the early 1980s. See their *Export of Meaning: Cross-Cultural Readings of "Dallas"* (New York: Oxford University Press, 1990). On the differential cultural appropriation of *Oshin* in Belgium and Iran, see Hamid Mowlana and Mehdi Mohesnian Rad, "International Flow of Japanese Television Programs: The *Oshin* Phenomenon," *Keio Communication Review* 14 (1992), 51–68. Stuart Cunningham and Elizabeth Jacka make the very useful point that how a given soap opera is received in another culture can only be understood in relation to the mix of foreign and domestic programming available. In other words, they argue, the transcultural appeal of soaps' stories and their serial structure are not sufficient explanations. See their "Neighbourly Relations? Cross-Cultural Reception Analysis and Australian Soaps in Britain," *Cultural Studies* 8 (October 1994), 509–25. Stephen Crofts adduces ten reasons for the success of *Neighbours* around the world, among them: an emphasis on the "everyday" and suburban domesticity, the foregrounding of women in key plotlines, and an appeal to teenage viewers. See his "Global Neighbours?" in *To Be Continued*, 98–121. Daniel Miller's work on *The Young and the Restless* in Trinidad is summarized in "The Consumption of Soap Opera: The Young and the Restless in Trinidad," in *To Be Continued . . . Soap Operas Around the World*, 213–33.

Select Bibliography

Allen, Robert C. "On Reading Soap Operas: A Semiotic Primer." In *Regarding Television: Critical Approaches—An Anthology*, edited by E. Ann Kaplan, 97–108. Frederick, Md.: University Publications of America, 1983.

———. *Speaking of Soap Operas*. Chapel Hill: University of North Carolina Press, 1985.

———. *To Be Continued . . . Soap Operas Around the World*. London and New York: Routledge, 1995.

Ang, Ien. *Watching "Dallas": Soap Opera and the Melodramatic Imagination*. London: Methuen, 1985.

Barnouw, Eric. *A History of Broadcasting in the United States*. 3 vols. New York: Oxford University Press, 1965.

Basinger, Jeanine. *A Woman's View: How Hollywood Spoke to Women, 1930–1960*. Hanover, N.H. and Middletown, Conn.: University Press of New England and Wesleyan University Press, 1993.

Biracree, Tom. *Soap Opera Mania: Love, Lust, and Lies from Your Favorite Daytime Dramas*. New York: Prentice Hall, 1994.

Brooks, Peter. *The Melodramatic Imagination: Balzac, Henry James, Melodrama, and the Mode of Excess*. New York: Columbia University Press, 1985.

Brooks, Tim and Earle Marsh. *The Complete Directory to Prime Time Network TV Shows*. New York: Ballantine Books, 1995.

Buckman, Peter. *All For Love: A Study in Soap Opera*. London: Secker & Warburg, 1984.

Buxton, Frank and Bill Owen. *The Big Broadcast 1920–1950*. New York: Avon Books, 1972.

Carroll, Noel. *Theorizing the Moving Image*. Cambridge: Cambridge University Press, 1996.

Cassata, Mary and Thomas Skill. *Life on Daytime Television: Tuning-In American Serial Drama*. Norwood, N.J.: Ablex, 1983.

Chayefsky, Paddy. *Television Plays*. New York: Simon & Schuster, 1955.

Copeland, Mary Ann (contributing author). *Soap Opera History*. Lincolnwood, Ill.: Publications International Ltd., 1991.

Dunning, John. *Tune In Yesterday: The Ultimate Encyclopedia of Old-Time Radio, 1925–1976*. Englewood Cliffs, N.J.: Prentice Hall, 1976.

Edmonson, Madeleine and David Rounds. *The Soaps: Daytime Serials of Radio and Television*. New York: Stein & Day, 1973.

Feuer, Jane. "Melodrama, Serial Form and Television Today." *Screen* 25 (1984): 4–16.

Fiske, John. *Television Culture: Popular Pleasures and Politics*. New York: Methuen, 1987.

Fulton, Eileen. *As My World Still Turns: America's Soap Opera Queen Tells Her Own Story*. New York: Carol Publishing Group, 1996.

Fuqua, Joy V. "'There's a Queer in My Soap!': The AIDS/Homophobia Story line of *One Life to Live*," in *To Be Continued . . . Soap Operas Around the World*, edited by Robert C. Allen, 199–212. London and New York: Routledge, 1995.

Gilbert, Annie. *All My Afternoons: The Heart and Soul of the TV Soap Opera*. New York: A&W, 1976.

Gledhill, Christine. *Home Is Where the Heart Is: Studies in Melodrama and the Woman's Film*. London: British Film Institute, 1987.

———. "Speculations on the Relationship between Soap Opera and Melodrama." *Quarterly Review of Film and Video* 14 (1992): 103–24.

Goldenson, Leonard with Marvin J. Wolf. *Beating the Odds: The Untold Story Behind the Rise of ABC: The Stars, Struggles and Egos That Transformed Network Television*. New York: Charles Scribner's Sons, 1991.

Greenfield, Jeff. *Television: The First Fifty Years*. New York: Harry N. Abrams, 1977.

Groves, Seli. *The Ultimate Soap Opera Guide*. Detroit: Visible Ink Press, 1995.

Groves, Seli and the editors of the Associated Press. *Soaps: A Pictorial History of America's Daytime Dramas*. Chicago: Contemporary Books, Inc., 1983.

Harrington, C. Lee and Denise D. Bielby. *Soap Fans: Pursuing Pleasure and Making Meaning in Everyday Life*. Philadelphia: Temple University Press, 1995.

Harvey, Robert C. *The Art of the Funnies: An Aesthetic History*. Jackson: University Press of Mississippi, 1994.

Higby, Mary Jane. *Tune in Tomorrow*. New York: Cowles, 1966.

Johnson, Edgar. *Charles Dickens: His Tragedy and Triumph*. New York: Penguin Books, 1986.

Kammen, Michael. *The Lively Arts: Gilbert Seldes and the Transformation of Cultural Criticism in the U.S.* New York: Oxford University Press, 1996.

Kaplan, Fred. *Dickens: A Biography*. New York: Avon Books, 1988.

Kaplan, E. Ann, ed. *Regarding Television: Critical Approaches—An Anthology*. Frederick, Md.: University Publications of America, 1983.

LaGuardia, Robert. *"Ma Perkins" to "Mary Hartman": The Illustrated History of Soap Operas*. New York: Ballantine, 1977.

———. *The Wonderful World of TV Soap Operas*. New York: Ballantine Books, 1977.

———. *Soap World*. New York: Arbor House, 1983.

Lahue, Kalton C. *Continued Next Week: A History of the Moving Picture Serial*. Norman: University of Oklahoma Press, 1964.

Lazarsfeld, Paul and Frank Stanton. *Radio Research, 1942–43*. New York: Duell, Sloan and Pearce, 1944.

Leibman, Nina C. *Living Room Lectures: The Fifties Family in Film and Television*. Austin: University of Texas Press, 1995.

Lemay, Harding. *Eight Years in Another World*. New York: Atheneum, 1981.

Lichty, Lawrence and M. C. Topping, eds. *American Broadcasting*. New York: Hastings House, 1975.

Lund, Michael. *America's Continuing Story: An Introduction to Serial Fiction, 1850–1900*. Detroit: Wayne State University, 1993.

MacDonald, J. Fred. *Don't Touch That Dial!: Radio Programming in American Life from 1920 to 1960*. Chicago: Nelson-Hall, 1979.

Marc, David and Robert J. Thompson. *Prime Time, Prime Movers: From "I Love Lucy" to "L.A. Law"—America's Greatest TV Shows and the People Who Created Them*. Boston: Little, Brown & Co., 1992.

McNeil, Alex. *Total Television: A Comprehensive Guide to Programming from 1948 to the Present*. New York: Penguin Books, 1996.

Modleski, Tania. *Loving With a Vengeance: Mass-Produced Fantasies for Women*. New York: Routledge, 1984.

Mumford, Laura Stempel. "Plotting Paternity: Looking for Dad on the Daytime Soaps." *Genders* 12 (1991), 45–61.

———. *Love and Ideology in the Afternoon: Soap Opera, Women, and Television Genre*. Bloomington: Indiana University Press, 1995.

Newcomb, Horace. *TV: The Most Popular Art*. New York: Anchor Books, 1974.

———. *Television: The Critical View*. 4th ed. New York: Oxford University Press, 1987.

Nochimson, Martha. *No End to Her: Soap Opera and the Female Subject*. Berkeley and Los Angeles: University of California Press, 1993.

Poll, Julie. *As the World Turns: The Complete Family Album*. Los Angeles: General Publishing Group, 1996.

Porter, Dennis. "Soap Time: Thoughts of a Commodity Art Form." *College English* 38 (1977), 782–88. Reprinted in *Television: The Critical View*, 3rd ed., edited by Horace Newcomb, 122–31. New York: Oxford University Press, 1982.

Rose, Brian, ed. *TV Genres: A Handbook and Guide*. Westport, Conn.: Greenwood, 1985.

Ruthledge, Dr. John. *The Guiding Light*. Chicago: Guiding Light Publishing Co., 1938.

Schatz, Thomas. *Hollywood Genres*. New York: Random House, 1981.

Schemering, Christopher. *The Soap Opera Encyclopedia*. New York: Ballantine Books, 1985.

———. *Guiding Light: A 50th Anniversary Celebration*. New York: Ballantine Books, 1988.

Seldes, Gilbert. *The Public Arts*. New York: Simon & Schuster, 1956.

Smulyan, Susan. *Selling Radio: The Commercialization of American Broadcasting, 1920–1934*. Washington, D.C.: Smithsonian Institution Press, 1994.

Soap Opera Digest. New York: Network Publishing Corp.

Soap Opera Magazine. Tarrytown, N.Y.: SOM Publishing, Inc.

Soap Opera Weekly. New York: K-III Magazines.

Soares, Manuela. *The Soap Opera Book*. New York: Harmony Books, 1978.

Spence, Louise. "Life's Little Problems . . . and Pleasures: Watching Soap Operas." *Dissertation Abstracts International* 51 (1991).

Spigel, Lynn. *Make Room for TV: Television and the Family Ideal in Postwar America*. Chicago: University of Chicago Press, 1992.

Steadman, Raymond William. *The Serials: Suspense and Drama by Installment*. 2nd ed. Norman: University of Oklahoma Press, 1977.

Stuart, Mary. *Both of Me*. New York: Doubleday & Co., 1980.

Thompson, Robert J. *Television's Second Golden Age: From "Hill Street Blues" to "ER."* New York: Continuum, 1996.

Timberg, Bernard. "The Rhetoric of the Camera in Television Soap Opera." In *Television: The Critical View*, 4th ed., edited by Horace Newcomb, 164–78. New York: Oxford University Press, 1987.

Waggett, Gerard J. *The Soap Opera Book of Lists*. New York: Harper Paperbacks, 1996.

Wakefield, Dan. *All Her Children: The Real Life Story of America's Favorite Soap Opera*. Garden City, N.Y.: Doubleday, 1976.

Warner, Gary. *All My Children: The Complete Family Scrapbook*. Los Angeles: General Publishing Group, 1994.

———. *General Hospital: The Complete Scrapbook*. Los Angeles: General Publishing Group, 1995.

Watson, Mary Ann. *The Expanding Vista: American Television in the Kennedy Years*. New York: Oxford University Press, 1990.

Westheim, Arthur Frank. *Radio Comedy*. New York: Oxford University Press, 1979.

Williams, Carol Traynor. *"It's Time for My Story": Soap Opera Sources, Structure and Response*. Media and Society Series. Westport, Conn.: Praeger, 1992.

Zenka, Lorraine. *Days of Our Lives: The Complete Family Album*. New York: Regan Books/HarperCollins, 1995.

Acknowledgments

The Museum of Television & Radio enjoyed the generous cooperation of the entire soap opera creative community in the research for this exhibition. Heartfelt thanks to everyone for their time and consideration.

The interviews conducted by Ron Simon and Ellen O'Neill, portions of which are reprinted throughout this book, were invaluable to the research for the entire exhibition. Thank you to the following who took time from their busy schedules to be interviewed: Susan Bedsow-Horgan (Executive Producer, *One Life to Live*); Bill Bell, Jr. (President, Bell-Phillips Television); Bradley Bell (Head Writer/Executive Producer, *The Bold and the Beautiful*); William J. Bell and Lee Phillip Bell (Creators, *The Young and the Restless, The Bold and the Beautiful*); R. Scott Collishaw (Producer, *Another World*); Ken Corday (Executive Producer, *Days of Our Lives*); Carolyn Culliton (Associate Head Writer, *The City*); Richard Culliton (Head Writer, *General Hospital*); Anthony Geary ("Luke Spencer," *General Hospital*); Don Hastings ("Bob Hughes," *As the World Turns*); Francesca James (Executive Producer, *All My Children*); Charles Keating ("Carl Hutchins," *Another World*); Claire Labine (Creator, *Ryan's Hope*); Michael Laibson (Executive Producer, *Guiding Light*); Harding Lemay (former Head Writer, *Another World*); Bill Mickley (Production Designer, *As the World Turns*); Agnes Nixon (Creator, *One Life to Live, All My Children, Loving*); Jay O'Neill (Technical Director, *Days of Our Lives*); Wendy Riche (Executive Producer, *General Hospital*); Edward Scott (Executive Producer, *The Young and the Restless*); Roy Steinberg (Producer, *Guiding Light*); Mary Stuart ("Jo Tate," *Search for Tomorrow*); Gary Tomlin (Director, *One Life to Live*); Mimi Torchin (Editor-in-Chief, *Soap Opera Weekly*); John Valente (Executive Producer, *As the World Turns*); John C. Zak (Producer/Director, *The Bold and the Beautiful*).

Thank you to the following people for their generous assistance with arranging and conducting set tours and helping to schedule the interviews: Paulette Cohen (Publicist, *Days of Our Lives*); Louis Grieci (Production Manager, *Another World*); John Keeler (Unit Manager, *Guiding Light*); Gilbert Parker (William Morris Agency); Jonathan Renes (Publicist, *As the World Turns*); Sid Sirulnick (Production Manager, *As the World Turns*); Janet Storm (Director of Program Publicity, DMB&B); Gillian Strum (Publicist, *Another World* and *As the World Turns*); Frank Tobin of the Frank Tobin Agency and his colleagues David Sperber and Charles Sherman.

Thanks to Sallie Schoneboom at ABC Daytime for her help in obtaining permission from Susan Lucci, Erika Slezak, and Robin Strasser to reprint excerpts from their participation in Museum seminars.

The Museum of Television & Radio gratefully acknowledges all of the individuals and companies that donated programming used in the preparation of this book and accompanying exhibition, including:

Harriet Abraham, Marge Ponce, Angela Shapiro, and ABC, Inc; Larry Auerbach; Jack Sullivan and Broadway Video; CBS Inc.; Keith Charles; Janet Rider, Ed Zimmerman, and Columbia Television; Susan Dansby; Barbara Brady, Philip Dixson, and D'Arcy, Masius, Benton, & Bowles; Rhonda Friedman; Ira Gallen; Martin Halperin; Carole Henson and ITV; Harding Lemay; David Parker and the Library of Congress; J. Fred MacDonald; Bruce Minnix; NBC Entertainment; Agnes Nixon; Pacific Pioneer Broadcasters; Ed Rider and Amy Fischer of the Procter & Gamble Archive; Mary Stuart; Millee Taggart; Dan Einstein and UCLA Film and Television Archive; Leonard Valenta; Nancy Wiard; Nancy Wicker.

We thank Noah Arceneaux, William Boddy, John Dunning, Sonny Fox, Nelson Hoineff, J. Fred MacDonald, Julie Poll, Brian Rose, Ed Trach, Bernard Timberg, and Gary Warner for sharing their insights and expertise on soap opera.

We could not have asked for a more committed publisher than Harry N. Abrams, Inc. Thank you to Paul Gottlieb for his enthusiasm for the project, Bob Morton our patient and helpful editor, and Robert McKee, the book's designer.

We would especially like to thank Procter & Gamble for sponsoring this exhibition. It was their commitment to the history of the genre that enabled the Museum to take the first serious look at this important part of broadcasting history. We would also like to thank the American Federation of Television and Radio Artists (AFTRA) for providing additional generous support.

The three reprinted essays from "Soapland" by James Thurber are from *The Beast in Me and Other Animals*, by James Thurber. Copyright © 1948 by James Thurber. Copyright © 1976 by Rosemary A. Thurber. Reprinted by arrangement with Rosemary A. Thurber c/o the Barbara Hogenson Agency.

The acquisition of photographs for a project of this scope is an enormous undertaking and was only successful because of the help and support of the following individuals and organizations: Stav Birnbaum, Corbis-Bettmann; Patricia Carroll and Mimi Torchin, *Soap Opera Weekly*; John Filo, CBS Photo; Joel Ghivelder, TV Globo; Michael Henry, Broadcast Pioneers Library, University of Maryland; Kathy Hutchins; Ann Limongello, ABC, Inc.; Howard Mandelbaum and Ron Mandelbaum, Photofest; Protele; Charles Sherman and David Sperber, Frank Tobin Agency; Janet Storm and Cindy Marshall, D'Arcy, Masius, Benton, & Bowles; April Swieconek, NTV America; and Ray Whelan, Jr., Globe Photos.

An exhibition and publication of this magnitude required the efforts and talents of the entire Museum staff. The following people in particular were integral to the completion of this book and the exhibition:

In the Curatorial Department: Susan Fisher, Vice President; Abbey Benowitz, Curatorial Assistant; in the Publications Department: Jack CK Chen, Designer; Kitty May, Managing

Editor; in Technical Services: Steve Blot, Project Engineer; and Ann Marie Aversano, Andrea Begor, James Kreyling, and Tracy Martin, Tape Transfer Technicians; in the Registrar's Office: Hunter Brown, Registrar; in Research Services: Jonathan Rosenthal; in the Education Department: Dale Zaklad, Director; Ritty Burchfield, Coordinator, Satellite Seminars; Lisa Baim, Assistant Coordinator, William S. Paley Television Festival; in Public Relations: Diane Reed, Director, and Jane Leet, Senior Publicist; in Development: Tina Forleiter, Director; LoriJeane Moody, Grants Coordinator; Barbara Tarter, Coordinator, Corporate Relations; for Business Affairs: David Greenstein, Vice President; in the President's Office: Michelle Stoneburn, Vice President; and in Public Affairs and Programs: Diane Lewis, Vice President.

THE EXHIBITION TEAM

Above all, this publication and exhibition would not have been possible without the talents and dedication of the staff of the Editorial and Curatorial Departments. In particular, Roberta Panjwani, Associate Editor, and Lynn Messina, Editorial Assistant, who contributed greatly to the editing of the manuscript. In Curatorial, Ken Mueller, Radio Manager, who created the companion listening series to the screenings; and Allen Glover, Researcher; Barry Monush, Curatorial Assistant; Leah Oppenheim, Assistant to the Vice President of Curatorial Services; and Raj Kaup, Curatorial Assistant, all of whom fact checked articles and viewed countless hours of programs to help conceptualize the screening series.

About the Contributors

ROBERT C. ALLEN is the James Logan Godfrey Professor of American Studies at the University of North Carolina, Chapel Hill. His considerable work in the study of soap operas includes his books *Speaking of Soap Operas* and *To Be Continued . . . Soap Operas Around the World*, for which he served as editor; as well as book chapters and articles, including "On Reading Soaps: A Semiotic Primer" in *Regarding Television* and "The Guiding Light: Soap Opera as Economic Product" in *American History/American Television*. Mr. Allen's other books include *Channels of Discourse: Television and Contemporary Criticism*, which he edited; *Film History: Theory and Practice*, which he coauthored; and *Horrible Prettiness: Burlesque and American Culture*.

JANE FEUER is professor of English at the University of Pittsburgh, where she teaches in the film studies program at the graduate and undergraduate levels. Her books include *The Hollywood Musical*; *Seeing through the Eighties: Television and Reaganism*; and she coauthored (with Paul Kerr) *MTM: Quality Television*. She has written for *Harper's* and *American Movie Classics Magazine* and has served as a consultant for ABC Daytime television and the New York Center for Visual History.

LAURA STEMPEL MUMFORD is a writer and independent scholar in Madison, Wisconsin. Her publications include *Love and Ideology in the Afternoon: Soap Opera, Women, and Television Genre*, and articles on television in *Camera Obscura*, *Quarterly Review of Film and Video*, and *Genders*. For ten years Ms. Mumford wrote about media, culture, and style for Madison's weekly newspaper, *Isthmus*, and she is currently at work on a book of critical essays.

RON SIMON is curator of television at The Museum of Television & Radio. Previous exhibitions that he has curated for the Museum include *Jack Benny: The Radio and Television Work*; *Witness to History*; and *The Television of Dennis Potter*. He serves as an adjunct professor at Columbia University and has lectured and consulted at the Smithsonian Institution, the Whitney Museum of American Art, the Museum of Modern Art, and Hunter College. Mr. Simon is a member of the Editorial Board of *Television Quarterly*.

LOUISE SPENCE teaches media studies at Sacred Heart University, Fairfield, Connecticut. The coauthor of *In Search of Oscar Micheaux* (with Pearl Bowser), her work on film and television has appeared in *Quarterly Review of Film Studies*, *Screen*, *Movies and Methods*, *The Journal of Film and Video*, and *To Be Continued . . . Soap Operas Around the World*. Ms. Spence is the recipient of a 1995 N.E.H. research grant and was a 1992 MacDowell Colony Fellow.

ROBERT J. THOMPSON is associate professor at the S. I. Newhouse School of Public Communications at Syracuse University, an occasional visiting professor at Cornell University, and the former director of the N.H.S.I. Television and Film Institute at Northwestern University. He is the author of *Television's Second Golden Age: From "Hill Street Blues" to "ER,"* and the coauthor (with David Marc) of *Prime Time, Prime Movers: America's Greatest TV Shows and the People Who Created Them*. Mr. Thompson's articles have appeared in such publications as *The Journal of American Culture*, *Television Studies*, *Psychology Today*, *The Chronicle of Higher Education*, *Feedback*, *Popular Music and Society*, and *Television Criticism*.

Photograph Credits

Please note that every effort was made to provide correct photo identifications and credit lines; any error or omission herein is unintentional. Also note, the dates given for the photos found on pages 14 and 15 are approximate.

Jacket front: (clockwise from left) © ABC; Courtesy Paulette Cohen/© Columbia Pictures Television; Courtesy DMB&B/© Robert Milazzo; Courtesy Frank Tobin Public Relations/© Columbia Pictures Television; and (center photo) © ABC; jacket back: (clockwise from left) Courtesy CBS; Courtesy CBS; Courtesy Frank Tobin Public Relations; Courtesy CBS; Courtesy CBS; © ABC; p. 2: (clockwise from top left) © ABC; Courtesy Frank Tobin Public Relations/© Columbia Pictures Television; Courtesy Photofest (CBS); © ABC; Courtesy Globe Photos/© Columbia Pictures Television; p. 3: (clockwise from left) © Barry Morgenstein/Provided by *Soap Opera Weekly* Magazine; Courtesy Frank Tobin Public Relations; Courtesy DMB&B; © ABC; p. 4: (left to right) Courtesy Photofest/© ABC; Courtesy Photofest; Courtesy Globe Photos/© Columbia Pictures Television; © Hutchins-Michelson/Columbia Pictures Television; p. 5: (left to right) Courtesy CBS/© Columbia Pictures Television; Courtesy Photofest (CBS); Courtesy Globe Photos; p. 6: © ABC; p. 9: Courtesy Library of American Broadcasting, University of Maryland, College Park; p. 10: Courtesy Photofest/© Columbia Pictures Television; p. 11: Courtesy Photofest; p. 12: Courtesy CBS; p. 13: Courtesy NBC; p. 14: (clockwise from top left) Courtesy Photofest; Courtesy DMB&B/© E.J. Carr; Courtesy Globe Photos; Courtesy DMB&B/© E.J. Carr; Courtesy Photofest; Courtesy Photofest; p. 15: (clockwise from top left) Courtesy Photofest; © ABC/Photo by Vern Evans; Courtesy Frank Tobin Public Relations/© Columbia Pictures Television; Courtesy Photofest; p. 17: (top) Courtesy CBS; (bottom) Courtesy Julie Pool; p. 18: Courtesy CBS; p. 19: Courtesy CBS; p. 22: Courtesy Photofest; p. 23: Courtesy CBS; p. 24: (clockwise from left) Courtesy Photofest (CBS); Courtesy Photofest; Courtesy Photofest (CBS); p. 25: Courtesy CBS; p. 26: Courtesy Photofest; p. 27: Courtesy NBC/Globe Photos; p. 28: Courtesy Photofest; p. 29: (top) Courtesy Photofest, (bottom) © ABC; p. 30: (top) © ABC; (bottom left) Courtesy Globe Photos/Photo by Steve Fenn; (bottom right) © ABC; p. 31: Courtesy Frank Tobin Public Relations; p. 34: © ABC; p. 35: Courtesy Frank Tobin Public Relations; p. 38: © ABC; p. 39: Courtesy Frank Tobin Public Relations; p. 40: Courtesy CBS; p. 41: Cover-drawing by Mary Petty/© 1948 The New Yorker Magazine, Inc.; p. 43: NBC; p. 44: (left) Courtesy Photofest; (right) Corbis-Bettmann; p. 45: Courtesy CBS; p. 47: Courtesy CBS; p. 49: Courtesy Photofest; p. 51: Cover-drawing by Edna Eicke/© 1948 The New Yorker Magazine, Inc.; p. 52: Courtesy Photofest; p. 54: Courtesy Photofest; p. 55: Courtesy Photofest; p. 56: Courtesy CBS; p. 57: Courtesy Photofest; p. 59: Cover-drawing by Constantin Alajalov/© 1948 The New Yorker Magazine, Inc.; p. 61: Courtesy CBS; p. 63: Courtesy Photofest; p. 65: Courtesy Photofest; p. 66: Courtesy Photofest; p. 69: Courtesy CBS; p. 72: Courtesy Photofest; p. 73: Courtesy Photofest; p. 74: (top) Courtesy CBS; (bottom) © ABC; p. 75: Courtesy Frank Tobin Public Relations; p. 76: Photo by Irv Haberman/Courtesy CBS; p. 78: Courtesy Frank Tobin Public Relations; p. 79: (top) Courtesy Photofest; (bottom) Courtesy Paulette Cohen/© Columbia Pictures Television; p. 82: Courtesy Photofest/Photo by Craig Sjodin/ABC; p. 83: Courtesy Photofest; p. 84: Courtesy Photofest; p. 85: Courtesy Globe Photos; p. 86: Courtesy DMB&B/© Cathy Blaivas; p. 87: Courtesy Globe Photos; p. 88: Courtesy CBS; p. 89: Courtesy CBS; p. 90: Courtesy Paulette Cohen/© Columbia Pictures Television; p. 91: Courtesy DMB&B/© Cathy Blaivas; p. 92: Courtesy Globe Photos; p. 94: Courtesy Photofest/Photo by Monty Brinton/© Columbia Pictures Television; p. 95: (top) Courtesy DMB&B; (bottom) Courtesy Photofest/Photo by Ann Limongello; p. 97: (top) Courtesy Globe Photos/Photo by Chris Haston; (bottom) Photo by Kimberly Butler/© ABC; p. 98: Courtesy Globe Photos; p. 100: Courtesy Frank Tobin Public Relations/Photo by Bernard Fallon; p. 101: (top and bottom) © ABC; p. 102: Courtesy Photofest; pp. 104–6: © ABC; p. 108: Courtesy Photofest (NBC); p. 109: (top and bottom) © ABC; p. 110: © BBC; p. 112: Courtesy Globo TV Network, Brazil; p. 113: Courtesy Photofest; p. 114: Courtesy Protele; p. 115: © Nippon Television Network Corp.; p. 118: Courtesy Frank Tobin Public Relations; p. 119: Courtesy Photofest/© Grundy Television Pty Ltd.; p. 120: Photo by Donna Svennevik/© ABC; p. 125: Courtesy Photofest; p. 126: Courtesy Photofest (CBS); p. 129: Courtesy Photofest; p. 130: Courtesy Photofest (CBS); p. 133: Courtesy CBS; p. 134: Courtesy Photofest; p. 137: © ABC; p. 138: Courtesy Photofest; p. 141: Courtesy Globe Photos/Photo by Ed Geller; p. 142: Courtesy Globe Photos/Photo by Chris Haston/© Columbia Pictures Television; p. 145: Courtesy Photofest; p. 146: © ABC; p. 149: Courtesy Photofest/© ABC; p. 150: Courtesy Frank Tobin Public Relations/Photo by Randy Tepper/© Columbia Pictures Television; p. 154: Courtesy Photofest (ABC); p. 156: Courtesy Photofest (ABC); p. 157: Courtesy Photofest (ABC); p. 159: Courtesy Photofest (NBC); p. 160: Courtesy Globe Photos; p. 163: NBC/Globe Photos/Photo by Alice S. Hall

Captions for pages 2–5: p. 2: (clockwise from top left) *One Life to Live:* Nora Buchanan (Hillary B. Smith), Hank Gannon (Nathan Purdee), Rachel Gannon (Sandra P. Grant), Drew Buchanan (Victor Brown), R. J. Gannon (Timothy Stickney); *The Young and the Restless:* Danny Romalotti (Michael Damien) and Christine "Cricket" Blair (Lauralee Bell); *As the World Turns:* Chris and Nancy Hughes (Don MacLaughlin and Helen Wagner); *General Hospital:* Stone Cates (Michael Sutton) and Robin Scorpio (Kimberly McCullough); *Days of Our Lives:* Tom and Alice Horton (Macdonald Carey and Frances Reid); p. 3: (clockwise from left) *Another World:* Carl and Rachel Hutchins (Charles Keating and Victoria Wyndham); *The Bold and the Beautiful:* The Forresters (clockwise from left) Kristen (Teri Ann Linn), Thorne (Jeff Trachta), Eric (John McCook), Ridge (Ronn Moss), and Stephanie (Susan Flannery); *Guiding Light:* Hart Jessup (Michael Hilliard), Dinah Marler (Wendy Moriz), and Roger Thorpe (Michael Zaslow); *All My Children:* Amy Tyler (Rosemary Prinz), Phoebe Tyler (Ruth Warrick), and Phillip Brent (Richard Hatch); p. 4: (left to right) *One Live to Live:* Dorian Lord (Robin Strasser); *Another World:* John Randolph (Michael Ryan) and Pat Matthews (Beverly Penberthy); *Days of Our Lives:* Julie Olson (Susan Seaforth Hayes) and Doug Williams (Bill Hayes); *Days of Our Lives:* Marlena Brady (Deidre Hall); p. 5: (left to right) *The Young and the Restless:* Lance Prentiss (John McCook) and Lorie Brooks (Jaime Lyn Bauer); *As the World Turns:* Bob Hughes (Don Hastings); *One Life to Live:* Bo (Robert S. Woods), Asa (Philip Carey), and Clint (Clint Ritchie) Buchanan

Index

Note: This index is referenced by character names, which appear within quotation marks. Actors are cited when they appear in a photograph. Page numbers in *italics* refer to illustrations and captions.

"Abbott, Jack," 151
"Abbott family," 151
Abernathy-Lear, Gloria, 93
Adams, Evangeline, 56
Adventures of Kathlyn, The, 13
African-American characters, 36, 93, 96, 99, 106, 128, 147, 162; *30, 94, 97, 98, 108, 163*
Against the Storm, 64
"Alden family," 156, 157
"Aldrich, Dr. Steve," 139
"Aleata, Caroline" (Deborah Courtney), *83*
"Alexander, Raven," 135
Allen, Robert C., 67–68, 89, 93
All in the Family, 36
All My Children: 33, 71, 113, 156; *29, 30, 34, 79, 85, 95, 97, 104, 120, 121, 149;* audience of, 78, 80, 83, 84, 92, 93; bible of, 28, 34, 148; debut of, 36, 148; gay characters in, 96, 107, *109;* lineage of, 123; MT&R seminar on, 102; social issues in, 26, 93, 99, 101, 103, 106, 148–49; write-up of, 148–49
"Ames, Amy" (Jada Rowland), 131; *130*
"Ames, Valerie Hill" (Lori March), 131; *130*
"Ames family," 131
Amos 'n' Andy, 13, 15, 42; *13*
Anderson, Sherwood, 51
"Andrade family," 158
Andrews, Robert Hardy, 18, 42, 48–49, 50, 53, 68, 70
"Andropoulos, Steve" (Frank Runyeon), 132; *89*
"Angelique" (witch), 144
Another World, 16, 28, 34, 36, 71, 121, 123, 140–41; *28, 84, 86, 91, 95, 141*
Arley, Jean, 127
Arnheim, Dr. Rudolf, 60
As the World Turns: 16, 26, 36, 71, 150, 158; *14, 24, 74, 76, 77, 89, 133;* audience of, 79, 91, 93; creation of, 22, 26, 142; debut of, 72, 135; innovations in, 26, 132; lineage of, 121, 123; social issues in, 106; write-up of, 28, 132–33
Atkinson, Brooks, 43
audience: activities of, 84; African-American, 93; changing demographics of, 137, 147, 148; collective memory of, 36, 37–38; college students in, 89, 92, 148; emotional investment of, 26, 80, 95, 96, 103, 117, 132, 135, 151, 155; fans in, 89, 95–96; fantasies of, 85, 116–17;

feedback from, 56–57, 83, 91; gay males in, 95–96; gifts from, 62, 63–64; implied, 89, 91–93, 99; isolation of, 84; men in, 89, 93, 95–96, 135; periodicals for, 85, 86, 93; research on, 77–85, 89–96; size of, 42, 51; surveys of, 60–62; women in, 89, 92–93, 99; *20*
Aunt Jenny's True Life Stories, 20; *21*
Australia, serials in, 113, 115, 117; *119*
auteur theory, 67

Backstage Wife, 19, 50, 62, 63, 70, 122; *63*
"Baker, Jeff," 28, 132
"Baldwin, Scotty," 136
"Bancroft, Iris Cory," 140
"Banning, Meta Bauer" (Ellen Demming), *14*
"Bannister, Reed," 62
"Barr, Robert," 158
"Barrett, Brenda" (Vanessa Marcil), *82*
"Bates, Lotty," 156
"Bauer, Bert" (Charita Bauer), 32, 33, 128, 129; *14, 15, 24, 129*
"Bauer, Bill" (Lyle Sudrow), 128; *14*
"Bauer, Ed" (Martin Hulswit), *24*
"Bauer, Mike" (Don Stuart; Glenn Walken), 129; *14, 24*
"Bauer, Papa" (Theo Goetz), *129*
Baumer, Marie, 50
"Baxter, Angie," 148
Beech-Nut Company, 44
Bell, Bradley, 91, 161
Bell, Lee Phillip, 36, 71, 150, 161; *75*
Bell, William J.: 22, 25, 32, 34, 81, 140, 142, 143, 150, 151, 161; *31, 75;* as Phillips protégé, 16, 33, 36, 38, 71, 121, 123, 128
Bell, William J., Jr., 118
"Bellini, Dr. Nick," 139
Ben Casey, 32
Berg, Dr. Louis I., 20, 59–60
Berg, Gertrude, 15, 42–43; *43*
"Bergman, Janet," 124
"Bergman, Marge" (Melba Rae), 124; *22*
"Bergman, Stu" (Larry Haines), 124; *22*
Berle, Milton, 20
Betty and Bob, 68, 122
Big Sister, 20, 54, 60–62, 64
Bill the Barber, 49
"Blair, Christine (Cricket)" (Lauralee Bell), *150*
Bochco, Steven, 37
Boddy, William, 81
"Bodine, Brian," 148
Bold and the Beautiful, The, 36, 77, 81, 96, 118, 123, 161; *35, 78, 92, 100, 118, 160*
"Brady, Marlena Evans" (Deidre Hall), 143; *90, 142*
"Brady, Roman" (Wayne Northrop), 143; *90*
"Brandon, Charlotte" (Lesley Woods), *72*

"Brandon, Ray" (Staats Cotsworth), *72*
"Braxton, Stephanie," 92
Brazil, *telenovelas* in, 111, 117, 119; *112*
"Brent, Charlie," 148
"Brent, Phillip" (Richard Hatch), *29*
"Brewer, Jessie" (Emily McLaughlin), 136; *14*
"Brewer, Dr. Phil" (Roy Thinnes), 136; *14*
Bríco, Leonardo, *112*
Brighter Day, The, 71, 122
"Brinthrope, Lord Henry," 54
"Brinthrope, Sunday" (Vivian Smolen), *18*
"Brooks, Chris," 161
"Brooks, Lauralee," 151
"Brooks, Leslie," 150–51
"Brooks family," 150
"Brown, Ellen," 54
Brown, James Harmon, 157
"Buchanan, Asa" (Philip Carey), *146*
"Buchanan, Bo" (Robert S. Woods), *146*
"Buchanan, Clint" (Clint Ritchie), *146*
"Buchanan, Cord Roberts" (John Loprieno), *146*
"Buchanan, Drew" (Victor Brown), *30*
"Buchanan, Nora" (Hillary B. Smith), *30*
"Buchanan family," 147; *146*
"Burns, Betty" (Patricia Dunlop), *63*

"Cabot, Rosanna" (Yvonne Perry), *14*
Cadenhead, Julie Pars, 81
Calmer, Ned, 50
Cantor, Muriel, 70
"Capwell, Eden" (Marcy Walker), 158; *14, 87*
"Capwell family," 158
Carlson, Emmons C., 46
Carrington, Elaine, 42, 44–45, 56–57, 62, 64, 68, 70, 122; *44*
"Carrington, Iris," 141
"Carter, Sheila" (Kimberlin Brown), *78*
"Cassen, Doug" (Nat Polen), 76, *77*
"Castillo, Cruz" (A Martinez), 158; *14, 87*
"Cates, Jagger" (Antonio Sabato, Jr.), *82*
"Cates, Stone" (Michael Sutton), 107, 108, 137; *109*
"Chancellor, Katherine" (Jeanne Cooper), 151; *15*
"Chancellor, Phillip," 150–51
"Chandler, Julie," 148
Chase, Allan, 143
Chayefsky, Paddy, 31
Cheers, 37
Cheyenne, 32
China, serials in, 111, *112*
Cinderella story, 70
City, The, 123, 157; *157*
"Coleridge, Jillian," 152
"Collins, Barnabas" (Jonathan Frid), 144; *145*
"Collins, Quentin," 144
Collishaw, R. Scott, 26, 140

comedy, 140, 155, 161

comic strips, 12–13; *12*

"Conrad, Carol (Chichi)" (Teri Keane), 54

"Cooney, Dixie" (Cady McClain), *97*

Corday, Betty, 143

Corday, Ken, 81, 142

Corday, Ted, 22, 24, 26, 32, 121, 123, 143; *23*

Coronation Street, 99, 113, 116, 117; *113*

"Cortlandt, Melanie," 148

"Cortlandt, Nina" (Taylor Miller), 85

"Cory, Mac" (Douglass Watson), 140–41; *91*

"Cory, Maggie" (Robyn Griggs), 95

"Cory, Rachel Davis" (Victoria Wyndham), 28, 36, 140–41; *28, 91, 141*

Couple Next Door, The, 122

"Crabtree, Archie" (John Stratton), *113*

"Craig, Cathy" (Amy Levitt), 99, 147; *102*

"Craig, Jason" (Tony Addabbo), *163*

"Crawford, Betsy" (Elizabeth Kemp), *83*

Crawford, Joan, 131

Crosby, Percy, 49

Cruisinberry, Jane, 121

Culliton, Carolyn, 80, 96, 157

Culliton, Richard, 33, 91, 115

"Curtin, Walter," 140

Curtis, Dan, 144

"Dale, Margaret (Meg)," 127

"Dale, Vanessa" (Audrey Peters), 127, 131; *126*

Dallas, 37

"Dallas, Stella," 20

"Dane, Marco," 147

Dark Shadows, 144; *145*

David Harum, 54; *55*

"Davidson, Bill" (Arthur Hughes), 53, 55, 62, 64; *49*

"Davis, Althea," 139

"Davis, Harry" (John Raby), 65

"Dawson, Rosemary" (Betty Winkler), *52*

Days of Our Lives: 28, 36, 71; *27, 79, 90, 142*; creation of, 142, 143; influence of movies on, 32, 150; lineage of, 121, 123; social issues in, 101–2; write-up of, 143

"Delaney, Michael" (Chris Bruno), 96, 107–8; *109*

"de la Parra, Luis" (Rogelio Guerra), *114*

Dickens, Charles, 12–13, 38, 111; *11*

"Dillon, Laurel," 107

"Dillon, Tim" (Tommy Michaels), *109*

"DiMera, Stefano" (Joseph Mascolo), *79*

"Dixon, Andy" (Scott DeFreitas), *133*

"Dixon, John," 132, 133

Dobson, Bridget Hursley and Jerome, 121, 128, 132, 136, 158

Doctors, The, 139, 140; *24, 138*

"Donovan, Douglas" (Bryan Cranston), *156*

"Donovan, Kerry," 55, 62

"Donovan, Mike" (James Kiberd), 156; *156*

"Donovan, Nancy," 56, 62

"Donovan, Noreen" (Marilyn McIntyre), *156*

"Donovan, Rose" (Terri Keane), *156*

"Donovan, Stacey," 157

"Donovan family," 156; *156*

Dragnet, 37

"Drake, Adam," 135

"Drake, Dr. Noah" (Rick Springfield), 6

Duffy's Tavern, 52

Dunning, John, 68

"Duvall, Mary," 158

Dwyer, Charles, 13

Dynasty, 37

EastEnders, 99, 113, 116; *110, 111*

Edge of Night, The, 22, 72, 121, 135; *134*

Ellis, Ralph, 124

Emmy awards, 128, 139, 141, 143, 153

Esensten, Barbara, 157

"Evans, Maggie" (Kathryn Leigh Scott), *145*

Fagundes, Antonio, *112*

Falken Smith, Pat, 136, 143

Faraway Hill, 20

"Fenelli, Jack," 152

"Fenmore, Lauren" (Tracey E. Bregman), *78*

Fernwood 2-Night, 155

Fischer, Vera, *112*

Fisher, Harry Conway "Bud," 13

Flesch, Dr. Rudolph, 64

"Forbes family," 156

Forever Fernwood, 155

"Forrester, Eric" (John McCook), *100*

"Forrester, Felicia" (Colleen Dion), *100*

"Forrester, Kristen" (Teri Ann Linn), *100*

"Forrester, Ridge" (Ronn Moss), 161; *35, 100*

"Forrester, Stephanie" (Susan Flannery), *100*

"Forrester, Thorne," 161

"Forrester family," 161

"Foster, Greg," 161

"Foster, Jill," 150

"Foster, Snapper" (William Grey Espy), 11, 161; *10*

"Foster family," 150, 161

Foyle, Kitty, 54

"Frame, Steve," 140

"Frazier, Martha," 128

Freud, Sigmund, 84–85

"Friday, Joe," 37

Front Page Farrell, 122

Funt, Julian, 62

"Furillo, Capt. Frank," 37

"Gallant, Felicia," 141

"Gannon, Hank" (Nathan Purdee), *30*

"Gannon, Rachel" (Sandra P. Grant), *30*

"Gannon, R. J." (Timothy Stickney), *30*

"Gardner, Jenny" (Kim Delaney), 148; *149*

"Gardner, Opal," 148

"Garrison, Clarke" (Dan McVicar), *100*

General Hospital: 34, 37, 128; *6, 14, 15, 26, 38, 82, 137*; AIDS/HIV issue in, 107, 137; *109*; audience of, 79, 80; creation of, 32, 136, 139; lineage of, 121, 122; social issues in, 106, 137; *98, 99*; write-up of, 136–37

General Mills, 46, 49

General Mills Hour, The, 18

Generations, 93, 96, 162; *97, 163*

Gibson, Charles Dana, 13

"Goldberg, Molly" (Gertrude Berg), 42; *43*

Goldbergs, The, 15, 42–44, 53; *43*

"Gook, Sade" (Bernardine Flynn), *47*

"Gook, Vic" (Art Van Harvey), *47*

"Gorrow, Vivien," 140

Gothic romance novel, 144

"Grant, Dick" (James Lipton), 73

"Grant, Felicia" (Linda Dano), 86

"Grant, Nancy" (Lisa Wilkinson), *29*

"Gray, Carla" (Ellen Holly), 36, 106, 147; *106*

"Gray, Sadie," 106

Great Britain, serials in, 99, 111, 113, 116, 117; *110, 113*

Griffin, Sean, 93, 96

Guiding Light: 16, 32, 53, 71, 93, 142; *14, 15, 17, 23, 24, 72, 73, 88, 89, 129*; duration of, 8, 18, 116; lineage of, 33, 34, 36, 46, 122, 123, 128, 158; on radio, 13, 122, 128; to television, 26, 128; write-up of, 18, 128–29

Gumps, The, 13, 15; *12*

"Hall, Ed" (Al Freeman, Jr.), *106*

Hall, Sam, 144

Hamburger Katie, 54

"Hardy, Simone Ravelle" (Stephanie Williams), 106; *98, 99*

"Hardy, Dr. Steve" (John Beradino), 136; *26*

"Hardy, Dr. Tom" (David Wallace), 106; *98, 99*

"Harper, Ben" (Christopher Reeve), 83

Harper's Monthly, 13

"Hart, David" (Brian Farrell), 83

"Hart, Spencer," 58

"Hartman, Heather" (Claudia Lamb), *154*

"Hartman, Mary" (Louise Lasser), 155; *154*

"Hartman, Tom" (Greg Mullavey), *154*

"Harum, David" (Cameron Prud'homme), *55*

"Harvey, Peter" (Sidney Smith), *52*

"Hastings, Nathan" (Adam Lazarre-White), 94

Hawkins Falls, 22

Hawthorne, Nathaniel, 13

"Hayes, Taylor" (Hunter Tylo), 161; *35*

"Henderson, Brandy," 135

Henry, William E., 60

Hill Street Blues, 37

"Hoffman, Dr. Julia," 144

"Holden, Kathy Roberts" (Susan Douglas), 128; *73*

"Holden, Max" (James DePaiva), *101*

"Horton, Alice" (Frances Reid), 143; *27, 142*

"Horton, Bill and Laura," 143

"Horton, Marie," 143

"Horton, Michael," 102

"Horton, Tom" (Macdonald Carey), 143; *27, 142*

Hoshi no Kinka (Heaven's Coins), 115

"Hubbard, Dr. Angie" (Debbi Morgan), 93; *157*

"Hubbard, Jesse," 148

"Hughes, Bob" (Don Hastings), 24, 26, 72, 133; *133*

"Hughes, Chris" (Don MacLaughlin), 133; *24, 133*

"Hughes, Edith," 132

"Hughes, Frannie" (Julianne Moore), *133*

"Hughes, Kim" (Kathryn Hayes), *133*

"Hughes, Margo Montgomery" (Hillary Bailey Smith), 132; *133*

"Hughes, Nancy" (Helen Wagner), 133; *24, 74, 133*

"Hughes, Penny," 28, 132, 148

"Hughes, Tom" (Gregg Marx), *133*

"Hughes family," 132–33; *133*

Hummert, Frank and Anne, 18–19, 22, 36, 42, 46, 48–49, 68, 70, 71, 122; *19, 40, 41*

Hunt, Eugenia, 124

"Hunter, Addie," 143

"Hunter, Jeremy" (Jean LeClerc), *95*

"Hunter, Susan," 143

Hursley, Doris and Frank, 32, 121, 122, 136, 158; *25*

"Hutchins, Carl" (Charles Keating), 36, 77, 141; *141*

I Led Three Lives, 32

India, serials in, 111, 112, 113

Internet, soap chat on, 84, 91, 93, 96

"Invisible People, The" (Thurber), 41

"Ivorytown, Rinsoville, Anacinburg, and Crisco Corners" (Thurber), 41, 51–58, 68

Jackson, Charles, 54

"Jacobs, Robin," 102

James, Francesca, 85

James, Henry, 13

Japan, serials in, 112, 117, 119; *115*

"Jeeter, Jimmy Joe," 155

"Jenny, Aunt" (Edith Spencer), 20; *21*

"Jessup, Hart" (Michael Hilliard), *14*

"Johnson, Jacob" (Darnell Williams), *157*

Joyce Jordan, M.D., 54, 58

Just Plain Bill, 42, 49, 53, 54, 56, 58, 62, 64, 122; *49*

"Kane, Erica" (Susan Lucci), 28, 36, 96, 99, 102, 148; *34, 95, 120, 121*

"Kane, Joan," 131

Kape, Michael, 93, 95–96

"Karr, Mike" (Forrest Compton), 135; *134*

"Karr, Nancy" (Ann Flood), 135; *134*

"Karr, Sara Lane," 135

"Karras, Dr. Christina" (Robin Strasser), *29*

"Kasnoff, Mike" (Shawn Christian), *14*

Kenney, H. Wesley, 143

Ke Wang (Yearnings), 111, 116

"King Fish," 42

Koestenbaum, Wayne, 96

Korea, serials in, 111, 117

"Kramer, Carolyn" (Claudia Morgan), *61*

"Kransky, Rose," 18

"Kuramoto, Aya" (Noriko Sakai), *115*

Labine, Claire, 107, 108, 112, 121, 127, 137, 152

Ladies' World, The, 13

LaGuardia, Robert, 121

Laibson, Michael, 26, 101

L.A. Law, 37

Lampropoulos, Candy, 78, 80, 81

"Lane, Jack," 72

"Larkin, Raymond" (Victor Kilian), *154*

Latin American countries, *telenovelas* in, 111–13, 116, 117, 119; *112, 114*

Laytons, The, 64

Lazarsfeld, Dr. Paul S., 20, 60

Lear, Norman, 155

Lederer, Hanni, 78–79, 81

Lemay, Harding, 70, 117, 140

Lesan, David, 23

Levien, Alisa, 121

Lewis, David P., 20

Life Can Be Beautiful, 16, 53, 54, 58; *54*

Lipton, James, 121

"Listening Women, The" (Thurber), 41, 59–64

"Lockridge, Augusta" (Louise Sorel), *159*

"Lockridge, Laken" (Julie Ronnie), *159*

"Lockridge, Minx" (Dame Judith Anderson), *159*

"Lockridge family," 158

"Logan, Brooke" (Katherine Kelly Lang), 161; *35, 92*

"Logan family," 161

Lone Journey, 58

Lonely Women, 46

"Lord, Dorian," 29, 147

"Lord, Victor," 147

"Lord, Victoria" (Erika Slezak), 36, 103, 104, 105, 147; *105*

Lorenzo Jones, 53, 122

Los Ricos Tambien Lloran (The Rich Also Cry), 113; *114*

Love Is a Many Splendored Thing, 99

Love of Life, 122, 127, 152; *83, 126*

Loving, 71, 81, 123, 156–57; *74, 156*

Loving with a Vengeance (Modleski), 91–92

"Lowell, Claire" (Barbara Berjer), *76, 77*

"Lowell, Ellen" (Patricia Bruder), 132; *76, 77*

"Lowell, James T." (William Johnstone), 132; *76, 77*

"Lowell family," 132

"Lynley, Margo" (Lauren Koslow), *100*

MacDonald, J. Fred, 70

"McFadden, Wally" (Jack Magee), *30*

"McGuire, Sally" (Lee Crawford), 11; *10*

"Malone, Dr. Jerry" (Sandy Becker), 58; *56*

Manners, J. Hartley, 54

"Manning, Walter," 54

Ma Perkins, 8, 13, 20, 22, 49, 52, 54, 57, 58, 122, 124; *57*

"Marceau, Chief Bill," 135

"March, Audrey," 136

"Marick, Dimitri" (Michael Nader), *34*

Marland, Douglas, 73, 115, 128, 133, 136, 139, 156, 157; *74*

"Marshall, Adam" (Kristoff St. John), *163*

"Marshall, Henry" (Taurean Blaque), 97

"Marshall, Ruth" (Joan Pringle), 97

"Martin, David," 143

"Martin, Dixie," 107

"Martin, Joe" (Ray MacDonnell), *104*

"Martin, Tad" (Michael E. Knight), 96; *97*

"Martin, Tara," 148

"Martin family," 148

Mary Hartman, Mary Hartman, 37, 155; *154*

Mary Noble, Backstage Wife, 19, 50, 62, 63, 70, 122; *63*

Masters, Edgar Lee, 51

"Matthews, Alice Frame" (Jacqueline Courtney), 140; *84*

"Matthews, Bill," 140

"Matthews, Liz" (Irene Dailey), 28

"Matthews family," 140

Mayer, Paul Avila, 121, 127, 152

Meltz, Lee, 84

Menser, Clarence L., 43, 49

Mexico, *telenovelas* in, 111, 117, 119; *114*

Mickley, Bill, 83, 103

Miller, Daniel, 119

"Miller, Lisa" (Eileen Fulton), 36, 132; *74*

Mr. Keen, Tracer of Lost Persons, 50

Modleski, Tania, 91–92

"Montgomery, Margo" (Hillary Bailey Smith), 132; *133*

Monty, Gloria, 37, 131, 136; *38*

"Moody, Luna" (Susan Batten), *101*

"Moore, Lenore," 140

Morales, Marilyn, 80, 81

Morley, Christopher, 54

Morse, Carlton, 15, 121

"Moynihan, Mother," 17, 18, 111
Mrs. Wiggs of the Cabbage Patch, 53
Mutt and Jeff, 13
Myrt and Marge, 44; *44*

"Nagai, Shuichi" (Takao Osawa), *115*
"Nagai, Takumi" (Yutaka Takenouchi), *115*
Neighbours, 113, 115, 117; *119*
"Nelson, Greg" (Laurence Lau), 148; *149*
"Nelson, Toby" (Carl Eastman), *54*
"Newman, Nikki Reed" (Melody Thomas Scott), 37, 104, 151; *39*
Newman, Robert, 62
"Newman, Victor" (Eric Braeden), 33, 37, 151; *39*
"Newman, Victoria," 104
New Yorker, The: covers of, *41, 51, 59;* "Invisible People," 41; "Ivorytown, Rinsoville," 41, 51–58, 68; "Listening Women," 41, 59–64; "O Pioneers!," 41–50, 67, 73; "Sculptors in Ivory," 41
Nicholson, Erwin, 135
Nixon, Agnes: 22, 28, 33–34, 92, 103, 124; *30, 74;* as Phillips protégée, 16, 33, 38, 71, 74, 121, 123, 140, 147; and social issues, 26, 34, 36, 74, 105, 128, 147, 148–49, 156
"Noble, Larry" (Ken Griffin), 62; *63*
"Noble, Mary" (Vivian Fridell), 19, 63; *63*
"Novack, Joe," 152

"Ogden, Hilda" (Jean Alexander), *113*
"Olson, Julie," 143
O'Neill, Jay, 32
One Life to Live: 156; *30, 101, 102, 105, 106, 146;* audience of, 81, 95; creation of, 34, 105, 147; lineage of, 71, 122–23; MT&R seminar on, 29, 105; social issues in, 36, 99, 103, 104, 106, 107; write-up of, 147
One Man's Family, 15, 121
"O Pioneers!" (Thurber), 41–50, 67, 73
O Rei do Gado (The Cattle King), 112
Orr, Peggy, 84
Ortiz, Diana, 84
Oshin, 119
Our Gal Sunday, 16, 18, 19, 54, 58, 70, 122; *18*
Our Private World, 132
Our Town, 51

Painted Dreams, 17, 18, 20, 22, 46, 68, 111, 122; *66, 67*
"Palmer, Missy," 140
"Parker, Kathy," 124
Patterson, Joseph, 13
Peg o' My Heart, 54
Pepper Young's Family, 44, 56–57, 62, 68, 122; *66, 67*
"Perkins, Ma" (Virginia Payne), 13, 20, 57; *57*
"Perkins family," 158

Peyton Place, 37, 71
Phillips, Irna: 11, 16–18, 34, 42, 45–46, 68–72, 103, 111, 132, 140, 142, 143; *9, 17, 45, 69;* basic formula of, 17, 71, 132, 148, 152; protégés of, 12, 16, 33, 36, 38, 71, 74, 121, 122–23, 128, 140, 147; and sponsors, 25, 32; and television, 20, 22, 26, 31, 68, 71, 121
"Phillips, Scott and Kathy," 124
Pickwick Papers, The (Dickens), 12–13
Pingree, Suzanne, 70
"Polly, Aunt" (Charme Allen), 55
Por Estas Calles (In These Streets), 117
Portia Faces Life, 54, 58, 63–64
"Powers, Maggie" (Lydia Bruce), 139; *24*
"Powers, Dr. Matt" (James Pritchett), 139; *138*
Procter & Gamble, 16, 25, 26, 32, 33, 42, 44, 46, 53, 56, 132, 135, 140, 141, 148

"Quartermaine, A. J." (Sean Kanan), 82
"Quartermaine, Alan" (Stuart Damon), 37, 136; *137*
"Quartermaine, Edward" (David Lewis), *137*
"Quartermaine, Jason" (Steve Burton), 82
"Quartermaine, Lila" (Anna Lee), *137*
"Quartermaine, Monica" (Leslie Charleson), 37, 102, 136; *137*
Queen's Throat, The (Koestenbaum), 96

race, 106–7, 147, 162; African-American characters, 36, 93, 96, 99, 106, 128, 147, 162; *30, 97, 98, 108, 163;* audience and, 93
radio: moving to television from, 64, 71, 124, 128, 150; pacing of plot in, 53; production credits in, 67, 68; serial narratives on, 13–20, 41–50, 51–58, 59–64, 121; *122*
"Radio's Daytime Serial" (F. Wilder), 60
Radio Writers Guild, 45
Ramayan, 113
"Rampal, David," 148
"Ramsay, Maria" (Dasha Blahova), *119*
"Ramsay, Max" (Francis Bell), *119*
Ramsey, William, 46, 56
Rauch, Paul, 140
"Raven, Paul," 127
"Reardon, Bridget" (Melissa Hayden), *14*
"Reardon, Nola," 128
"Reed, Nikki," 37, 104, 151
Reilly, Jim, 143
"Reynolds, Kim," 132
"Reynolds, Sam," 124
Rhymer, Paul, 15, 42, 43–44, 68
"Richardson, Greg," 158
Riche, Wendy, 108, 116
Richton, Addy, 53
Right to Happiness, The, 46, 58, 60, 122; *61*
Riley, Jim, 28, 32
"Riley, Pierce," 96

Rittenberg, Lucy, *23*
"Rivera, Angela" (Randy Brown), 95
"Rivera, Thomas" (Diego Serrano), 95
Road of Life, The, 32, 46, 54, 122
"Roberts, Cord" (John Loprieno), *146*
"Roberts, Joe" (Herb Nelson), *14*
"Roberts, Kathy" (Susan Douglas), 128; *73*
Rofel, Lisa, 116
"Romalotti, Danny" (Michael Damien), *150*
Romance of Helen Trent, The, 16, 54, 57, 71, 122
Rosemary, 44, 52, 57, 122; *52*
Russell, Gordon, 144, 147
Russia, serials in, 111, 113, 117
"Ruthledge, Rev. Dr. John," 17, 18, 26, 128; *17*
"Ruthledge, Mary," 18
"Ryan, Frank," 152
"Ryan, Johnny" (Bernard Barrow), *153*
"Ryan, Maeve" (Helen Gallagher), *153*
"Ryan, Mary," 152
Ryan's Hope, 121, 152–53; *153*
"Ryan, Siobhan," 152

St. Elsewhere, 37
"St. John, Karen," 20
Sam 'n' Henry, 15
"Sanders, Leora" (Lizbeth MacKay), 101; *104*
Santa Barbara, 121, 158; *14, 87, 159*
"Saybrooke, Marty," 104
Schemering, Chris, 121, 156
"Scorpio, Robert" (Tristan Rogers), *38*
"Scorpio, Robin" (Kimberly McCullough), 107, 108, 137; *82, 109*
Scott, Edward, 33
"Sculptors in Ivory" (Thurber), 41
Search for Tomorrow, 22, 26, 32, 33, 121, 122, 124–25, 127; *15, 22, 125*
Secret Storm, The, 37, 121, 122, 131; *130*
"Sentell, Travis," 125
serial narratives, 11–39; anonymity in, 67; basic formula for, 71, 74, 91–92; bitch goddesses in, 36; budgets for, 116; character shifts in, 102–3; classic, 121–63; closed, 112–13, 115–16, 117; comedy in, 140, 155, 161; in comic strips, 12–13; conversations in, 116; crimes in, 58; family as center of, 70, 152, 156, 157; gaps between episodes in, 116, 117, 119; illnesses in, 57–58, 63, 102, 103–4, 106, 107–8, 128, 137, 156, 162; influence of movies on, 32, 36; international, 111–19, 161; and leisure time, 81; lineages of, 121; *122–23;* moral types in, 56–57; narrators in, 58; naturalism in, 99; ninety-minute segments of, 141; plot recapitulation in, 53, 92–93; production credits of, 67, 68; on radio, 13–20, 41–50, 51–58, 59–64, 121; research on, 60–61, 77–85, 89–95, 116, 119, 121; sex and, 56, 108, 143, 147, 151; social issues in, 26, 34, 36,

53–54, 71, 74, 98–109, 127, 128, 131, 137, 147, 148–49, 151, 156, 162; social stratification in, 54–56, 99, 136, 150–51, 161; social value of, 91; soliloquy in, 58; in a specific culture, 117, 119; storytelling dynamics of, 26, 33, 92, 101–4, 106, 108, 112–13, 115–17, 139, 140, 143, 150–51; supercouples in, 143; symbolism in, 62, 63; syndication deals of, 131; on television, 20–39; write-ups of, 124–63

Serling, Rod, 31

sexual identity, 95–96, 107–8, 147

Seymour, Dan, *21*

Seymour, Robert, 12

"Shayne, Reva" (Kim Zimmer), 88, 89

"Sheffield, Jason," 107

"Sheffield, Kevin," 107, 108

"Shepherd, Devon" (Tricia Pursley), *30*

"Shumway, Cathy" (Debralee Scott), *154*

"Shumway, George" (Philip Bruns), *154*

"Shumway, Martha" (Dodie Goodman), *154*

Siegel, Charlotte, 79–80

"Simpson, Carolee," 139

Skippy, 49

"Slater, Lily," 156

Slesar, Henry, 135

"Sloan, Tina," 128

"Sloane, Shana," 156

"Smith, Ellis," 128

Smith, Sidney, 13

"Snyder family," 133

Soap, 37

Soap Opera, The (Cantor and Pingree), 70

Soap Opera Digest, 84

Soap Opera Encyclopedia, 121

Soap Opera Now, 93, 95

Soap Opera Now Online, 93

soap operas, *see* serial narratives

Soap Opera Weekly, 86

Soap Opera World, 121

Soap Summits, 106

Speaking of Soap Operas (Allen), 67–68, 89

"Spectra, Sally," 161

Spence, Louise, 93

"Spencer, Bill" (Jim Storm), *100*

"Spencer, Bobbie" (Jacklyn Zeman), 136; *6*

"Spencer, Caroline" (Joanna Johnson), 161; *92, 100*

"Spencer, Laura Vining" (Genie Francis), 37, 136, 143; *38*

"Spencer, Luke" (Anthony Geary), 37, 136; *38*

sponsorship, 32, 42, 44, 80–81, 84, 93; *see also* Procter & Gamble

Stedman, Raymond W., 68, 70

"Steele, Graham," 56

Steinberg, Roy, 128

Stella Dallas, 19, 54, 122

"Sterling, Bruce" (Ronald Tomme), 127; *126*

"Stewart, Betsy" (Meg Ryan), 132; *89*

Stolen Husband, The, 48, 122

Stone, Lynn, 53

Story of Mary Marlin, The, 56, 121

Sussman, Sally, 162

Sweet River, 54

"Tate, Arthur," 124

"Tate, Jo" (Mary Stuart), 22, 124, 125, 131; *15, 22, 125*

"Tate, Patti" (Lynn Loring), 124; *15*

Taylor, Elizabeth, 137

telenovelas, 111–13, 116, 117, 119; *112, 114*

television: cable, 37, 117; daytime vs. prime time, 31–32, 37, 103, 116, 136, 155, 156; director's role in, 113; executive producer's role in, 37; half-hour segments on, 26, 135, 161; hour-long segments on, 140, 151; lighting for, 32; location shots in, 37, 71, 99, 103; moving from radio to, 64, 71, 124, 128, 150; serial narratives on, 20–39, 121; *123*; visual look for, 26, 71, 136, 150, 161; *160*

Terry and Mary, 49

Texas, 141

This Child of Mine, 37

"Thorpe, Roger," 128

Three Girls Lost, 48

Thurber, James, *New Yorker* essays by, 41–50, 51–58, 59–64, 67–68, 70, 71, 73

Time magazine, 143

Today's Children, 18, 46, 70, 122

Tomlin, Gary, 28, 32, 113, 158

Torchin, Mimi, 86

Tovrov, Orin, 139

"Travis, Nicole," 135

"Trent, Helen," 54, 57

Turkey, serials in, 111, 117

Twain, Mark, 13

"Tyler, Amy" (Rosemary Prinz), *29*

"Tyler, Chuck," 148

"Tyler, Phoebe" (Ruth Warrick), 148; *29, 79*

"Tyler family," 148

Untouchables, The, 32

Valiant Lady, 122

Valles, Awilda, 81

"Vaughan, Hayley," 148

Vendig, Irving, 124, 135

Venezuela, serials in, 117

Vic and Sade, 43–44, 53, 68, 124; *47*

Vidal, Gore, 31

"Villareal, Mariana" (Veronica Castro), *114*

"Vincente, Tony," 124

"Vochek, Noreen," 156

"Vochek family," 156

"Wainwright, Julia," 158

Wallace, Art, 144

Walpole, Helen, 50

"Walton, Liza," 124, 125

"Warner, Dr. Cliff" (Peter Bergman), 93; *85*

Warner, W. Lloyd, 60

"Wayne, Dr. John," 61, 62

"Wayne, Ruth," 54, 62

Weaver, Sylvester "Pat," 20

"Webber, Dr. Lesley Williams" (Denise Alexander), 136; *6*

"Webber, Mike" (David Mendenhall), *6*

"Webber, Dr. Rick" (Chris Robinson), 136; *6*

"Wells, Susan Price" (Joan Tompkins), *55*

"Wexler, Karen" (Cari Shayne), *15, 82*

"Wexler, Rhonda" (Denise Galik-Gurey), *15*

WGN, 13, 15, 16, 18, 46, 68, 111

When a Girl Marries, 44, 53, 64, 122; *65*

Where the Heart Is, 152

"Whitmore, Sam" (Kelly Rutherford), *163*

Wilder, Frances Farmer, 60

Wilder, Thornton, 51

Williams, Carol Traynor, 71

"Williams, Doug," 143

"Williams, Paul," 151

"Williams family," 151

Winsor, Roy, 22, 32, 37, 121, 122, 124, 127, 131

"Winters, Drucilla" (Victoria Rowell), *94*

"Winters, Neil," 107

"Winters, Victoria," 144

"Wolek, Karen" (Judith Light), 147; *101*

Woman in White, 33, 46, 54, 58, 60, 122

"Young, Larry (Pepper)" (Curtis Arnall), 66, 67

"Young, Mary" (Marion Barney), 66, 67

"Young, Peggy" (Elizabeth Wragge), 66, 67

"Young, Sam" (Jack Roseleigh), 66, 67

Young and the Restless, The: 118, 143, 161; *10, 11, 15, 39, 94, 150*; audience of, 37, 93; lineage of, 32, *123*; and social issues, 36, 71, 104, 107, 151, 162; write-up of, 150–51

Young Dr. Malone, 54, 56, 58; *56*

Young Widder Brown, 54, 57, 122

Zak, John C., 71